THE STANLEY GIBBONS BOOK OF STAMPS
and Stamp Collecting

THE STANLEY GIBBONS
BOOK OF
STAMPS
and Stamp Collecting

James Watson
(Revised by John Holman)

Designed by Philip Clucas MSIAD
Produced by Ted Smart and
David Gibbon

GRANTA EDITIONS

ACKNOWLEDGMENTS

The portrait of King George V (now at St. James's Palace) is reproduced by gracious permission of Her Majesty the Queen.

Several items from the Post Office and Phillips collections are reproduced by permission of the National Postal Museum.

The following institutions, companies and individuals kindly made stamps and other material in their care available for photography and/or helped in other ways in the preparation of this book. The publishers here record their gratitude for such willing assistance.

Post Office Headquarters, Photographic Library
The National Maritime Museum, Greenwich
The Royal Philatelic Society, London
Bruce Castle Museum, London
Victoria Art Gallery, Bath
Isle of Man Post Office Authority
Swedish Post Office, Stockholm

Russell Bennett, Kathy Cooper, John Curle, James Negus and Richard Watkins of Stanley Gibbons

Archie Page and Frank Brench, former Editors of Post Office's *Philatelic Bulletin*
Peter Johnson, Railway Philatelic Group
Stuart Rossiter, former Editor *The London Philatelist*
George Beal, former Editor *Stamp Collecting*
Herbert Grimsey, British Philatelic Federation

Robson Lowe Ltd	Clive Abbott	Prof. Richard Guyatt
Harrison & Sons Ltd	Collis Clements	Edward Hughes
De La Rue & Co., Ltd	Gordon Drummond	Andrew Restall
Francis J. Field Ltd	M. C. Farrar-Bell	Sally and Walter Clucas.
L. N. Williams	David Gentleman	

Picture Research by Hanni Edmonds (Colour Library International) and John Holman (formerly of Stanley Gibbons Publications)

Featuring the Photography of Clive Friend F.I.I.P.

STANLEY GIBBONS BOOK OF STAMPS

Published by Granta Editions, 47 Norfolk Street, Cambridge CB1 2LE.

Granta Editions is an imprint of The Book Concern Ltd.

Text copyright © Stanley Gibbons Publications Ltd. 1990.
Photographs copyright © Colour Library Books Ltd. 1980 and
Stanley Gibbons Publications Ltd. 1990.
This edition copyright © Granta Editions.

Design and production in association with
Book Connections, 47 Norfolk Street, Cambridge.
Printed and bound in Barcelona, Spain.
ISBN 0 906782 47 3

S.G. Item No 2780
The colour illustrations of stamps are as faithfully reproduced from the originals as photographic and printing techniques permit; they are enlarged or defaced to comply with Post Office regulations.

Preface to the Second Edition

This book was written by the late James Watson in 1979 and first published in 1981. It was immediately praised as one of the best introductory books ever on the subject of stamps and stamp collecting. The praise was not only for the many carefully chosen colour illustrations but for the easy-to-read and invigorating text. That was not surprising as James Watson was one of Britain's best-known and best-liked philatelic writers. During his years at Stanley Gibbons he built up an enormous knowledge of stamp design, printing and, in particular, varieties. He was not, however, a specialist collector himself and was always able to take a broad view of the subject. In his many writings he always tried to inform the reader, interest him in the subject, not bore him with unnecessary detail and complicated explanations. Stamps were to be enjoyed and those who knew Jim knew he enjoyed studying and writing about stamps. His enthusiasm showed in his words.

In the decade since Jim wrote this work much has changed in the stamp world. Stamps keep pouring from postal administrations and new types of stamps are regularly introduced for the benefit of the letter-writing public and/or stamp collectors. Details of these have been added to the text. The opportunity has been taken to update most chapters, to include illustrations of recent issues and in particular to augment the chapters on Stamp Books and Magazines and Philatelic Organizations and Societies. The chapter on Stamps for Investment has been dropped as inappropriate in a book designed primarily for newcomers to the hobby. Stamp investment is a controversial and complicated matter, not really suited to such a book as this as any opinions rapidly become out of date. Collectors interested in investment should consult the various columns on this subject in stamp magazines. In its place we have added a chapter on the history of Stanley Gibbons, as in 1990 we celebrate the 150th anniversary of the birth of the founder of the firm, Edward Stanley Gibbons, the 125th anniversary of the first Gibbons stamp catalogue and the centenary of *Gibbons Stamp Monthly*.

It has been a pleasure for me to prepare this new edition, for two reasons. It was one of the first projects I worked on when I joined Stanley Gibbons in 1980, finding the stamps for photography for the illustrations. Secondly I was fortunate to work, albeit for a short while, with Jim Watson before his retirement in 1981. Not only did I appreciate his wide knowledge of philately but also his gentle manner, his sense of humour and his friendly way. All who knew him were saddened when he died in 1987 but remember him through his writings. I hope that many more collectors will come to appreciate him through this second edition of his finest book.

John Holman

In January 1990 the British Post Office commemorated the 150th anniversary of Penny Post and the first adhesive postage stamps with five 'special definitives' showing Queen Victoria and Queen Elizabeth II. The colours of the 20p and 15p stamps recall the Penny Black and Two Pence Blue of 1840.

CONTENTS

1
The History of the Postal Service

When Columbus discovered the New World in 1492 and, a few years later, Vasco da Gama rounded the Cape and pioneered the sea route to India, neither of these gallant adventurers had the means of communicating the news of their exciting discoveries to their Spanish and Portuguese masters. Then, after many months, when the voyagers returned home, the news would have been conveyed by couriers on horseback to all points of Europe, many of them no doubt belonging to the vast network of posts operated by the Counts of Thurn and Taxis.

The dak runner from mail-transport set, India 1937 (SG 251).

Foot messengers had been employed since before Roman times, and the native bearers of Africa, the Inca 'postmen' of Peru and the *dak* runners of India are familiar to us on modern postage stamps. Organized postal services came into existence with the great surge of civilization which developed in the 15th and 16th centuries – the revival of learning, especially reading and writing, inspired by the Reformation, the great religious revolution led by Martin Luther, and the beginnings of the Renaissance – the rebirth of literature and the arts. Köster, Gutenberg and Caxton set up printing presses, and printed books began to

Opposite: A large block of Penny Blacks; the stamp – incorporating Queen Victoria's portrait – which introduced Sir Rowland Hill's grand scheme of uniform penny postage.

appear – William Caxton established a print shop in Westminster, London, in 1476, and before he died in 1491 he printed between 80 and 100 different titles.

Regular messenger services were established in Britain by the reigning monarchs, and the 'relay' system, by which letters and despatches were carried by 'post to post' horsemen to far distant destinations, is said to have been inaugurated by Edward IV in 1482. Government officials, wealthy merchants and the clergy frequently had to devise their own services, while for the general population at that time there were no facilities for the conveyance of mail.

The foundations of an organized postal service were laid by Henry VIII, who was in constant communication with his ministers, and with the Pope and countries abroad. About the year 1512, he appointed the first 'Master of the Posts', Sir Brian Tuke, whose most important duty, as supervisor of the Royal Posts, was to overhaul the 'relay' system and establish a series of stages or 'posts' along the primitive main roads leading from London to other towns in the kingdom, to the principal ports and to Scotland. The 'posts' or posthouses were usually inns or taverns spaced at intervals of 10 or 20 miles, and the reluctant innkeepers were obliged to have horses – and sometimes riders – ready on demand, day and night, for the king's messengers to continue their journeys.

When Queen Elizabeth ascended the throne in 1558, Thomas Randolph became 'Master of the Queen's Posts' and was responsible for both the inland posts and overseas mails, competing against the private mails handled by the Merchant Adventurers of London. The carriage of private letters was grudgingly permitted, but accepted only if the destination was along the carrier's route and with the assurance that the postage fee would be paid on delivery. Elizabeth, however, sat uneasily on her throne – she was afraid of foreign intrigues, and aware that private letters despatched abroad could avoid censorship. Her fears culminated in 1588 when England was attacked by the 'invincible' Spanish Armada, and in 1591 she finally established the monopoly of the Royal Posts by proclamation.

In 1609, James I made a similar – and equally futile – attempt to ban the conveyance of inland private letters (the so-called 'by-letters') by other than the official post, hoping to regain some of the considerable revenue enjoyed by more efficient 'pirate' enterprises. The merchants promptly appointed their own postmaster, Mathew De Quester, a Flemish merchant living in England, to take care of letters to and from the Continent.

De Quester organized a most efficient mail service, not only linking the English towns, but extending his activities to France and the Low Countries. The official 'Master of the Posts', Lord John Stanhope, was busily occupied establishing posts *en route* to Scotland and to Ireland, and was never able to outwit

General Letter Office commemorated 300 years later with postboy design, Great Britain (SG 619).

the De Questers, father and son. When, in 1619, De Quester was appointed Postmaster of England for Foreign Parts, Stanhope took him to the High Court – the result was a victory for neither. While Stanhope's claim was acknowledged, De Quester was permitted to keep his title and continue with his expanding postal service, which lasted until 1632. Charles I appointed Thomas Witherings, a mercer by trade, and one William Finell, to take control of the Foreign Posts, in the same year.

Witherings had been originally employed to take care of Charles's French wife, Queen Henrietta Maria – dealing with her correspondence and messages, and arranging her lodging during her travels – which ideally fitted him for the task of reorganizing the foreign mails. He started the first regular postal service to the Continent, with a daily packet-boat sailing between Dover and Calais. Then, in 1635, he assumed control of the whole of the postal services, inland and foreign. He was authorized by royal proclamation to 'settle' daily 'running posts' from London to Dover, Edinburgh, to Chester and Holyhead (for Ireland), Norfolk, Yarmouth, Oxford, Bristol, Exeter and Plymouth. He imposed a fixed charge for letters, 2d. for a single-sheet letter under 80 miles from London, 4d. between 80 and 140 miles, and 6d. above 140 miles in

England and Wales. Thomas Witherings was the first real pioneer of the British postal service, and certainly one of its most successful administrators. His career was terminated by the Civil War, but he laid the foundations of the state postal service which led to the establishment of the General Letter Office in 1660.

The Thurn and Taxis Post

While the postal systems of Britain were suffering the pangs of creation in the 16th and 17th centuries, the Counts of Thurn and Taxis (originally Tour and Tassis) were building up a huge network of postal services across Europe, defying the competition of rivals and overcoming appalling conditions on the roads, often little more than cart-tracks, where bandits and robbers abounded.

It all began when Roger de Tassis was employed by the Hapsburg Holy Roman Emperor, Frederick III, to extend the existing courier service of the Holy See to the Tyrol. This important link was further extended to Brussels when relays of horse posts replaced the slower foot-messengers. When Frederick died in 1493, he was succeeded by his son, Maximilian I, and it was Maximilian's son, Philip I (Philippe le Beau), who appointed Roger's son, François de Tassis, as Captain and Master of the Posts in the Low Countries, in 1500. Five years later François was further commissioned to set up a royal courier service linking Brussels and the Low Countries with the courts of Austria, France and Spain. Thus François became the first Grand Master of the Imperial Posts, an office which was to be inherited by his successors, father to son, for more than 300 years.

For his services, François was to receive an annual payment of 12,000 livres, but the money was not always forthcoming as the imperial treasury was financing the numerous wars which ravaged Europe at that time. François seized the golden opportunity – he sought and obtained permission for his couriers to carry private letters, a privilege confirmed by Emperor Charles V in 1516. In this manner he not only made substantial profits, but established a reliable and dependable public postal service. Also confirmed was the hereditary monopoly of the Taxis family, now ennobled, and when François died in 1517, he was succeeded by his nephew, Jean Baptiste, a descendant of the 'la Tour' (Torre or Thurn) side of the family.

The continuing story of the Thurn and Taxis Post is one of expansion and development – and eventual decline as some countries chose to opt out of the postal monopoly. Jean Baptiste was followed by his sons, François, who died within a year, and Leonard who, with one break of seven years, held office from 1536 to 1612, and consolidated the family postal services by establishing new routes and regularizing the pay and conditions of the couriers who, by that time, num-

*Above: Thurn and Taxis 1852/9, from
1965 West German stamp (SG 1403).
Below: Belgium honours the family,
1952/60 (SG 1399, 1680, 1712).*

bered about 25,000. His successors, Lamoral, Leonard François and Lamoral Claude, survived the Thirty Years War though they lost the postal monopoly in northern Germany, where several states formed their own postal services. Eugene Alexander was invested with the title of Prince, *circa* 1686, and was designated Postmaster-General.

Under the control of Anselm Francis, Alexander Ferdinand, Charles Anselm and Charles Alexander, the princely post reached its peak of operations during the 18th century. But the French Revolution and Napoleon's successes in Europe deprived them of the greater part of their services and revenues. Belgium, France and the Netherlands started their own posts, and the Thurn and Taxis network was reduced to parts of northern and southern Germany, its headquarters being Frankfurt-on-Main. The Thurn and Taxis administration issued its own postage stamps in 1852, but Prince Maximilian Charles of Thurn and Taxis finally relinquished postal services and stamps to Prussia in 1867. It was the end of the greatest postal system of its time the world had ever known.

Only in France was there a postal service comparable to that which Thomas Witherings had pioneered in Britain – in 1653 the Comte de Villayer established a local post in Paris on the lines of the British penny posts. He sold franked or 'stamped' wrappers which enclosed the letters, set up collection boxes in Paris streets and undertook the delivery of letters and parcels to any address in the city.

Henry Bishop and his 'Mark'

When Oliver Cromwell became head of the government as self-styled Lord Protector of England in 1653, he appointed Captain John Manley as Master of the Posts. Then, by an Act of 1657, he created the office of Postmaster-General and appointed John Thurloe to the new post. Following the Restoration and the return of Charles II to the throne in 1660, Cromwell's Act was deemed unlawful – Charles passed an Act of his own and appointed Colonel (later Sir) Henry Bishop, 1605-91, as Postmaster-General. Bishop fought for the Royalists in the Civil War, and it is said that when Cromwell's 'Ironsides' were searching for him at his home in Henfield, Sussex, they failed to discover his hiding-place by which his little dog stood guard. A painting of Bishop holding the dog exists today at Parham House, an Elizabethan mansion in Sussex.

Henry Bishop, first Postmaster-General, on an advertising label for the London 1960 International Stamp Exhibition.

Henry Bishop was the typical country squire/professional soldier of the period, but the office of Postmaster-General was a tough assignment, even for him. He was contracted to 'farm' the mails – that is, pay £21,500 a year for the privilege of collecting (and keeping) the postal fees – and his immediate task was to speed up deliveries and, in short, reorganize the entire postal system. To this end, he introduced a novel device to record the acceptance of letters at the receiving houses. 'A stamp is invented', he announced, 'that is putt upon every letter shewing the day of the moneth that every letter comes to this office, so that no letter Carryer may dare to detayne a letter from post to post, which before was usual'. That was in August 1661.

Hitherto, all marks had been in manuscript and these generally indicated the amount of postage to be collected, or recorded that the postage had been 'Paid' in red ink. Never before had dates been endorsed on letters which were often held for examination by post office 'spies', commissioned by a jittery government.

These small, circular handstamps, known to philatelists as 'Bishop marks' – forerunners of the present-day postmarks – were patterned in two segments, the upper half indicating the month (eg 'OC' for October), and the lower segment, the day of the month, or vice versa. First used in London, the Bishop marks were in constant use, in various forms, throughout Britain until 1787, when they began to be phased out.

Bishop established a ring of receiving houses around the City of London where letters could be handed in for conveyance to the General Post Office, which was located at the 'Swan', one of the first public posthouses, in Bishopsgate. But he was harried by the numerous illicit posts, the corruption of his own officials who held back letters while pocketing the fees, and the open abuse of the 'free franking' privilege by peers and members of parliament. Bishop's revenues suffered accordingly, and he became involved in expensive litigation. Three years after his appointment, he gave up the onerous task and retired.

The new Postmaster-General was Daniel O'Neale and, from 1663, the Post Office revenues were settled on the King's brother, James, Duke of York, later James II, who took an active interest in the further development of the postal services. Then came two major setbacks – the Great Plague, in which 30 of the 45 people employed in the London Post Office died, in 1665, and the Great Fire which followed in 1666 and which caused the Post Office to change its headquarters several times. As the City recovered from these disasters, the postal traffic began to increase in volume – Lord Arlington became Postmaster-General in 1667 and, by 1674, the total amount of postal revenue he had to pay annually to the Duke of York, under his farm or contract, had risen to more than £40,000.

The government continued its attempts to suppress all private posts, even appointing special police to detect smugglers. It was a complete shock to the authorities when one, William Dockwra, a City merchant, set up his own (and at first, successful) postal service in London.

Dockwra's Penny Post

The incentive for William Dockwra and his colleagues (who called themselves 'the undertakers') to start an independent postal service was the fact that there was no local post within London or for that matter any other town. Letters were conveyed only from post town to post town, and delivery thereafter was uncertain and expensive. In March 1680, Dockwra opened his Penny Post with a head office in Lime Street, 'just around the corner' from Bishopsgate in London, and a few hundred yards from the General Post Office which had moved to Lombard Street, and

A Bishop Mark of 1766; dated the 20th November.

appointed several hundred 'receivers', at whose houses letters could be left for collection every hour and taken to central or suburban offices for distribution.

Dockwra charged 1d. for letters delivered within the City, and 2d. for the suburbs. Prepayment was compulsory and he accepted letters for delivery to the General Post Office and onward transmission, also packets up to 1lb in weight. Later in 1680, he introduced his own distinctive postmark – a small triangular handstamp with the words 'Penny Post Paid' along its sides, and an initial letter representing the collection

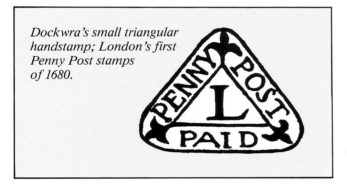

Dockwra's small triangular handstamp; London's first Penny Post stamps of 1680.

office, eg 'L' for Lime Street, in the centre. In addition, each letter was impressed with a small, heart-shaped time stamp recording the hour at which the letter left the office for delivery. There were 12 deliveries a day in central London, and in the evenings letter-carriers walked the streets ringing a bell to enable people to post their letters in his bag – the origins of the 'bell-man'.

The Dockwra triangular postmarks – there are three types – are of the greatest rarity today. Few have survived the centuries.

After two years, just when Dockwra was beginning to reap a substantial profit, he was prosecuted by James, Duke of York, for infringing his postal monopoly (and depriving him of revenues), and in November 1682, his 'pirate' service was closed down. The Post Office thereupon took over the organization and most of its personnel, and continued to run the Penny Post on similar lines from December in the same year. Similar triangular 'paid' marks were used though, strangely, these were inscribed 'Peny Post Payd' and included the day of the week as well as the

A bell-man of the early 19th century evoked in a Rowlandson drawing dated 1819.

office of origin, represented by code letters. These marks continued in use until 1794, when the Penny Post was reorganized and new date stamps were introduced.

Meanwhile, Nathaniel Castleton was appointed Controller of the new Government Penny Post, but after years of increasing chaos and inefficiency, he was replaced by the unrepentant William Dockwra, who had received compensation (in the form of a pension) for his previous dismissal, from William III and Mary, in 1697. Eventually Dockwra, too, was accused of mismanagement ('fiddling' the receipts) and lost both office and pension. Thereafter he faded from public life.

The Penny Post continued to flourish. An Act of 1711 during the reign of Queen Anne regularized the basic penny rate of postage, and limited the distance such letters could be carried to within a radius of ten

Ralph Allen, postal pioneer, a painting in the Bruce Castle Museum, London.

miles from the General Post Office. In 1765, Penny Posts were authorized for provincial towns and cities, and in 1773, Peter Williamson set up a private Penny Post in Edinburgh. Bristol, Birmingham and Manchester established their Penny Posts in 1793, and others quickly followed, amounting to more than 2,500 by 1840. In 1794, there were further changes in the rates and regulations of the London Penny Post and, in 1801, the service came to an end as such when an Act of Parliament decreed that letters should, in future, be charged 2d. for both town and country districts.

Ralph Allen — Entrepreneur

Ralph Allen, as shown on 1935 Philatelic Congress of Great Britain souvenir label.

The Post Office Act of 1711 was not solely confined to the control of the Penny Posts — it also embraced the country services which, by that time, formed a disorganized and haphazard network of posts across England and Wales, and Scotland, too. Postmasters were required to account for all letters passing through their offices, but corruption was widespread — letters were lost, mishandled or undercharged at every stage. The greatest losses occurred in the passage of by(e)-letters, conveyed from one town to another, say Reading to Oxford, by-passing London, and the newly-designated cross or 'cross-road' letters carried along the remote cross-country post roads linking the main roads.

It was in 1720 that one Ralph Allen, youthful postmaster of Bath who had already proved himself a capable organizer, persuaded the Postmaster-General to give him control of the provincial posts. He became the supervisor of the by- and cross-road letters throughout the country, and agreed to pay £6,000 a year to the Post Office under a seven-year 'farm' contract. Postmasters were required to keep records and make returns on all postal traffic, and to employ postmarks bearing the name of the despatching office. For the first few years Allen lost money, but in 1734 he renewed his efforts and began to prosper. He set up 'every day' posts between London and other main cities, and eventually regular postal services provided daily deliveries all over the country.

Ralph Allen was born in 1694, the son of a Cornish innkeeper. At the age of 11 he was helping his grandmother, postmistress of St Columb, thence he moved to Exeter and, in 1710, to Bath where, just two years later, he became deputy postmaster and subsequently postmaster. He was a dedicated pioneer of the posts and became a great benefactor of the city of Bath, of which he was Mayor in 1742. When he died in 1764, the Post Office took over his postal network. Allen had become a wealthy man and the Post Office acquired a profitable enterprise — 'The Bye and Cross Road Letter Office'. But the carriage of mails was still a painfully slow and dilatory process. Letters were borne, as of yore, by postboys on horseback from stage to stage: the roads were poor — Macadam had yet to make his roads and his fortune — and wayside robbery was rife. It was the era of the stage-coach and the post-chaise, yet, surprisingly, no one had thought of transporting the mails across country, town to town, by carriage and horses. That is, not until 1782.

John Palmer — Coachman Extraordinary

Another gentleman of fashionable Bath whose name stands out in postal history was John Palmer, born there in 1742. Coming of age, he joined his father in a project to open a theatre in Bath — in the event, it was, at that time, the first provincial theatre — and travelled to London to petition for the necessary royal patent. He was successful and later the Palmers opened a second theatre in Bristol. Running the two theatres necessitated frequent travel by coach between the two cities, and regular journeys to London to find and engage the leading stage players of the day. Invariably his coach overtook the postboys and their laden horses — it was, he realized, quicker for him to travel by coach than to have a letter conveyed to London, a difference of a day.

The more Palmer thought about this, the more he became sure in his own mind that the mails had to travel by coach. 'The Post at present', he declared, 'instead of being the swiftest is almost the slowest conveyance in the country'. The idea of mail-coaches became an obsession to Palmer and he impulsively abandoned his theatres, travelling once again to London to further the project. He obtained access to William Pitt, then Chancellor of the Exchequer, who accepted Palmer's proposals and, despite strong opposition from the Post Office, authorized a trial run, Bristol to London.

So, on 2 August 1784, a gleaming 'diligence', drawn by four selected greys, set off from the Swan Tavern, adjacent to the Corn Exchange, Bristol, at 4pm, bound for Bath and London with the Royal Mail — Britain's first mail-coach. The coach reached the Swan with Two Necks in London at 8am the next morning — exactly on schedule and in a record time of 16 hours. On this and on the return journey the coachman was accompanied by an armed guard and four passengers. Following this success, William Pitt, who had meanwhile become Prime Minister, authorized

John Palmer: Inventor of mail-coaches, Surveyor and Comptroller General of Mails 1786-92.

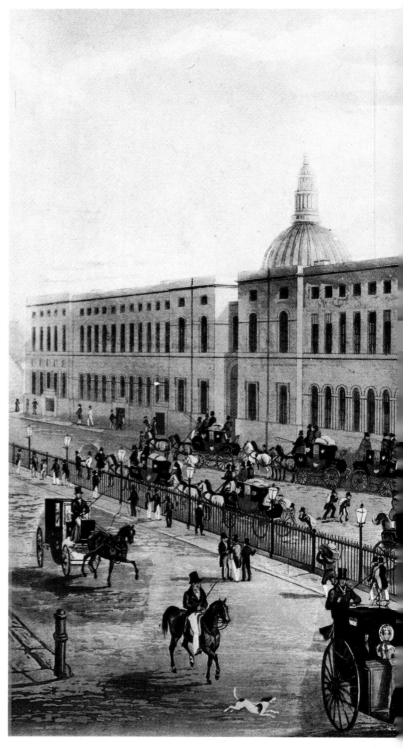

extensions of the mail-coach service to other post roads. Within weeks coaches were running to Norwich, Liverpool and Leeds, and by the end of the year, to many other towns.

For the next 50 years, the mail-coaches travelled the length and breadth of the country, rolling over the hills and dales with the strident call of the posthorn heralding the approach to town and village. Fine new roads were laid by John Macadam, new lightweight coaches were built by Besant and Vidler, and prosperity came to the great coaching inns. The gaily-liveried coaches were given names according to their destination, such as 'The Wonder' (to Holyhead), 'The Cumbrian' (to Glasgow) and 'Quicksilver', the fastest coach of all, running from London to Devonport. And when, in September 1839, the Post Office moved to a fine new building in St Martin's-le-Grand in London, crowds gathered each evening to watch the coaches depart *en masse* with 'a sound of trumpets, a trampling of hoofs and a thundering of wheels'.

John Palmer continued to supervise coach operations as an officer of the Post Office – he was appointed Comptroller General of the Mails in 1786 at an annual salary of £1,500, but eventually he antagonized the Post Office and was dismissed in 1792 – he won a pension of £3,000, and subsequently a grant of £50,000. He died in 1818, having founded and lived to see the golden era of the mail-coach.

The original Bath mail-coach, pioneered by Palmer, depicted on an old print.

Above: A painting of the New General Post Office, with the Royal Mails preparing to depart.
Left: George Stephenson's Locomotion *on a British stamp of 1975 (SG 984).*

By 1835, there were about 700 Royal Mail coaches, and 3,300 stage-coaches, connecting every place of importance throughout the country, all averaging ten miles or more an hour and running reliably to time-tables. But their days were numbered – the 'iron horses' of the railroad were beginning to snort and puff along experimental tracks and, in 1825, the first train, with George Stephenson, its creator, at the controls of 'Locomotion', carried several hundred passengers between Stockton and Darlington.

The sailing packet,
the Windsor Castle,
engaging the French
in 1805.

Four 19th century mail packet boats from a Jamaica 1974
miniature sheet (SG MS384).

Mail was first carried on the pioneer Liverpool and Manchester Railway in 1830 at the suggestion of Sir Francis Freeling, then Secretary to the Post Office, and in 1838 a travelling post office (a converted horse-box) was put into service between Birmingham and Warrington on the Grand Junction Railway – an idea which Rowland Hill, the great postal reformer of the 19th century, had conceived for road coaches in 1826. The first TPOs had no means of exchanging mail-bags en route – the train had to slow down while bags were thrown out and incoming bags were grabbed from a pole. Later, more sophisticated equipment was introduced, employing nets, both on the train and at the side of the line, to scoop mail-bags and permit the exchange at high speed. In this modern era of high-speed trains, the practice has been discontinued.

1794 Mail boat Earl of Chesterfield *on a Guernsey stamp of*
1972 (SG 67).

Just as the rapid development of the railways brought about the equally rapid decline of the mail-coach – the last of them had been taken off the roads by 1846 – so the steamboat gradually began to replace the sailing packet which had voyaged around the world transporting mail for more than a century. In 1838, Samuel Cunard offered to the Lords of the Admiralty

'to furnish steamboats of not less than 300 horse-power to convey the mails from Liverpool to Halifax and Boston and back, twice each month . . .' Cunard's Boston packet service, forerunner of modern transatlantic mail transport, continued until 1868.

Sir Rowland Hill KCB

One man's passion, persistence and zeal brought about a virtual revolution in Britain's inefficient and much-maligned postal services. That man was Rowland (later Sir Rowland) Hill, 1795-1879, the former schoolmaster, administrator and inventor, who was born in Kidderminster, Worcestershire, the third son of Thomas Wright Hill, who managed a school in Birmingham.

Rowland was a fertile inventor (though most of his ideas came to naught) and a compulsive campaigner. When the Hill family moved to Tottenham, North London, in 1827, to open their model school at Bruce Castle, he continued teaching there. Newly married and not in the best of health, he had time to contemplate his future and pursue his numerous inventions – an improved steam engine, a screw propeller (instead of paddles) for steamboats and a rotary printing press, intended to print newspapers on a

continuous roll of paper. The press was the forerunner of modern rotary presses, but at that time newspapers were subject to a stamp tax which had to be individually impressed. The Treasury refused to permit the stamping to be done mechanically in the press, a disappointment which roused Hill's interest in government revenues and taxes.

In 1833, he gradually began to relinquish his duties as a teacher at Bruce Castle – he was ambitious for a more arduous and rewarding occupation, and he became interested in a project for the colonization of South Australia. Bruce Castle, an ancient manor house dating from the time of Henry VIII and named after Robert the Bruce of Scotland, remained the family home for many years. The building eventually became a local museum, while the grounds came into use as a public park. In 1927, the Morten postal history collection was lodged there and has since been augmented by the Tottenham Corporation. Bruce Castle was substantially restored in the early 1960s, and is now an established postal history museum.

Through his interest in South Australia, Hill became acquainted with Edward Gibbon Wakefield, who was promoting the scheme for the colonization and population of South Australia, then uninhabited, and in 1835 he was appointed Secretary of the South Australia Commission, which was largely responsible

*Three essays by Charles Whiting
submitted as part of the
Treasury competition for the
design of the first postage
stamp, 1839.*

for the territory being formed into a British province in 1836 and becoming a Crown Colony five years later.

At about that time – the mid-1830s – Hill began to study the postal service and its ponderous, complex methods of collecting and delivering letters, and of assessing and collecting the due amounts of postage. Postage rates were based on the number of sheets forming the folded letter, and on the distance it had to travel. Envelopes, just coming into use, cost more, and post office clerks had to examine each missive, check its destination and route, and mark the appropriate fee on the letter. Postage was collected on delivery and this practice resulted in numerous abuses, delays and refusals. If the charge was exorbitant – as it invariably was – the addressee refused to take delivery, causing a loss to the Post Office. Letters were often coded so that the recipient could 'get the message' without taking delivery, and sometimes the plodding letter-carriers were waylaid and robbed of the cash they had collected on their rounds.

Another abuse which rankled Hill – and the general public – was the privilege, established in the mid-17th century, accorded to members of parliament (of both Houses) of having their letters 'franked' by their own signatures for free delivery through the post. The 'franks' were liberally distributed among associates and relatives. Never before – or since – had an MP so many friends! So Rowland Hill had plenty to occupy his mind when evolving his master plan for the posts, setting down his criticisms, quoting postal statistics and extracts from parliamentary reports.

'Post Office Reform – Its Importance . . .'

Rowland Hill published his memorable pamphlet, 'Post Office Reform: Its Importance and Practicability' in January 1837. Initially it was a 'private and confidential' document intended for and directed to the government – especially for the official Commission of Inquiry which had been set up in 1835 at the instigation of Robert Wallace, MP, to examine the running of the Post Office. Hill's main proposals, after he had listed the deficiencies of the existing administration, were: the introduction of a uniform basic postage rate of one penny per half-ounce in weight, and a penny for each additional half-ounce, regardless of the number of sheets a letter contained or of the distance it was required to travel; and the pre-payment of the postage.

Later, Hill appeared before the Commission and proposed the sale of franked, or stamped, postal stationery – letter-sheets, wrappers and envelopes – to the public and, almost as an afterthought, the issue of 'small stamped labels' – 'bits of paper just large enough to bear the stamp, and covered at the back with a glutinous wash which the user might, by applying a little moisture, attach to the back of a letter'. As we shall see, Hill was quite wrong in his anticipation

that the public would prefer the postal stationery to the stamps, nevertheless, after publishing further editions of 'Post Office Reform' and the appointment of a parliamentary committee to examine his proposals, he issued yet another pamphlet in May 1839 – 'On the Collection of Postage by means of Stamps'. His ideas won public support and enthusiasm, and in July 1839, bowing to public pressure, the Chancellor of the Exchequer formally announced the Penny Post.

Despite Hill's own prophecy that the inevitable fall in revenue would not be recovered for several years, the 'Penny Postage' bill passed through Parliament without opposition and was granted the Royal Assent by the young Queen Victoria on 17 August 1839.

The Queen expressed 'great satisfaction' with the proposed 'reduction of the postal duties' which, she said, would be 'a relief and encouragement to trade' and, by facilitating intercourse and correspondence, would be 'productive of much social advantage and improvement'. The Lords of the Treasury wasted no time in putting Hill's reforms in hand – they sponsored a competition in which the public were invited to submit suitable designs for the stamps and postal stationery – letter-sheets and envelopes – and appointed Rowland Hill as adviser to the Treasury to introduce the postal reforms and supervise their implementation.

The Treasury Competition brought more than 2,600 entries, of which four were awarded prizes of £100, though none was considered suitable for use. One of the winners was Henry Cole, himself an active campaigner for educational and social reforms – subsequently Cole was appointed to assist Hill and played an active role in the preparations for the new stamps and stationery. It was Cole who negotiated with William Mulready, R.A., in the creation and design of the ill-fated 'Mulready' letter-sheets and envelopes, and who suggested to his friend, John Calcott Horsley, the idea for what is now generally accepted as the first Christmas greetings card (which Horsley designed and sent to Cole) in 1843.

Another competitor was James Chalmers, a Dundee bookseller and publisher who, years before, had essayed stamped 'labels' for use as postage, but he was only one of many who claimed to have 'invented' the adhesive stamp. Another was Laurenz Koschier, the centenary of whose death was commemorated by Austria with a special 'Europa' stamp in 1979. It seems that the idea, and the design, of Britain's new stamps just emerged from a host of suggestions and essays, and that Hill himself elected the use of the Queen's portrait as their main feature, adopting the size and format of contemporary tax labels. Thus were born the Penny Black and Twopence Blue.

A preliminary step towards the reduction of postal charges and, incidentally, the abolition of 'free franking' and the time-wasting assessment of the

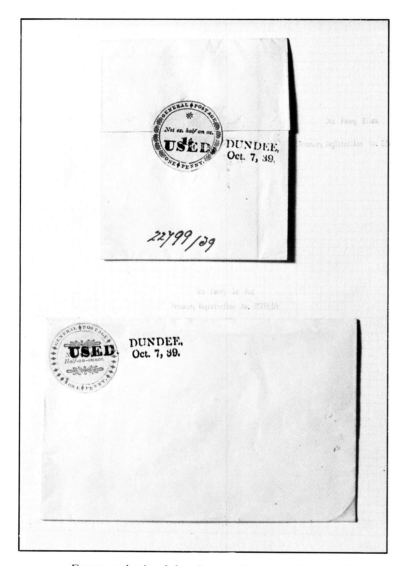

Essays submitted by James Chalmers for the Treasury competition.

number of sheets in a letter, was effected in December 1839 when a 'compromise' postage rate of fourpence an ounce was introduced, applicable everywhere except in London where the local rate came down to one penny, and existing 'penny posts' in other towns. Then, on 10 January 1840, Hill's grand scheme – uniform penny postage – was introduced throughout the country. The stamps, letter-sheets and envelopes had not been printed in sufficient quantities for their release at that time, hence letters were accepted with the cash over post office counters and marked 'Paid' with a handstamp. This practice was permitted to continue until 1853, when the use of adhesive stamps became compulsory.

'A Life Well Spent'

While Rowland Hill enjoyed the confidence of the Treasury, his relations with the Post Office were far from cordial. The Secretary of the Post Office,

Colonel Maberly, and his colleagues resented Hill's radical changes in the operation of the postal service. They were as unco-operative as they dared, but Hill successfully by-passed their opposition and carried through his master plan. All went well until September 1842 when, following the defeat of Lord Melbourne's Liberal Government in the general election, Hill was dismissed from his position at the Treasury. His services to the out-going government were barely acknowledged and there was a public outcry over his dismissal: this was expressed in tangible form four years later, in June 1846, when he was presented with the sum of £13,000, raised by public subscription.

Meanwhile, Hill turned his attention to the railways and became Chairman of the London & Brighton Railway Company – he lived in Brighton after leaving the Treasury and he was able to contribute many ideas for improved services as a regular commuter to London. Then, in November 1846, following another change of government, Hill was offered – and accepted – the post of Secretary to the Postmaster-General. It was not the supreme post, but nevertheless he picked up the reins and suggested, or brought into use many innovations, all directed towards a more efficient operation of the postal service. At last, in 1854, he was appointed Secretary to the Post Office, and for the next ten years he was able to consolidate many of the improvements he had inaugurated, while at the same time introducing new schemes aimed at speeding-up the deliveries of mail.

In 1860, Rowland Hill was made a Knight Commander of the Order of the Bath by Queen Victoria in recognition of his outstanding services to his country in reorganizing the posts and introducing the world's first adhesive postage stamps. Then in 1864, he was overtaken by ill-health and was forced to retire from the Post Office. At last his achievements were fully acknowledged, and he was granted a pension equal to his full salary for the remainder of his life, and an award of £20,000 from the Exchequer. He wrote his memoirs, based on the famous diaries which were eventually lodged in the postal museum at Bruce Castle, and which were published – *The Life of Sir Rowland Hill and the History of Penny Postage* – in 1880, the year following his death.

The last of the many honours accorded to him was the Freedom of the City of London in 1879 – later that year, on 27 August, he died at his Hampstead home, and the nation mourned his demise. Sir Rowland, who was 84, was given a state funeral and lies buried in St Paul's Chapel, Westminster Abbey. So passed a 'man of great genius, sagacity, perseverance and industry', one who devoted some 40 years to postal reforms which changed and improved communications beyond all recognition, and who pursued him aims with foresight, energy and tenacity. For 'The Father of the Penny Post', it was truly 'a life well spent'.

The statue of Sir Rowland Hill outside the Chief Post Office in the city of London.

Two of the stamps issued in 1979 marking the centenary of the death of Sir Rowland Hill (St. Vincent and Guyana).

In retrospect, it can be seen that many of Hill's ideas, other than a uniform postal rate and the use of adhesive stamps, were adopted, bore fruit at a later date or were the inspiration for others to develop. 'A letter-box for every house' was one of his original campaigns, and the first post-boxes in the streets of London were erected in London in 1855, following the success of an experimental pillar-box set up in St Helier, Jersey, on the suggestion of Anthony Trollope, the novelist and Post Office surveyor's clerk. He promoted an underground railway to speed the mails across London – a pneumatic railway was in experimental use for several years from 1863, but the Post Office railway did not materialize until 1927. At long last, in 1854, Hill succeeded in integrating the operations of the London and General Posts, and, in 1856, he divided London into the now familiar postal districts – N, NW, W, WC etc., each with its own receiving and sorting office.

His own son, Pearson Hill, joined the Post Office in 1850 and is best remembered for his experimental machine cancellations of 1857-8, and his invention of the 'duplex' combined datestamp and canceller which was in constant use from 1858 until about 1909. Pearson's son, Colonel Henry Warburton Hill, was a distinguished soldier with a CMG, also a DSO and other medals to his credit. He, too, wrote a fascinating book – *Rowland Hill and the Fight for Penny Post,* published in 1940.

Several statues were erected to the memory of Sir Rowland Hill. The one most familiar to Londoners stands outside the main entrance of the King Edward Building which, completed in 1910 and standing within a stone's throw of St Martin's-le-Grand, houses the Chief Post Office and the National Postal Museum. From his lofty vantage-point he is still spiritually in charge of postal operations, and surveys all that goes on around him.

The famous 'Wyon head' – a medal produced to mark Queen Victoria's visit to the City of London, 1837.

2
The First Stamps

To say that Rowland Hill 'invented' the adhesive postage stamp is to revive a controversy which has persisted ever since Britain issued the world's first stamp – the famous Penny Black – on 6 May 1840 (the Twopence Blue followed two days later – on 8 May). We have seen how the Treasury Competition brought a multiplicity of suggested designs, mostly unacceptable, but it seems that Hill was greatly influenced in his evolved design by the sketches submitted by Benjamin Cheverton – who advocated the embossing of 'a female head of the greatest beauty, to be executed by Mr. Wyon', as a precaution against forgery. The female head in his drawings was that of the Queen, based on the portrait of the sovereign engraved by William Wyon for the commemorative City Medal of 1837, the prototype for the issued stamps. Cheverton received £100 in the Treasury Competition for 'consultation'.

William Wyon, born in Birmingham of a famous family of medallists, came to London seeking fame and fortune in 1815. He became Chief Engraver at the Royal Mint in 1828, and subsequently Engraver of Seals to the Queen, and a member of the Royal Academy. His portrait medallion head of the young Queen Victoria appeared on the early coinage of her reign, but it was the City Medal head which Rowland Hill instructed the stamp printers, Perkins, Bacon and Petch, to use as a basis for the engraved die – the stamps were to be printed by the line-engraving process. Henry Corbould was commissioned to prepare a watercolour sketch of the Queen's head, taken from the medal which had been struck in honour of her visit to the Guildhall in the City of London upon her accession.

The printers, meanwhile, busied themselves with

Above, top; Henry Corbould, whose sketch of the young Queen Victoria was used as the model for the Sovereign's head on the Penny Black and Twopence Blue (above).

preparations for engraving the supplementary parts of the stamp design which, complying with Rowland Hill's specifications, were to include an engine-turned background, intricate 'banknote'-style borders, small ornaments in the form of 'stars' in the upper corners, and an alphabetical sequence of capital letters in the lower corners – all precautions against forgery. The rose engine or lathe, and the unique steel-plate printing process (described in Chapter 5) were specialities of the Perkins, Bacon company, having been brought to England by Jacob Perkins when he arrived from the United States in 1819.

The corner letters served to identify the location of every stamp on the plate, or printed sheet, of 240 stamps, arranged in 20 horizontal rows of 12. The first stamp in the top row was lettered AA, the last in the row, AL; the first in the second row was BA, progressing to BL; and so on down the sheet to TA and TL at the beginning and end of row 20. The letters were hand-punched in the corner squares of the design in the final stages of plate-making. An additional safeguard was the inclusion of a special 'Crown' watermark in the handmade paper on which the stamps were printed.

From Corbould's drawing, Charles Heath and his son, Frederick, engraved the Queen's profile (the portrait which was to be used on stamps, as it transpired, throughout her reign), utilizing the blank space on the master die which had been initially prepared by the printers. The inscription 'POSTAGE' appeared at the top of the stamp and 'ONE PENNY' (or 'TWO PENCE') at the foot, while each sheet of stamps was inscribed across the margin 'Price 1d. per Label, 1s. per Row of 12, £1 per Sheet. Place the Labels ABOVE the Address and towards the RIGHT HAND SIDE of the

Charles Heath (1785-1848). Engraver of the Master Die for the world's first adhesive postage stamp.

Letter. In Wetting the Back be careful not to remove the Cement.' The 'cement' was, of course, the gum on the back of the stamps, which were imperforate and had to be removed from the sheet by scissors or a knife.

Perhaps the most striking feature of the new stamps was the omission of the country name. Since Great Britain was the only country issuing stamps in 1840 and they were, in effect, 'locals' – valid only in the United Kingdom – the Queen's head must have been considered sufficiently authoritative. This omission, almost unique among stamp-issuing countries, has been continued as a tradition by Great Britain ever since.

A block of 1d. black stamps from the corner of a sheet showing marginal inscription – details of the selling price.

The printers worked day and night to build up stocks and maintain supplies. They produced an average of about six million 1d. blacks each month – reputedly 68 or 70 million altogether – at a cost to the government of 6d. per thousand. Eleven different plates were laid down and used for the 1d. black, two only for the 2d. blue. The postage rate on an ordinary letter – 1d. per half-ounce – had been established on 10 January 1840 ('uniform penny postage'), and the Post Office had anticipated the greater demand for the 1d. stamps when they were first made available to the public on 1 May. Printing of the 2d. stamps (for one-ounce letters) did not commence until the beginning of May. The new stamps sold well and were at once accepted by the public, much to the surprise of Rowland Hill, who had expected greater use to be made of his letter-sheets and envelopes, issued on 6 May.

Designed by William Mulready, these elaborately decorative items of postal stationery were, in modern parlance, an 'instant flop'. The uniform design showed Britannia with the British lion at her feet, 'presiding over the ocean' and greeting the peoples of the world who were ranged on either flank in groups, including Chinese, a Laplander and Red Indians, with space below for the address. The Mulready letter-sheets and envelopes were greeted with scorn and ridicule, and numerous Victorian-style caricature envelopes appeared, lampooning Mulready's designs. The 1d. envelope was withdrawn in January 1841, the 2d. envelope in the following April, and the letter-sheets in 1844.

In addition to the ordinary postage stamps, Rowland Hill ordered special 1d. blacks for official use, replacing the 'free franking' privileges which had been withdrawn with the introduction of uniform

The VR 1d. black designed for use on mail posted from government departments. The idea of this special stamp for official mail was abandoned after only a few sheets had been used.

Above: A yellow Maltese Cross cancellation, used at Horsham, Sussex. Right: William Mulready, the designer of the decorated envelopes. Lower right: a Victorian lampoon of the Mulready envelope.

penny postage in January 1840. These stamps were printed with the letters 'VR' ('Victoria Regina') in the upper corners in place of the 'stars'. After some 3,500 sheets had been printed, the idea of special stamps for government offices was abandoned and they were never brought into use. A few specimens are known to exist unused and postally used, and are extremely rare. They are listed in the stamp catalogues as 'Prepared for use, but not issued'.

The first postmark canceller used on the 1d. black and 2d. blue stamps was in the shape of a Maltese Cross, applied in red ink, a colour long used by the Post Office to indicate that postage had been paid. Prior to the issue of the stamps, postmasters were told 'not to fail to provide yourself with the necessary supply of Red Composition by that time' (6 May). The stamps, however, were not printed with fugitive inks, and numerous cases of them being cleaned and re-used came to the notice of the Post Office – the one kind of fraudulent use Rowland Hill had not anticipated! So, in February 1841, the colour of the 1d. stamps was changed from black to red-brown, with the ink made fugitive by the addition of prussiate of potash. The 2d. blue was similarly treated – white lines were added to the design to distinguish the new printing – while black ink was used thereafter for postmarking.

The Maltese Cross cancellations remained in use until 1844 and are known in other colours besides red

and black – blue, magenta and yellow crosses are extremely rare. The 1d. red stamps lasted, in various forms, almost 40 years and are probably the most common Victorian stamps. Perforated stamps first appeared in February 1854, following experiments by Henry Archer. The classics of British stamps, however, have always remained the 1d. black and 2d. blue.

The Primitives

Other countries of the world were slow to follow Britain's lead in the issue of postage stamps. Brazil and the Swiss cantons of Geneva and Zurich produced their first stamps in 1843; none is recorded for 1844, and in 1845, Basle (another Swiss canton) and the United States' postmasters issued stamps. There followed Mauritius and the United States (Government issues) in 1847, the Bermuda postmasters' stamps in 1848 and Bavaria, Belgium and France in 1849.

Numerous countries, colonies and states issued stamps between 1850 and 1860, and all these early issues are the 'primitives' or 'classics' of the collector's world. Primitives only qualify as such if they were conceived, designed and produced in their countries of origin, and the dies *and* plates were hand-engraved, or designs lithographed or type-set, by local craftsmen. Therein lies the fascination of the primitive stamp.

US Postmasters' Provisionals, 1845-1847

These stamps and envelopes were issued by the post-masters of certain cities and towns in the United States to facilitate the prepayment of postage, prior to the introduction of the general issues in 1847. Most are rare – in some cases only a single copy is known to exist; some are neat, well-printed labels, others mere hand-stamps, and stamped envelopes are known.

The five cent black on buff stamp of Alexandria, Virginia, was issued by Postmaster Daniel Bryan in 1846 – it was inscribed 'PAID 5' in the centre with the town name in typical Mid-Western lettering around the circular design. Postmaster Martin F. Revell of Annapolis, Maryland, issued a stamped envelope in 1846, the imprinted red stamp featuring the American Eagle with '5 PAID' printed alongside it. Postmaster James M. Buchanan, of Baltimore, used his own signature on envelopes and stamps in 1845.

Only one copy is known of the crude five cent stamp issued by Postmaster Worcester Webster at Boscawen, New Hampshire – the known copy, uncancelled on an envelope, subsequently passed through many famous hands, including Ferrary and Arthur Hind. The Brattleboro, Vermont, five cent black on buff, issued by Postmaster Frederick N. Palmer, was an unostentatious little stamp, printed from a copper plate reproducing the postmaster's initials, while the solitary existing Lockport, New York, five cent red and black, issued by Postmaster Hezekiah W. Scovell, was a crude oval handstamp. The five cent black on azure stamp produced by the Millbury, Massachusetts postmaster, Colonel Asa H. Walters, was circular in shape, bearing a likeness of George Washington. All these stamps were issued in 1846.

In 1845, the New Haven, Connecticut, postmaster, E.A. Mitchell, issued five cent envelopes handstamped in red or blue, with his own signature in purple (on the red) or black (on the blue). Postmaster Robert H. Morris of New York commissioned the banknote engravers, to print five cent black stamps from a steel plate, professional style. The die for the head of Washington was identical to that used for the current banknotes and, although hardly primitives in the accepted sense, these stamps were the forerunners of the US general issues of 1847 which are strikingly similar in appearance. Morris issued his stamps in 1845 – most copies were initialled in red ink, 'R.H.M.', or by his deputy, Alonzo Castle Monson ('A.C.M.').

Welcome B. Sayles, the Postmaster of Providence, Rhode Island, issued five cent and ten cent stamps in a small, rectangular design in 1846.

Perhaps the most famous of the US Postmasters' stamps are the St Louis (Missouri) 'Bears' – 5, 10 and 20 cents – printed in black on coloured wove paper, and issued by Postmaster John M. Wimer in November 1845. The design featured the Missouri arms with two standing bears as supporters – hence the popular nickname. The rarest of them is the 20 cents: only 20 are known.

The famous 1d. and 2d. 'Post Office' stamps of Mauritius – the first issue of 1847 (SG 1 and 2).

Mauritius 'Post Office', 1847

The first British colony to issue stamps was a beautiful, remote island in the Indian Ocean – Mauritius. Inhabited by the French for almost a hundred years, the island was occupied by the British in 1810, and formally ceded to Great Britain under the Treaty of Paris in 1814. In 1847, the Governor of Mauritius, Sir William Gomm, ordered stamps through the Crown Agents, from Perkins, Bacon and Co., who were preparing to supply various British colonies with stamps in a uniform 'Britannia' design. But when the stamps showed no prospect of being delivered, an engraver of Port Louis, J. Barnard, was commissioned to engrave a copper plate and print stamps modelled on the British 1d. red and 2d. blue. It is said that he was urged to complete the work quickly as the stamps were required by Lady Gomm to be used on invitations to a ball at Government House. (A stamped envelope containing an invitation is in the Royal Philatelic Collection.)

Barnard printed 500 each of the 1d. orange-red and 2d. blue stamps directly, one at a time, from the plate, and they were placed on sale on 21 September 1847. The entire issue was sold in a few days and nothing was heard of them until years later. They are now among the rarest stamps in the world.

The 'Britannias' were not placed on sale in Mauritius until 1854, and in the interim there were

Bermuda, Postmasters' stamp,
signed by W. B. Perot, Postmaster
of Hamilton (1848) (SG O1).

A modern issue of Mauritius depicting the famous 2d. 'Post Office' stamp and the Post Office building as it was before 1870 (SG 419).

more primitives – stamps very similar to the 'Post Office' types inscribed 'POST PAID', issued in 1848, and a deplorable series engraved by Lapirot, re-engraved by Sherwin and lithographed by Dardenne, all in 1859.

Bermuda Postmasters' Stamps, 1848-1861

William B. Perot, Postmaster of Hamilton, Bermuda, issued his own crude stamps from 1848 onwards, and these, too, are now among the greatest rarities. Though rated as provisionals rather than primitives, the stamps are of great historic interest and reflect life and times in the colony. Perot was allowed to keep the fees he collected for postage on local letters, and he installed a special box where letters (and pennies) could be deposited after normal hours. Often the letters outnumbered the pennies and, as he had no means of identifying the culprits, he decided to produce his own stamps.

While postmarking letters with his little handstamp, the idea of using the postmarker occurred to him. The circular cancellation was already inscribed 'Hamilton Bermuda' and with the year – he made imprints of the postmark on sheets of paper, wrote 'One Penny' and his signature on each, and cut them to size. Thereafter his customers were obliged to purchase the 'Perot' stamps before he would accept their letters for the post. J.H. Thies, the postmaster at St Georges, Bermuda, used his Crown Circle 'Paid' handstamp as a postage stamp in 1860, and it is interesting that Perot adopted a similar mark for his last recorded issue in 1861. Neither of these stamps indicated the amount of postage paid.

New South Wales 'Sydney Views', 1850

The famous 'Sydney Views', the first stamps of New South Wales, Australia, were designed by Robert Clayton of Sydney. The 'view', forerunner of the

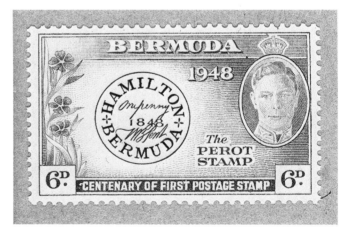

A Bermuda stamp marking the centenary of Perot's post, 1949 (SG 129); and a stamp of 1959 depicting Bermuda's Post Office c. 1848 (SG 156).

colony's badge, showed Sydney Harbour with, in the foreground; a statuesque group of immigrants 'sitting on their luggage at the quayside', and a ship in the bay. It was an original, attractive design, enhanced by fine engraving and rich colours. The frame, with its familiar lettering and corner 'stars', was clearly derived from Britain's 1d. red and 2d. blue.

Each of the three values – 1d., 2d. and 3d. – was produced from a single plate, engraved on copper by Clayton, John Carmichael and H.C. Jervis respectively. These plates were exceedingly soft so that the earliest impressions were fine and clear, the later printings showing signs of extreme wear with correspondingly faint impressions. The numerous stamps subsequently printed from renewed and re-engraved plates on various types of paper provide a fine field of philatelic study of shades and varieties.

First stamps of New South Wales and Victoria commemorated by Australia, 1950 (SG 239-40).

The 'Sydney Views' were followed in 1851 by the 'Laureated' issues which 'restored the monarchy' in the sense that New South Wales had been unique at that time in not portraying the Queen on her first stamps. The 1d. and 2d. stamps showed a rather 'chicken-necked' profile of Her Majesty wearing a 'crown of laurel', and the plates were engraved by Carmichael, and later, Jervis.

Victoria 'Half Lengths', 1850

The State of Victoria was so eager to issue its own postage stamps that it produced dies, plates and stamps though still legally part of New South Wales, and, furthermore, continued to do so through the years to about 1912 with only three exceptions. Thomas Ham's unique design for Victoria's first stamps showed the Queen seated, wearing a crown and holding the orb and sceptre – a full-face portrait which has been described as a 'pleasant, plump, nursery story-book Queen'. Ham engraved the dies on a single piece of steel and printed the stamps by the lithograph process from transfers.

Hawaii, one of the 'Missionary' issue of 1851 (SG 3).

The stamps are known as the 'Half Lengths' because of the nature of the portrait – in 1852 Thomas Ham engraved another design for Victoria (which by then had become a separate colony), showing a full-length portrait of the Queen seated on the coronation chair, known to philatelists as the 'Queen on Throne' stamps. This design was subsequently adapted and improved by Perkins, Bacon in 1856.

British Guiana 'Cottonreels', 1850-1851

For simple charm, the famous type-set 'Cottonreels' of British Guiana are probably unique. Much of that charm evolves from the coloured wove papers upon which the 'postmark-style' design was printed in black. A single-lined circle enclosed the country name, 'BRITISH GUIANA', and the face values – 2, 4, 8 or 12 cents. The stamps were printed in sheets at the offices of the *Royal Gazette* in Georgetown, and they were first issued on 1 July 1850. Their nickname was derived from the similarity of the stamps to the end-papers of reels of cotton.

To discourage forgery, the stamps were initialled by the postmaster or his clerks before they were issued, in variously coloured inks, sometimes in pencil. All the 'Cottonreels' are rare and the difference in value between the 'cut-round' and the highly prized 'cut square' stamps is very considerable. An envelope with a used pair of the two cents, ex-Ferrary, is in the Royal Philatelic Collection.

Hawaii 'Missionaries', 1851

The famous Hawaiian 'Missionaries' were authorized by a local government bill with the object of improving postal traffic between Hawaii and the United States, and the onus of providing the stamps fell upon a local store-keeper, printer and publisher, H.M. Whitney, who was appointed postmaster and given full rein to run the postal service for his own profit. There were two denominations – two cents and three cents – for internal use, and 13 cents for letters going abroad.

The stamps were type-set and printed in blue on thin, brittle strips of paper and were a typical printer's concoction – the bold figure of value within a square of squiggles and fancy type, the inscription 'Hawaiian Postage' at the top and the face value repeated at the foot. They were issued in October 1851, and, in November 1852, a second printing of the 13 cents was issued with the country name changed to 'HI & US Postage' – 'Hawaiian Islands and United States Postage'. The Hawaiian 'Missionaries' acquired their nickname because of the extensive use of them by the American missionaries in Hawaii in their correspondence to friends and relations. The stamps now rank among the world's greatest rarities.

Trinidad 'Lithographs', 1852-1860

Trinidad, first of the West Indian colonies to issue postage stamps, employed a design originally intended for Mauritius, depicting the seated figure of Britannia, produced by Perkins, Bacon, and issued in August 1851. A year later, the Trinidad authorities ran short of the engraved stamps, and ordered provisional issues from a local printer. The stamps were lithographed from a die engraved by Charles Petit, who made a passable imitation of the Britannia stamps – at first he produced some fine impressions, but, as they were frequently brought into use to meet shortages of the Perkins, Bacon stamps until 1860, the quality sadly deteriorated. The stamps bore no face values – they were identified by their colours which differed from those of the regular stamps – and the postage rate was, in fact, 1d. for inland letters.

Réunion, 1852

If the Mauritius 'Post Office' stamps were inspired by Britain's 1d. red, then it is likely that the idea and the format for the first stamps of neighbouring Réunion, one of France's oldest colonies, were likewise derived from the original French issues of 1849. The 15 and 30 cent black stamps were type-set and printed by M. Lahuppe, the local printer in St Denis, the island's capital, and, like the famous 'Missionaries' of Hawaii, displayed liberal use of printers' fancy type and ornament – floral and geometrical patterns framed by printers' rules. They were inscribed 'Ile de la Réunion – Timb. Poste' in tiny lettering at top and foot.

Tasmania, 1853

The first adhesive stamps of Tasmania, issued on 1 November 1853, were inscribed 'Van Diemen's Land' – Abel Tasman, the Dutch navigator who dis-

Australia – 1953 stamp commemorating the centenary of the first Tasmanian postage stamp (SG 271).

covered the island in 1642, was in command of an expedition sent out by Van Diemen, Governor of the Dutch East India Company. They were 1d. blue and 4d. orange stamps, bearing a small, fanciful profile of Queen Victoria (barely recognizable as such), facing to the right. The 1d. was in the usual format of the times, the oval portrait set in a rectangular frame, while the 4d. was an octagonal design having an oval frame within. C.W. Coard engraved the stamps which were printed by H. and C. Best at the *Courier* newspaper office in Hobart.

India, 1854

On 1 July 1852 the so-called 'Scinde Dawk' stamps were issued under the authority of Sir Bartle Frere, Commissioner in Scinde (Sind). These small wax discs – they resembled seals – were embossed by De La Rue and are therefore not strictly primitives, though, nevertheless, they are quite rare. They were half anna stamps in white, blue and scarlet.

India's first real stamps were designed at the surveyor-general's office in Calcutta, and reproduced by lithography, the half anna blue and one anna red being issued on 1 October 1854. Again one sees the influence of contemporary British stamps in the simple, rectangular design – the same profile of the Queen derived from Wyon's head, the inscriptions 'INDIA' (top) and 'HALF ANNA' or 'ONE ANNA' at the foot, and the ornaments in the upper corners.

A fortnight later, on 15 October, an octagonal four anna stamp appeared, preceded by the two anna green in the normal format some few days earlier. The bizarre blue and red octagonal stamps – the first British stamps to be printed in two colours – were printed from head and frame plates. Inverted heads are known and rare.

Above, top: The world's most famous stamp, the 1c. black on magenta of 1856, British Guiana (SG 23).
Above: Guyana publicized its unique stamp in a commemorative issue of 1967 (SG 414).

British Guiana 'One Cent' Black on Magenta, 1856

'The World's Rarest Stamp' – a unique distinction – is the British Guiana one cent black on magenta issued in 1856. It is the only one of its particular kind in existence and it was discovered quite by chance. The story begins early that year when the current stamps became exhausted and further supplies of the regular 'Ship' issues from the printers, Waterlow and Sons of London, were delayed. The Georgetown postmaster ordered a provisional supply of one cent and four cent stamps from Joseph Baum and William Dallas, the publishers and printers of the local *Royal Gazette* (who also printed the earlier 'Cottonreels'). In an attempt to reproduce the existing design, they employed a printing block of a sailing vessel which normally headed their 'Shipping News' page, and included the motto *Damus Petimus que Vicissim* ('We give and we seek in turn').

Cape of Good Hope – 1d. and 4d. 'wood block' stamps of 1861. At the base of the page, Cape triangulars reproduced on modern South African commemoratives (SG 144 and 145).

The one cent stamp was used almost exclusively for the local delivery of newspapers, mainly the *Gazette* itself, and few people kept the wrappers. Consequently, nothing was heard of the type-set one cent provisionals until 1873, when a young schoolboy collector, L. Vernon Vaughan of British Guiana, came across a rather battered and grubby specimen amongst old family letters. It was initialled by Postmaster E.D. Wright (as was the custom) and postmarked 'Demerara AP 4 1856'. He sold it to a fellow collector, N. McKinnon, for six shillings and five years later he in turn sold his collection, including the mystery one cent, to a Liverpool dealer.

The dealer, Thomas Ridpath, soon afterwards sold the precious stamp to Renotière von Ferrary in whose possession it remained until the Ferrary sales in Paris in the early 1920s, when it was purchased by Arthur Hind, the American millionaire for a record 300,000 francs – about £7,300. After Hind's death the stamp was sold in America for $45,000 (1940), in 1970 for $280,000 and again in April 1980 at auction for $850,000 in New York.

Australia – 1954 commemorative for the centenary of the Western Australia 'Black Swan' stamp (SG 277).

Western Australia 'Swan', 1857

The first stamps for Western Australia, issued in 1854, were engraved and printed by Perkins, Bacon and Co. – they featured the colony badge, a black swan, in horizontal format with the same dimensions as the Penny Black. This primitive is the issue of 'temporisers' – 2d. and 6d. stamps in similar design, lithographed by A. Hillman, the local government printer, during a temporary shortage, in 1857. The design was similar to the regular 4d. Swan with the same clipped corners, but the printing was coarse and the lettering poor. The stamps were issued imperforate and rouletted, and the 2d. is known printed both sides.

Moldavia (Rumania), the 'Bulls' – from the 1858 issue (SG 1 and 3).

Moldavia 'Bulls', 1858

Moldavia, the ancient principality occupied in turn by the Russians, Austrians and Turks in the early 19th century, and now a province of Rumania, issued her first stamps on 15 July 1858. The stamps were among the most primitive ever issued, being handstruck one at a time on sheets of coloured paper, a sheet comprising two rows of eight stamps, 16 in all. The circular design featured a bull's head above a posthorn with the figures of value – 27, 54, 81 or 108 parales – within the horn's oval handgrip. The 'parale' was the local equivalent of the Turkish para and similarly represented the fortieth part of a piastre.

The Moldavian 'Bulls' were withdrawn on 31 October 1858 and the remainders were eventually destroyed. On 1 November the 'Bulls' reappeared in rectangular format, inscribed 'PORTO GAZETE' (for newspapers) and 'PORTO SCRISORE' (for letters) – again these were handstruck, imperforate stamps in new values relating to reduced postal rates – 5, 40 and 80 parales. In 1862, Moldavia united with neighbouring Wallachia to form the nucleus of Rumania as 'Moldo-Wallachia' – the bull this time shared stamp space with an emblematic figure representing Wallachia.

Cape of Good Hope 'Woodblocks', 1861

The Perkins, Bacon triangular stamps were imitated when, during an acute shortage of the 1d. and 4d. stamps in Cape Town, local provisionals, the so-called 'woodblocks' (due to their crude appearance) were engraved on steel by C.J. Roberts, and printed by typography from stereo plates prepared by Saul Solomon and Co. on laid paper. The 1d. vermilion and 4d. blue 'woodblocks' were issued between February and April 1861, during which time the 'missing' supply of new stamps from London was lying in a Cape Town harbour store awaiting clearance.

There were several printings and consequently numerous shades. In the course of these printings, when it became necessary to replace worn clichés, two of them, a 1d. and a 4d., were accidentally inter-

changed, resulting in the printing of both values, one stamp in every sheet, in the wrong colours. The 1d. in blue, and the 4d. in vermilion, are now extremely rare and valuable stamps. The Tapling Collection in the British Library has an impressive array of 'woodblocks', including the errors of colour, forgeries and reprints.

The first Japanese stamp of 1871 depicted on 1946 commemorative, marking the 75th anniversary of the Japanese postal service (SG 438).

Japan 'Dragons', 1871

The first stamps of Japan were separately hand-engraved on the plate and must therefore be classified as primitives, although they are among the best produced of them all. In Japan there were many engravers on wood, few who could engrave on copper. One of the few was Atsutomo Matsuda, who had made plates for the new paper currency and adapted the same designs to the stamps. There were four denominations – 48, 100, 200 and 500 mon – each featuring two dragons standing upright ('rampant'), facing inwards to the 'kanji' or Japanese characters representing the face values. Each stamp was slightly different, including some 'mild-looking dragons' and some angry ones. The stamps were issued on 20 April 1871.

'Primitive' Round-up

Numerous other countries produced their own first stamps, and there are undoubtedly primitives among them, in appearance if not by definition. Often they were mere labels, produced in a hurry for a provisional stamp début. In Fiji, for example, the *Fiji Times*

launched an 'express' postal service with the issue of type-set stamps in 1870. In the same year, Afghanistan issued her first stamps – the Afghan 'Lions'. These were circular in design, with the head of the lion in the centre, and they were each drawn separately on the litho plates, thus they differ in detail. Certain stamps of the Indian native states (the 'Feudatory States') were weird and wonderful creations, exotic and incomprehensible to Western eyes eg: Bhor (1879), Bundi (1894), Dhar (1897), Jammu and Kashmir (1866), Jind (1874), Poonch (1876) and Rajpipla (1880).

During the American Civil War (1861-5) the postmasters of the Confederate States (as the 11 southern states were known), remembering that some of their colleagues in other states had issued their own provisional stamps some 15 years earlier, followed suit. There were 38 of them in all, ranging from Athens, Georgia, to Victoria, Texas, and, later in 1861, these were followed by a general issue, as the Union issues continued to be denied to the 'Feds'.

South America was another lucrative source of the quaint and the primitive, notably the Buenos Aires, Cordoba and Corrientes forerunners of Argentine stamps (1856-58), the Uruguay 'Suns' of 1856 and 1859, Bolivia's 'Condor' (1866) and the early issues of Colombia from 1859. Peru's first government-sponsored stamps were issued on 1 March 1858, after the Pacific Steam Navigation Co. had handed over their provisional issues for general use.

The Classics

The word 'classic' is defined as 'a work of the highest class, rank or distinction', originally ascribed to the best Greek and Roman writers or to the old masters in music. Philatelists long ago adopted the word when referring to the early postage stamps, the main condition of its appellation being the quality of print and production. Britain's first stamps were the first classics – the real 'old masters' of the stamp world, and they set a standard which was an example and an inspiration to all other stamp-issuing countries.

The news of Britain's postal innovations of 1840 only gradually spread around the world, though as early as 1842 a firm of New York carriers inaugurated a local mail delivery service, the 'City Despatch Post', and produced stamps bearing an engraved portrait of George Washington. They were used at a time when ordinary pre-paid mail was carried only from post office to post office, even in the largest cities and towns, to enable letters to be delivered to the addressee – numerous other US carriers issued their own stamps for similar purposes from 1849 to about 1860.

Brazil's 'Bull's Eyes', 1843

The extraordinary thing about the first Brazilian stamps, issued on 1 August 1843, was that, somehow,

The 'Pack Strip' of Brazilian
Bull's Eyes, 1843 (SG 1 and 2).

the authorities acquired Perkins, Bacon-style equipment – including a transfer roller – and engraved dies from which they prepared plates of 54 stamps, each plate comprising panes of 18 of each value – 30, 60 and 90 reis. The designs featured large, ornamental figures of value within oval settings, hence their nickname, 'bull's eyes', and the arrangement of the stamps in the sheet permitted *se-tenant* pairs, that is, stamps of two different denominations joined together in a pair. A classic example was the 'Pack Strip' – it was owned by an American collector, Charles Lathrop Pack – which was a vertical strip of three containing a pair of the 30 reis *se-tenant* with the 60 reis, the most famous item in Brazilian stamps. The stamps bore no country name or other inscription.

These stamps were followed in 1844 by smaller, rectangular designs with italic or inclined numerals of value, the *Inclinados* or 'snake's eyes', and in 1850 by smaller versions of the original 'bull's eyes' which became known as the 'goat's eyes' or, if blue instead of the customary black colour, 'cat's eyes'. Small high-value stamps appeared in 1861 – it was not until 1866 that Brazil honoured Emperor Dom Pedro II with his portrait on stamps. There are two interesting theories as to why that honour was delayed. One was that, in 1843, there was no one in the Rio Treasury who was sufficiently skilled to engrave such a portrait in the time available; the other was that there was objection to the prospect of the Emperor's likeness being obliterated by postmarks!

The Swiss 'Cantonals', 1843-1845

Zurich won the distinction of issuing the first adhesive postage stamps in Europe, following Britain's lead, and the 'large numeral' four rappen (postal rate within the city) and six rappen (rate within the canton) were issued on 1 March 1843. The numerals were bold and 'fat', and, for security reasons, the stamps had a background diamond pattern lithographed within a 'Penny Black' format, and, as an additional safeguard, a ground of horizontal or vertical red lines. These were virtually Switzerland's first stamps.

Geneva's stamps appeared on 30 September 1843 – the idea of M. Candolle, who had been in England in 1839 when the first stamps were about to be issued there. The lithographed five cent stamps showed the arms of Geneva, and were issued in joined pairs, hence their sobriquet, 'Double Geneva'. Again, one five cent stamp was the cost of a letter within Geneva itself, ten cent within the canton, and the pairs of stamps had a 'bridge' across them inscribed 'Port Cantonal'. The Genevans, however, were uncertain how or when to use these 'dual-purpose' stamps – some pairs were cut through horizontally and single stamps were bisected and used thus – and a few months later the pairs were sold at a discount to encourage sales.

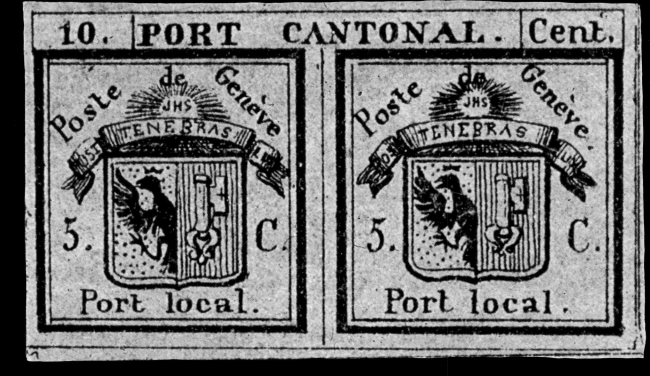

Switzerland 'Double Geneva'
Cantonal stamp, 1843 (SG G1).

Pair of Zürich Cantonal
stamps of 1843 (SG Z1).

The Swiss canton of Basle produced the first multicoloured stamp, issued on 1 July 1845. Inscribed 'STADT POST BASEL', it featured the so-called Dove of Basel – the bird, actually an eagle, was embossed on an engraved background resembling an inn-sign. The face value was two and a half rappen, and the stamp was delightfully coloured in carmine, black and blue.

The first Swiss Federal stamps, issued under the aegis of the newly-formed Federal Constitution, appeared in 1850.

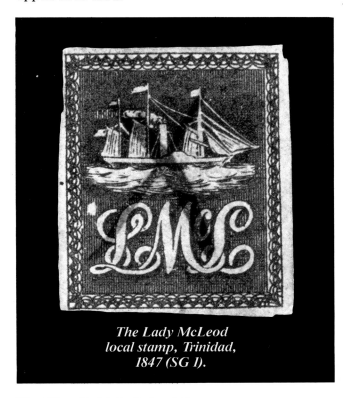

The Lady McLeod
local stamp, Trinidad,
1847 (SG 1).

The First British Colonials

Private enterprise and initiative which had led to the creation of the Mauritius 'Post Office' and Bermuda 'Perot' stamps also played a part in Trinidad, an island in the British West Indies, famous for its oil, asphalt, sugar and rum. Here, in April 1847, David Bryce, owner of the SS *Lady McLeod,* a coaster employed on the Port of Spain – San Fernando run, issued five cent stamps for the prepayment of the carriage of letters between the two ports, a distance of about 40 miles. The design of this attractive blue stamp showed the vessel at 'full steam ahead' in the upper half of the stamp, and the large script initials 'L Mc L' in the lower half. For many years, stamp collectors in other parts of the world did not know of its existence and it was at first regarded with suspicion: it is now a rare and valuable stamp. Trinidad's first Government-issued stamps appeared in 1851.

In 1850, the 'classic' sun rose over British Guiana, New South Wales and Victoria. The primitive forerunners of the stamps of these three colonies have already been described and, in the course of time, the London printers contributed regular supplies of less spectacular, though more professional, stamps. The Guiana sailing ship, in 'Penny Black' format, was current from 1853 to 1876, when smaller, neater 'ship' stamps, printed letterpress by De La Rue, replaced the Waterlow-printed lithographed issues. In the interim there was a local release of type-set stamps (1862) which consisted of frames without a central design. In New South Wales the ubiquitous 'Penny Black' head of the Queen (which will be referred to as the 'Wyon' head) took over, and one notes the name of E.H. Corbould as designer. Victoria continued with rather dull series of Victorian portraits, again Wyon-inspired.

During the next 20 years or so, it was the Wyon Medal and the Chalon Head which established the likeness of Queen Victoria on postage stamps to her loyal subjects. And it was the most loyal and progressive colony of Canada which broke the ice (and took the plunge) by using, on her first stamps the head taken from Alfred Chalon's magnificent full-length portrait of the young Queen.

British North America

Canada's first stamps of 1851 – 3d. Beaver, in red; 6d. Prince Albert, violet ranging to purple; and 12d. Chalon's 'Queen', in sombre, elegant black – were designed by Sir Sandford Fleming, the Scottish-born engineer who pioneered the Canadian Pacific Railway. The beaver was emblematic of Canada's early prosperity, in particular the activities of the Hudson's Bay Company's fur-traders; the inclusion of Prince Albert, the Queen's Consort, was an act of courtesy; and the beautiful 'Twelvepence Black' (as it is known) depicted a head and neck version of the Chalon portrait, which was to be the standard for numerous other colonies.

In 1837, on the occasion of Queen Victoria's first visit to the House of Lords after her succession to the throne, Her Majesty stood at the front of the grand staircase while the artist, Alfred Edward Chalon, sketched the young Queen in her robes of state. From this sketch, Chalon made three copies of the portrait: the first was given by the Queen to her mother, the Duchess of Kent, who later presented it to her son-in-law, the Prince Consort. The two other copies were presented to the King of Prussia (believed destroyed by the RAF during World War II), and to the King of Portugal; the latter is now in the possession of Robson Lowe of London.

The new Canadian stamps were engraved by Alfred Jones and printed by Rawdon, Wright, Hatch and Edson (later the American Bank Note Company) of New York. In 1855 a 10d. stamp depicting Jacques Cartier, the French navigator who took possession of Canada in the name of France, appeared. The Chalon head was repeated on the 7½d. (dual currency)

Nova Scotia, the 1d., 3d. and 6d. first issue.

'Canada Packet Postage' stamp of 1857, and again, with the five cent Beaver, as a 12½ cent stamp in 1859. In 1868 a new set of 'Queen's Heads' inaugurated the Dominion of Canada.

Meanwhile, both New Brunswick and Nova Scotia had issued their own stamps in 1851, both adopting diamond-shaped heraldic designs, although Nova Scotia's No. 1, a 1d. red-brown, included a charming adaptation of the Chalon head, set diamond-wise in a square format. The Chalon portrait was used for the two, five and ten cent stamps issued by New Brunswick in 1860 – on the original five cent issue, the Postmaster-General, Charles Connell, used his own portrait. It is said that 'the Queen was not amused' and the stamp was quickly replaced by the Chalon. Newfoundland started with an heraldic series in 1857 followed, in 1865, by a pictorial issue; Prince Edward Island issued Wyon-style 'Queen's Heads' in 1861, and a 4½d. (3d. sterling) 'Chalon Head' in 1870.

In Canada's far west, the two Crown Colonies of British Columbia and Vancouver Island joined forces to issue a single 2½d. stamp in 1860. De La Rue's engraver ingeniously found space around the prevailing Wyon head of the Queen for the preposterously-long inscription – 'British Columbia & Vancouvers Island – Postage – Twopence Half-penny'. Mystery surrounds the first (imperforate) stamp which was never officially brought into use. In 1865, the colonies went their separate ways, Vancouver Island issuing five and ten cent stamps repeating the Wyon motif, British Columbia having new 3d. stamps showing the Crown

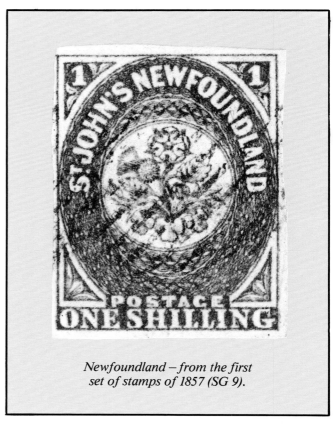

Newfoundland – from the first set of stamps of 1857 (SG 9).

and a large, decorative letter 'V'. When the two colonies were amalgamated in 1866, both issues came into general use in unified British Columbia, and provisionals were issued in 1868.

*The beautiful Chalon Head
on the first issue of Grenada.*

The British West Indies

The palm-fringed islands of the West Indies have been described as 'a string of pearls' adorning the Caribbean Sea. This well applies to the Leeward and Windward Islands, but other items of jewellery are spread farther afield – Jamaica and the Cayman Islands are far to the west, south of Cuba; the Bahamas and the Turks and Caicos Islands in the north, above Cuba and Hispaniola; and Trinidad and Tobago are the most southerly, virtually adjoining the mainland of South America. The early stamps of the British West Indies have a background history of swashbuckling piracy and naval adventure, conquest and eventual re-conquest, and gradual colonization and settlement.

Trinidad, discovered by Columbus in 1498, was the first of the West Indian colonies to issue stamps, in 1851. As described in the section on Primitives, they depicted 'Britannia and the sugar bags' and they were engraved by the indefatigable Perkins, Bacon and Co., imperforate and with face value (1d.) unspecified. The amalgamation with neighbouring Tobago came much later, in 1913, while Tobago's first stamps, Wyon-style, were issued in 1879.

The same design of Britannia was adapted for Barbados' first issues in 1852 – like those of Trinidad, the face values were not specified, but in this instance the different colours: ½d. green, 1d. blue, 2d. slate and 4d. red, enabled the largely illiterate native population to identify them. The English ship, *The Olive Blossom,* whose captain claimed Barbados for

James I in 1605, is depicted much later on a Barbados stamp, in 1906. The celebrated Chalon portrait of the Queen was introduced to the West Indies on the first stamps of the Bahamas, issued in 1859. It was a 1d. lake stamp inscribed 'Interinsular Postage', and it was followed in 1861 by 4d. and 6d. stamps bearing the same portrait in a more restrained setting.

Jamaica's first stamps in 1860 showed the Wyon head in a grand assortment of frames, 1d. to 1s. The diadem head was engraved by Joubert (Jean Ferdinand Joubert de la Ferté) for De La Rue who printed the stamps by typography with professional efficiency. In the same year, St Lucia issued her first stamps, and the printers, Perkins, Bacon, went to some lengths to produce a 'different' profile of the Queen, a new and gentler head engraved by Charles Henry Jeens. Again no values were expressed, and in 1863 De La Rue took over the printing. In 1861, Grenada issued 1d. and 6d. stamps bearing an outstanding version of the Chalon portrait, engraved by William Humphrys, an Irish-American and a leading engraver of the times. Grenada issued a revised Chalon head on the 1s. of 1875.

Also in 1861, the little island of Nevis, adjoining St Christopher in the Leeward Islands, came out with something different and original in stamp design – the badge of the colony, an allegory on the island's medicinal spring. There were four values – 1d., 4d., 6d. and 1s. – all with different frames, patently 'borrowed' from contemporary British stamps, and line-engraved by Nissen and Parker of London.

The first issues of St Vincent, also in 1861, were engraved masterpieces, combining the skills of Jeens, the engraver, and Perkins, Bacon, the printers. The Queen's profile, fuller-faced than the Wyon prototype, was placed against a graded oval background with a Penny Black-style 'banknote' frame. The colours – 1d. red and 6d. green, later augmented by 4d. blue and 1s. grey values – were rich and lustrous, the lettering beautifully proportioned and spaced. Antigua's first stamps, issued in 1862, had a portrait of the Queen comparable to that of St Vincent, but it was almost swamped by the heavy, lined background: another Jeens/Perkins, Bacon production.

When Columbus discovered the Virgin Islands he named them after St Ursula, the virgin saint, and her companion martyrs, reputed to have been massacred in Cologne. Thus the first stamps of 1866 show St Ursula herself, poorly lithographed by Nissen and Parker, from original dies by Waterlow. Later issues depicted the saint in statuesque form. The familiar Jeens head of the Queen appeared belatedly on the first stamps of the Turks Islands in 1867, and St Christopher used the formal diadem head for her first issues in 1870, typographed by De La Rue. It was the forerunner of the later keyplate types (whereby

Opposite page, above: Van Diemens Land (Tasmania) – A block of four 1d. stamps, first issued 1855, based on Corbould's water-colour of Queen Victoria. Opposite page, below: New Zealand, a pair of the 1d. in the first-issue design of 1855.

Ceylon's first stamp, 1857, a fine engraving of the Queen's head (SG 1).

Gambia – 6d. 'Cameo'.

South Australia – the Queen's head engraved for the first issue.

country names and values could be changed within the same design) in that the denomination at the foot was interchangeable.

Montserrat, the Leeward island discovered by Columbus in 1493 (he named it after a mountain in Spain), and whose inhabitants speak with a strong Irish accent derived from the original settlers, improvised her first issue of stamps in 1876 by over-printing the contemporary 1d. and 6d. stamps of Antigua. These remained in use until Wyon-head keyplate types were issued in 1880. Dominica's first stamps were modelled on those of St Christopher and came from the same stable – De La Rue. They were issued in 1874.

The Far-Flung Empire

Queen Victoria's reign was long and prosperous – it witnessed the spread of British imperialism and the rapid expansion of the Empire by exploration and conquest. Regular communications followed in the wake of the settlers' ships, post offices and postal services were established. First issues of postage stamps proceeded apace in all corners of the globe.

There were even British stamps in the North Sea – on the island of Heligoland which Britain seized from Denmark in 1807, and handed over to Germany in 1890 in exchange for Zanzibar. It was only 35 miles from the German coast, and the typographed stamps, with an embossed Hunnish version of the Wyon head of the Queen, were issued there in 1867. Cyprus (1880) and Gibraltar (1886) both used overprinted pro-visionals prior to having their own Wyon types, while Malta's first and only stamp for more than 20 years – the ½d. buff – issued in 1860, bore the

'standard' Wyon head in an octagon set on a kind of plinth. Jeens engraved, and Perkins, Bacon printed, the short-lived stamp issue for the Ionian Islands (1859), which were then under British care; the islands were ceded to Greece in 1864.

Africa's most distinctive first stamps, the Cape of Good Hope triangulars, 1d. red and 4d. blue, were issued in 1853. They were designed by Charles Bell, who pictured the seated figure of 'Hope' with her anchor (later the colony badge), engraved by Humphrys and superbly printed by Perkins, Bacon. The triangular stamps were intended for inland letters and were shaped thus so that the sorters could readily distinguish them from incoming mail from overseas. A 6d. lilac and a 1s. green were introduced in 1858. The Gambia, too, had distinctive stamps in 1869 – known as the 'Cameos', they featured the Queen's profile in embossed form on a background circle of contrasting colour, 4d. brown and 6d. blue, imperforate. Perforated 'Cameos' followed in 1880.

Some of the finest stamps of the 1850s came from New Zealand (1855), St Helena (1856) and Ceylon (1857). New Zealand, first stamps featured the Chalon head (they are also known as the 'full faces'), while the St Helena 6d. blue and the Ceylon 6d. purple-brown (forerunner of the so-called 'pence' issues) both displayed the profile of a very beautiful Queen. All these stamps were produced by the combined skills of William Humphrys, engraver, and Perkins, Bacon, printers, and they continued their successful endeavours by providing the first issues for South Australia (1855), and Chalon portraits for Tasmania (1855), following the primitives, and for Queensland (1860). The same team meanwhile furnished the

elegant 'Swans' for Western Australia in 1854, while Natal's Chalon stamps of 1859 were engraved by Jeens for Perkins, Bacon.

The first stamps for British Honduras (1866) showed the Queen wearing a full crown – engraved by Joubert and typographed by De La Rue, they remained in use for 25 years. The Falkland Islands' first stamps appeared in 1878 – the Queen's head was similar to that of the Canadian 1870 issue, 'Queen with bun' (or Chignon), and these were the first British Commonwealth – including British – stamps printed by Bradbury, Wilkinson.

During the 1860s and 1870s, the Wyon-inspired head of Queen Victoria became a 'standard' and commonplace feature of colonial stamp design. It appeared on Hong Kong's first definitives, with English and Chinese inscriptions (1862), and on the stamps of Sierra Leone (1859 and 1872), the Straits Settlements (1867), the Gold Coast (1875) and the Seychelles (1890). It was ubiquitous on Indian stamps – those inscribed 'East India' (1855 and 1860 to 1876), and the 'Empire' series from 1882. Only in the last years of Victoria's reign was there a decisive change of portrait on stamps – notably a painting by Heinrich von Angeli, and a photograph by W. and D. Downey of London. Both depicted a dignified, elderly Queen Victoria.

The First Europeans

It was almost ten years before the rest of Europe began to follow Britain's lead with the issue of postage stamps. France, Belgium and Bavaria issued their first stamps in 1849 – the symbolic head of Ceres, the Goddess of Corn, was engraved on the French stamps, and in 1852 that was replaced by the head of President Louis Napoléon, who was shown as Napoléon III, Emperor of the French, on stamps from 1853. Belgium also pictured her reigning monarch, Leopold I, King of the Belgians, on her first stamps. Known as the 'Epaulettes' (in reference to the King's uniform), they were engraved by J. H. Robinson, after a lithographed portrait by C. Baugniet. The Bavarian stamps were numeral types, square and practical.

In 1850, Hanover began with a single stamp bearing a large figure '1' (gutegroschen) on a shield and the crest of King Ernest Augustus; Prussia released stamps showing King Frederick William IV; Saxony emulated Bavaria with a large figure '3' (pfennigs) on a square stamp, and followed with stamp portraits of King Frederick Augustus II; and Schleswig-Holstein issued stamps bearing the arms of the combined duchies. Then came the stamps of Würtemberg and Baden (1851), both square 'numeral' types, and, in 1852, Brunswick, Oldenburg and Thurn and Taxis, followed by Bremen in 1855. A year later, Mecklenburg-Schwerin issued stamps which, like the 'Double Genevas', were divisible – into 'quarters'.

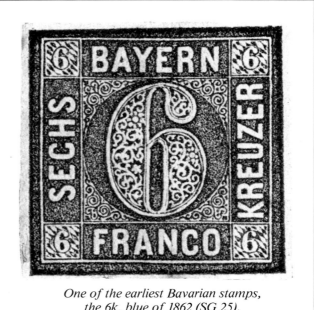

One of the earliest Bavarian stamps, the 6k. blue of 1862 (SG 25).

Block of Saxony's first stamp 1850.

Hamburg and Lübeck issued stamps in 1859, and in 1861 Bergedorf introduced stamps graduated in size according to their face values.

The first stamps of the great Austro-Hungarian monarchy made their début in 1850 – they bore the Austrian arms, but later issues portrayed Emperor Francis Joseph I, who also appeared (as King) on the first stamps of Hungary, under the dual monarchy, in 1871. Also worthy of mention are the arms-type stamps issued by Austrian Italy (Lombardy and Venetia) in 1850, and the unique Austrian newspaper stamps depicting Mercury, winged messenger of the gods, in 1851. Interesting, also, was the choice of

Finland, one of the first two stamps of 1856 (SG 1).

Hermes (or Mercury) as the subject of design by Greece for her first stamps in 1861 – these are now among the foremost classics of Europe.

Spain's 'Penny Black', issued in 1850, was a six cuartos stamp bearing a profile of the reigning Queen, Isabella II, looking left – the remaining values in this handsome issue showed the portrait reversed, looking to the right. Portugal's first stamps (1853) were embossed with a profile of Queen Maria, and the heads of successive monarchs were similarly embossed on Portuguese stamps until 1880. Denmark issued small, square German-style stamps in 1851, one showing the face value (two rigsbank-skillings) within a circle, the other, the armorial 'crown and crossed swords' of the Royal House of King Frederick VII. Similar stamps were issued for the Danish West Indies in 1855, the year in which Norway and Sweden, then a united kingdom under Oscar I, issued their first stamps, both arms-types. Iceland issued 'numeral' stamps in 1873.

Switzerland's familiar white cross on a shield appeared on her first regular stamps in 1850 – these were followed by the figurative 'Sitting Helvetias' in 1854, and the 'Standing Helvetias' in 1882. Luxembourg and the Netherlands showed different profile portraits of the same ruler on their first stamps of 1852 – Grand Duke William of Luxembourg was also King William III of Holland. Sardinia, whose King, Victor Emmanuel II, became the first ruler of united Italy, first issued stamps in 1851, as also did Tuscany, the independent Grand Duchy of northern Italy, with arms-type stamps featuring a crowned, squatting lion. The stamps of the Roman (or Papal) States, issued in 1852, showed the insignia of Pope Pius IX – the crossed keys of St Peter surmounted by the papal tiara or crown in various frames and shapes, printed in black on coloured papers. They were better and brighter than the rather staid arms-type designs which adorned the first stamps of Modena and Parma, the Italian grand duchies, in the same year.

The first stamps of Finland, issued in 1856, were original in format if not in subject – they were oval-shaped and showed the arms of the grand duchy and two posthorns. Russian domination is seen in

*Sweden, the 3 skilling-banco
yellow error of colour,
a celebrated rarity (SG 16).*

Finland's subsequent issues which, in a smaller arms-type, closely resemble, and are almost indistinguishable from, Russia's first stamps in 1858. They bore an embossed eagle, the crest of the Tsar, Alexander II, a design which continued in various forms until the turn of the century. The arms of the Two Sicilies were depicted on the first stamps of Naples, comprising the horse for Naples, the three legs with head of Medusa for Sicily, and the three *fleurs-de-lis* for Bourbon, in 1858. These were followed by a rather plain 'numeral' issue for Romagna (1859), and stamps for Sicily, picturing King Ferdinand II, in the

same year. The stamps issued for the Neapolitan Provinces in 1861 were succeeded by Italy's first regular issues in 1862. Both featured King Victor Emmanuel II.

Poland's first stamps in 1860 were arms-types almost identical to Russia's first issues (and the later Finnish stamps), and can only be distinguished by the inscriptions (Poland also was under Russian rule). Turkey's inaugural stamps of 1863 depicted the snail-like *tougra* or *paraph* of the Sultan of Turkey, Abdul-Aziz, and the Muslim crescent. In 1865, Rumania issued her first regular stamps bearing the likeness of Prince Cuza. When he was deposed in 1866, Prince

Strip of Norway's first issue, 1855.

Charles was proclaimed King and new stamps were issued bearing his portrait. Serbia's stamps in 1866 depicted the royal arms and Prince Michael, and the classic era of European stamps was rounded off by issues from the North German Federation (1868) and the German Empire (1872).

'Classic' Round-up

While the classic era of postage stamps is extended by philatelists to about 1870, there are important exceptions. Among these are the first issues of China, the stamps of the Imperial Customs Post, issued in 1878. These featured the Chinese dragon and the design closely resembles that of the local or municipal stamps issued by the treaty port of Shanghai several years earlier, in 1865. Egypt's first stamps with Arabic motif and inscriptions were issued in 1866, followed a year later by the popular 'Sphinx and Pyramid' series. Liberia, the 'Negro Republic' in West Africa, first issued stamps in 1860 – the figure of 'Liberty' seated on the harbour quay – and Persia (Iran) likewise in 1868, the uniform design depicting the country's arms – a lion with upraised sword and the sun.

The spread of Spanish influence overseas can be traced through the first issues of stamps in the Philippine Islands (1854), a charming duplication of Spain's third portrait series of Isabella, and in Cuba and Puerto Rico (1855), both of which had separate issues in 1873. Fernando Po, the Spanish island in the Gulf of Guinea, West Africa, issued a single 20 centavos de peso stamp in 1868.

Chile's first stamps (1853), and indeed all her postage stamps prior to 1910, showed Christopher Columbus – Perkins, Bacon printed the first issue. In

Austria, one of the Mercury newspaper stamps of 1851-56, 6k. red (SG N13).

1856, Mexico issued stamps depicting Father Miguel Hidalgo y Costilla, who led the 1810 revolution and whose stamps are known as the 'Hidalgos', and in 1859, Venezuela issued her first (arms-type) stamps. Nicaragua's first stamps (1862) showed her volcanic terrain, and Bolivar, a department of Colombia, issued some of the smallest stamps in the world in 1863. The first stamps of the Dominican Republic were issued in 1865, those of Ecuador in the same year.

n Stock Exchange Offices only.

		Postage Stamps to be affixed in this space.	Dated Stamp.
s.	d.		
...	...6...		
6			
...	......		
...	......		

3
Errors and Forgeries

There was a time when stamp collectors were generally regarded as eccentric (to say the least), and this image was enhanced when the 'mad hatters' of the hobby began to show a predilection for mistakes in stamp design and printing, and were prepared to pay high prices for the scarcer and more spectacular errors. The fact is that errors of design, and those caused by mishaps in the course of printing, hold a strong fascination for collectors, who are not so much concerned with prospective values as they are with pride of possession – owning something that other collectors have missed.

It is significant that many stamp errors relate to the earlier days of design and printing – when stamp designers were often craftsmen-engravers, and printing methods, particularly the time-honoured line-engraving process employing perhaps two separate printing plates, were susceptible to error. Modern design skills and sophisticated printing techniques have all but eliminated the possibilities of error, other than minor flaws. That, however, does not deter the modern collector from examining, hopefully, all the new stamps that come along!

Errors of Design

These occur when the artist-designer has been inadequately briefed, misinformed, mistaken or just careless – all things which could have been avoided and rectified by careful, thorough research. Maybe it wasn't always the fault of the artist, perhaps pressed to complete a series of sketches in a short time for an impatient postal administration. Design errors take

Australia – 1947 stamp inscribed 'Lieut. John Shortland R.N.', but erroneously showing his father (SG 219).

various forms – usually the subject depicted, or the captions and inscriptions, are incorrect, or there are errors of spelling and usage, especially of scientific and botanical names. Often there have been mistakes on maps reproduced on stamps.

The first questionable stamp design which comes to mind is the peculiar 'seal with paws' on a Newfoundland five cent stamp of 1865. Ordinary seals have flippers and there was some controversy for many years until it was established that the creature was a grey or saddleback seal, *Phoca groenlandica,* which has forefeet and inhabits the Newfoundland coast. Another Newfoundland stamp, one which somewhat stretched the long arm of coincidence, was the ten cent of 1897 showing 'Cabot's ship, the *Matthew,* leaving the Avon' – the vessel is an exact replica of Columbus's flagship, the *Santa Maria,* shown on a United States three cent commemorative of 1893, attributed to a Spanish engraving. The American Bank Note Company printed both stamps.

Still in Newfoundland and in the same series, Hans Holbein's portrait of Sebastian Cabot was used in error for that of his father, Jean – 'Hym that found the new isle' – on the two cent stamp; Sir Francis Bacon was portrayed as 'Lord Bacon' (six cent, 1910); and in 1928 the positions of Cape Bauld and Cape Norman on the Newfoundland coast were reversed (and later corrected) on a one-cent map of the country.

An amusing anachronism, one that was perpetuated in later issues, occurred on the first stamps of St Kitts-Nevis as a Crown Colony in 1903 – Christopher Columbus depicted in the act of discovering the islands, in 1493, through his telescope. The first telescope is said to have been constructed by Hans Lippershey, a Dutch spectacle-maker, in 1608. Also amusing was the Fiji 1½d. stamp of 1938 which showed a native outrigger canoe in full sail across a lagoon – with nobody in it. The absentee canoeist was restored in subsequent printings. A Bermuda 2d.

Opposite: The notorious 'Stock Exchange forgery' – one of the most daring and remarkable postal frauds ever known. It involved the extensive forgery of the Queen Victoria 1s. green and, although 'passed' by affixing hundreds of the stamps to telegraph forms, the deception remained undiscovered for 26 years.

stamp of 1936 was intended to represent the British racing yacht, *Viking* – instead the American yacht, *Lucie,* was depicted. And in 1955, a French stamp purporting to show the corvette, *La Capricieuse,* actually pictured the *Galathée.*

Another case of mistaken identity occurred in Australia, where, in 1947, stamps were issued for the 150th anniversary of Newcastle, New South Wales – the 2½d. stamp inscribed 'Lieut. John Shortland, R.N.' showed his father who bore the same name. Flags have often been misrepresented on stamps – a classic error was the Union Jack shown upside-down on a Jamaican 2½d. stamp of 1921 picturing the return of Jamaican volunteers from World War I – it was corrected in the same year. Sarawak's pictorials of 1950 were remarkable for two design errors – the two cent showing a tarsier, a kind of lemur, was inscribed 'The

Cook Islands – 1967, 4c. stamps inscribed WALTER LILY and correctly WATER LILY (SG 232, 233).

Tarsius' which is the genus to which it belongs; and the ten cent depicting a scaly ant-eater or Malayan pangolin, *Manis javanica,* minus its substantial tail which enables it to climb trees as shown. The stamp was replaced by a map in 1952. Similarly a North Borneo stamp of 1950, the 50 cent 'Clock Tower, Jessleton', was replaced with one bearing the corrected name, 'Jesselton', in 1952.

In 1956 the German Democratic Republic (DDR) issued stamps to commemorate the centenary of the death of Robert Schumann, the composer. His portrait was placed against a background of music which was soon identified by musicians as the song, *Wanderers Nachtlied I,* opus 4. 3, composed by Franz Schubert! The design was corrected within three months. And the French designer of a Mali (West Africa) stamp in 1971 was evidently not a racing man – his 'Epsom Derby' showed a steeplechase, probably the Grand National.

The spelling of New Zealand's 'Lake Wakitipu' (2½d., 1898) was corrected to 'Wakatipu' a few

months later, and when independent Malawi reprinted the Nyasaland stamps in 1964, they forgot to alter the caption of 'Lake Nyasa' on the 5s. stamp which was replaced by 'Lake Malawi' in 1965. Other examples of faulty captions include the Greek stamp of 1927 which portrayed the English admiral, Sir Edward Codrington, as 'Sir Codrington', later corrected, and the Cook Islands' four cent stamp of 1967 inscribed 'Walter Lily' for 'Water Lily'. This, too, was amended.

Geographical locations and maps are frequent sources of error. A tourist in Samoa couldn't find the 'Aleisa Falls' captioned on a 3d. stamp issued there in 1952, and it transpired that the picture showed the Malifa Falls, near Apia in Samoa. The Vernal Falls, in the Yosemite National Park, California, are shown on an 18 cent stamp issued by the Philippines in 1932 which is wrongly inscribed 'Pagsanjan Falls'. A Fiji map stamp of 1938 failed to identify the line of 180° longitude, while a similar Mauritius stamp of 1950 showed the line of latitude running through Port Louis as 21° 10′ S, when it should have been 20° 10′ S.

Territorial ambition inspired the Argentine Republic to issue a series of map stamps of South America claiming, by appropriate shading and boundaries, the 'Islas Malvinas' – the British Falkland Islands. The first stamp (1936) also embraced a part of Chile and, following protests from the Chilean authorities, the stamp was reissued without the country boundaries. In 1947 both Argentina and Chile issued Antarctic maps which swallowed up Graham Land, formerly one of the Falkland Islands Dependencies and now a part of British Antarctic Territory, while subsequent Argentine maps supported the claims, culminating in 1964 with an 'Antarctic Claims' issue which reproduced maps of the Antarctic islands including the 'Islas Malvinas'.

An apparent design error which could have occurred in the process of printing occurred on an Indian stamp in 1949. One of a series depicting archaeological statues and buildings, the one anna showed the 'Bodhisattva' (a candidate for Buddhism, or a future Buddha) in reverse as in a mirror. The corrected version, with the figure resting its right arm on its right knee, instead of left as before, was issued in the following year.

Errors in Printing

The select list of major printing errors dates from 1851 and it comprises three principal kinds of mishap – parts of a stamp design inverted, stamps printed in the wrong colour or with omissions of design, inscription or overprint. Virtually all of these are spectacular errors and many of them, especially those belonging to the classic era of postage stamps, are rare and valuable today. It is a strange anomaly of the stamp collecting hobby – comparable to no other form of 'collectables' – that mistakes are so highly prized. The reason is

*East German stamps depicting Schumann
and music. The lower original issue wrongly
showed music by Schubert (SG E264, E266).*

simply that, from the very first, stamps have been printed carefully, even laboriously, to high standards, and major errors have seldom occurred. Collectors are eager to acquire the few existing examples, especially if they pertain to their own sphere of interest, and consequently there are not enough to go round and high prices ensue.

Among the most valuable errors is the Baden (Germany) nine kreuzer stamp of the first issue of 1851 – the 'numerals' – printed in black on green paper instead of the normal dull rose paper of that denomination. Green was the normal coloured paper for the six kreuzer stamp and it is a reasonable surmise that a '6' was taken for a '9', the nine kreuzer stamps thus being printed in the wrong colour. Only two or three errors have survived – two of them are known on cover. A similar error occurred in Saxony in the same year (1851) when the half neugroschen stamp bearing the head of Frederick Augustus II in black was printed on pale blue paper instead of the normal blue-grey.

The famous 'Inverted Swan' of Western Australia, belonging to the lithographed issue of 1854, had, in fact, an inverted frame. Normally, with 'upside down' stamps, the printing of the component parts of the design are made from separate plates or stones, and relevance to adjoining stamps (and to the watermark, upright or inverted) establishes either the centre design or the frame as being inverted. The 4d. 'Swan', however, was printed in a single operation on a lithographic stone, and in one colour, blue. When the invert was discovered some 30 years later, its authenticity was in doubt as no one could understand how it had occurred. It eventually transpired that, in the course of laying down the lithograph plate, one of the special transfers for the frame was affixed upside-down in relation to the 'swan' – a fact which was proved when a damaged strip of three came to light in the 1930s, and one of the stamps, though torn, clearly showed the inverted frame. About a dozen 'Inverted Swans' are known and recorded. One is in the Royal Philatelic Collection, another in the Tapling (British Library) Collection.

As mentioned in the chapter on the Primitives, India issued lithographed stamps in 1854, the bicoloured (blue and red) four anna stamps being printed in two stages – the Queen's head and an octagonal frame. Examples with the head inverted are extremely rare. Also from the Primitives, the Cape of Good Hope 'woodblocks' include two striking errors of colour – 1d. blue and 4d. vermilion. These occurred when clichés of each value were accidentally transposed, the 1d. being inserted in the forme or 'plate' of the 4d. denominations and the 4d. in that of the 1d. values. The errors – which Stanley Gibbons sold for

Malawi stamps showing Lake Malawi, the top stamp is wrongly inscribed 'Lake Nyasa' (SG 225, 225a).

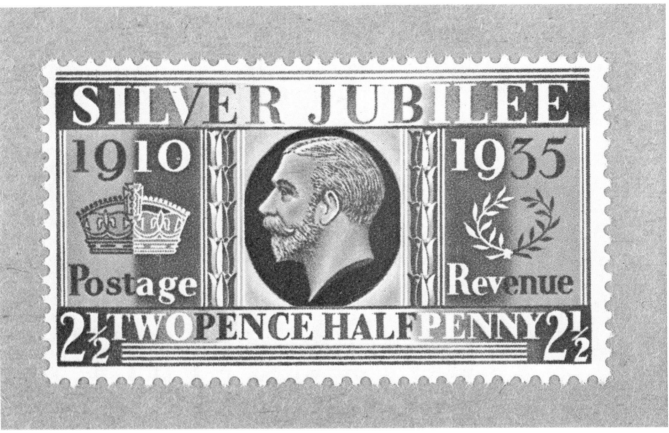

Above: Great Britain – 1935, 2½d. Silver Jubilee, but in Prussian blue (SG 456a).
Right: U.S.A. – 1962 Hammarskjöld memorial stamp correctly printed (lower stamp) and with error, yellow printing inverted (upper stamp) (SG 1202, 1203).

4s. each in 1864 – are now the most rare Cape triangulars.

Mystery surrounds the Barbados 'Britannia' 1s. of 1863 in blue – the colour of the 1d. – instead of the customary black. None were sold at post offices and few examples have survived. Another most striking error is the celebrated 'missing virgin' of the Virgin Islands – in which the black vignette picturing St Ursula is omitted. Jamaica has a stamp with an inverted frame – the 1s. 'Queen Victoria Statue' of 1920 – produced when a sheet was wrongly inserted in the press.

Errors of colour are recorded under the Neapolitan provinces of Italy and Sicily, while Spain's two reale blue (instead of red) is again rare and valuable. Issued in 1851, a year after the first stamps, few have been found, but the existence of a joined pair of the two and six reale stamps, both in blue (the normal colour of the six reale), proved that the error was genuine and that the wrong cliché had been inserted in the plate. The five reale in the same issue is known in chocolate-brown (instead of rose), and the two reale of

1855 exists in the colour of the 1 reale – blue instead of purple. A substituted cliché also produced Sweden's well-known 'Tretio' (30) error on the 20 öre 'numeral' stamp of the 1872-7 issue, which occurred during a late printing of the stamps in 1879.

Europe's rarest stamp is reputed to be the yellow Swedish three skilling banco, the first stamp in Sweden's first issue of 1855-8. In 1885, a schoolboy, Georg Backman, found a letter in some old correspondence bearing a three skilling banco stamp in an unusual colour, yellow, instead of the normal green. Young Backman sold the stamp to H. Lichtenstein, a Stockholm dealer, who, years later, sold it in turn to the great Ferrary. At the time of one of the Ferrary sales in 1922, it was established that the stamp was in the exact shade of the eight skilling banco of the same issue – and a cliché of the three skilling banco was inserted in error while the eight skilling banco stamps were being printed in 1857. Only one copy is known – hence it is a 'runner-up' to the unique British Guiana 'One Cent black on magenta' – and it has changed hands several times.

A 'rash' of inverted centres – later found to be inverted frames – occurred in the United States in 1901 when six stamps were issued for the Pan-American Exposition in Buffalo. The one cent 'Lake Steamer', two cent 'Empire State Express' and four cent 'Automobile' were all found inverted. But the most famous of US inverts is the Curtiss 'Jenny' biplane on a special 24-cent airmail stamp of May 1918. It was intended for use on letters carried on a new 'aeroplane mail service' between Washington, Philadelphia and New York, and on 14 May, the day before the first flight, Mr W. T. Robey, a stockbroker's clerk, bought a sheet of the new stamps in his local (Washington) post office and discovered, to his astonishment, that the aeroplane was upside-down on every stamp!

In modern times, such exciting 'finds' are few and far between. Captain Cook may be found inverted on the 1d. stamp featuring his portrait issued in 1932 by the Cook Islands; and an airmail overprint on a 10d. stamp was also inverted there in 1966. Then, in 1935, a collector bought some of the new King George V 'Silver Jubilee' 2½d. stamps at an Edmonton, North London, post office, and noticed that they were in a distinctive shade of blue, not the normal ultramarine. Thus were discovered the rare 'Prussian Blues' which were later found to have been colour trials released in error.

A whole sheet of the Aden 'Shihr and Mukalla' Universal Postal Union commemoratives of 1949 was found in a dealer's stock, with the '1 rupee' surcharge omitted, while the new issue buyer in another firm discovered, in a sheet of the 'Tangier'-overprinted stamps of 1957, a 9d. British stamp with the word 'Tangier' omitted – it had been printed on an intervening fold of the margin. In Canada, several copies of the five cent

A bogus label for fictitious kingdom of Sedang located in Indo-China.

'St Lawrence Seaway' stamps of 1959 were found with inverted centres, and, in the United States, when sheets of the four cent Dag Hammarskjöld commemoratives of 1962 were printed with the yellow colour inverted, the authorities printed thousands more with the same error 'to satisfy collectors' and, one suspects, to avoid speculation.

Errors of perforation and watermark, and printing flaws other than the errors of colour, inversion and omission already described, will be found in Chapter 6, 'Varieties and Printing Flaws'.

Intended to Deceive

Forgery! It's a word calculated to arouse apprehension in the mind of the novice stamp collector, awareness and caution in that of the experienced philatelist, yet these days it is possible to build up a collection of thousands of stamps and never encounter a forged stamp. It's not that forgeries – some of them very fine reproductions of the original stamps – do not exist any more, but rather that the great majority of them have been identified, documented and recorded in articles, books and catalogues. Most, if not all, of the important forgeries are known and can be attributed to their conspiratorial authors. Stamps were not

From a bogus set for Azerbaijan, U.S.S.R. In spite of their status they were later forged (lower stamp).

Bogus label, said to be for Odessa. This too had the accolade of being forged subsequently (lower stamp).

unique in this respect – forged works of art date from Roman times, and in the Middle Ages the paintings of the 'Old Masters' of Italy were blatantly copied by skilled artists and passed off as genuine originals, when demand exceeded the supply.

In philately there is a subtle distinction between forgeries and fakes. A forgery is defined as 'an imitation of a stamp intended to deceive': a fake is described as a genuine stamp which has been 'doctored' – by altering its colour, perforation, postmark or design detail to correspond to a rarer stamp, thus to defraud. Where a genuine stamp bears a fake overprint, surcharge or postmark, it is precisely described as 'genuine, with forged overprint (etc.)'. 'Bogus' stamps are labels which purport to be postage stamps but are not – unauthorized issues for existing, or even non-existent, countries. 'Reprints' are stamps printed again from the original plates after the official stamps ceased to be current.

Forgeries and fakes go right back to the first postage stamps. Rowland Hill recorded two 'poor imitations' of the Penny Black, but it was in Europe – Spain, Austria and Austrian Italy, Naples and Sardinia – that forged stamps (known to collectors as postal

forgeries) were produced on a large scale to defraud their respective post offices. In Spain, especially, the authorities were hard pressed to keep one step ahead of the forgers who, in the 1850s and 1860s, mass-produced passable imitations of successive issues of stamps. Forgeries of the 1850 issues of Austrian Italy (for Lombardy and Venetia) exist and are rare; similarly the stamps of Naples (1858) and the Neapolitan provinces (1861) are known and are usually found with genuine postal cancellations, rarely unused. Again, to deceive the postal authorities, the French 'Peace and Commerce' stamps of 1876, and the 'Sowers' of 1903, were extensively forged. Gradually, however, as stamp collecting became more and more popular, and the demand for the scarcer stamps increased, so the forger turned his attention to the collector for whom he produced what are termed philatelic forgeries.

The Master Forgers

Fouré, Fournier, Spiro, Sperati, De Thuin – they are all famous names in the philatelic history of fakes and forgeries. They operated during the 'classic' period of forgeries – from about 1860 to the early 1930s, in the

Three bogus labels: Top: Azad Hind – produced during World War II for the liberation of India. Centre: South Moluccas, part of Indonesia. Bottom: An old-time label with the doubtful distinction of being inscribed for both Labrador and U.S.A., but used in neither.

case of Sperati to 1953, De Thuin to the 1960s. Undoubtedly they made money, but most of them came to sticky ends, being branded as forgers and brought to court or, if they were lucky, having their equipment and 'stock' purchased by philatelic associations and societies for the protection of collectors.

Georges Fouré, a French teacher resident in Berlin, became a stamp dealer, founded a philatelic society and started a magazine, the *Berliner Briefmarken-Zeitung*, employing his native Gallic charm to market his 'home-made' rarities and 'hitherto unknown' varieties. Eventually he came under suspicion and was accused of producing fakes, especially those stamps whose colours he skilfully changed and the embossed envelopes which he manufactured on his own press. Finally, Fouré was denounced with such vituperation that he was forced to flee the German capital – he returned to Paris and faded into oblivion.

François Fournier of Geneva had a different technique, one in which he openly defied the authorities by trading in highly publicised 'facsimile' stamps. He was an expert philatelist and specialized in postmarking his 'stamps' with apparently genuine French and Swiss handstamps, all copied from the original stamps which he closely studied. While he sold his facsimiles as *objets d'art* (and not forgeries), tongue almost permanently in cheek, his customers, philatelists and dealers, were not so fastidious. His wares changed hands, with immense profits, as original stamps. Fournier brazenly issued warnings to collectors, urging them not to pay high prices for his facsimiles, and at the same time he started a 'repair clinic', undertaking to clean, repair and, if required, appropriately 'postmark' all the damaged stamps sent to him. Eventually, after his death, the Philatelic Union of Geneva purchased his equipment and stock, made up reference collections of the enormous range of forgeries and sold them to reputable dealers and societies for purposes of reference, in 1928.

The mass-production of stamp facsimiles was also the forté of Spiro Gebrüder of Hamburg, the famous Spiro brothers – jobbing printers who, from about 1860, started a profitable sideline on their lithographic presses, printing imitation postage stamps of Hamburg and other German cities, duchies and kingdoms, Spain and other countries, even the Cape of Good Hope triangulars. The Spiro forgeries were usually postmarked for the very good reason that the firm could not be accused of attempting to defraud the Post Office by marketing unused stamps – by implication the poor old stamp collector could be defrauded with impunity! After a few years, the Spiro forgeries were denounced in the philatelic press by a professional philatelist and writer, E.L. Pemberton, and the nefarious Spiro brothers finally, in the 1870s, abandoned their equally nefarious business. Many an old-time stamp collection will have had a Spiro 'souvenir' among its pages.

In more recent years, the 'uncrowned king' of the forgers was indisputably the notorious Jean de Sperati, who died in 1957, aged 73. For more than 30 years he produced excellent imitations – which he euphemistically called 'reproductions' – of rare stamps, more than 500 of them. Many were repeated (if they sold well) and, while many so-called experts were deceived into thinking the stamps were genuine, leading specialists and the expert committees of the (then) British Philatelic Association and the Royal Philatelic Society, London, shrewdly appraised them for what they were – very skilful forgeries. It is said that Sperati was so proud of his work that he initialled the backs of his stamps in pencil, knowing well that his signature could be rubbed out and the stamps sold as genuine issues.

Sperati forged one British stamp – the 2s. brown of 1867 – and numerous Commonwealth stamps, including the Australian £2 Kangaroo and early Mauritius, as well as prolific copies of early French,

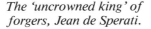

The 'uncrowned king' of forgers, Jean de Sperati.

German, Italian, Spanish and Swiss issues. He suffered a term of imprisonment for forgery and fraud, then in 1953 the British Philatelic Association acquired his entire remaining stock and equipment, displayed some of his stamps and published the *Sperati Story* with illustrations of his work. Some of the stamps were sold after having been indelibly marked as forgeries.

Another miscreant – Raul Charles de Thuin, a Belgian living in Mexico – deceived the experts for many years with his homemade versions of Latin-American stamps. In Mexico it was no offence to counterfeit obsolete stamps – he specialized in faking overprints and surcharges – and in 1947 the American Post Office tried in vain to curb his activities, seizing his letters and blocking US mail addressed to him. The dénouement came in December 1966, when the American Philatelic Society bought him out – stamps, dies and equipment – for a reputed £2,000. De Thuin agreed to 'retire' and wind up his business – not difficult at the age of 76!

Latin-American stamps were also the speciality of Samuel Allan Taylor, the 'Master Grafter' and leader of the infamous 'Boston Gang' of forgers in the United States in the 1860s. They issued 'stamps' for Santo Domingo (the Dominican Republic), Guatemala and Paraguay, those for the latter two countries appearing years before they officially started issuing stamps. Taylor was later prosecuted and, though never convicted, spent some time in prison. He died in 1913.

Bravado, panache and a kind of slapstick humour marked the activities of the 'London Gang' – Messrs Benjamin, Sarpy and Jeffryes – who openly ran a 'facsimiles' stamp shop in Cullum Street in the City of London, in the 1880s. Jeffryes printed them, while the other two were busy in their shop, often faking over-prints and surcharges on stamps in a back room for waiting customers. They were brought to trial and convicted in 1892, and the entertaining stories of the two 'gangs' and their misdeeds may be found in the Pelican book, *The Postage Stamp – Its History and Recognition*, by L.N. and M. Williams (London, 1956).

At least 15 identifiable forgeries are known of the Zurich four rappen of 1843, Switzerland being the first country (with Brazil) to issue stamps after Great Britain. The 'give-away' features were missing hyphens and red lines, extraneous stops, coarse impressions and, in one instance, immaculate line-engraving instead of the normal lithography.

The Austrian 'arms'-type stamps of 1850 provide examples of the forger's ingenuity – genuine stamps with forged impressions on the back. The one, three, and nine kreuzer stamps were printed on both sides as genuine errors, but not so the two kreuzer and the 2k. on 6k. and 2k. on 3k. which appeared in 1890. Identical 'arms' stamps were used for the first issues of Lombardy and Venetia, and in 1853 a band of expert forgers in Verona made first-class imitations of the 15c. red and 30c. brown, far superior to the original stamps!

The 'Stock Exchange' Forgery

One of the most daring and remarkable postal frauds ever known was the wholesale forgery of the British Queen Victoria 1s. green of 1867. Every forger needs an outlet for his handiwork and in this instance it was a clerk in the Stock Exchange Post Office in the City of London who 'passed' the forged stamps by affixing them to telegraph forms. In those days hundreds of telegrams were despatched each day by brokers to their clients, and large numbers of the 1s. stamps were used. Between 1872 and early 1874, nearly all the stamps sold by this clerk – whose identity was never traced – were forgeries, though this was not discovered until 26 years later.

Charles Nissen, a well-known philatelist, bought some of the telegraph stamps from a wastepaper dealer and found that they were all forgeries – the shade of green was different to the normal, the lines of shading were coarse and blurred, the corners were blunted and the 'stamps' were unwatermarked. In addition, some of the corner letters had impossible combinations which did not correspond to the methodical lettering of genuine sheets. Plate 5 of the current issue was the basis of the forgers' first imitations – when Plate 6 was officially introduced, they copied this, too. The latter is much the scarcer and better produced of the two.

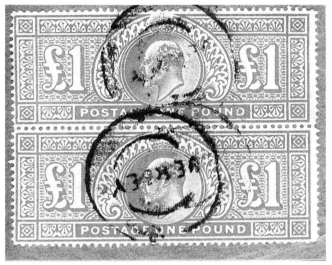

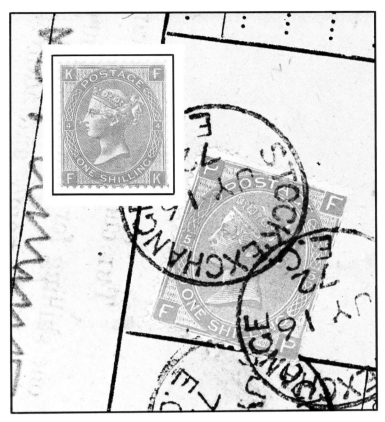

Top: A genuine Great Britain 1911 Edward VII £1 definitive and, beneath, a pair of 'Lowden' forgeries supposedly cancelled in 'Jersey'.

A forgery of the Great Britain 1867 1/- green used on a telegraph form at the Stock Exchange, London. The inset shows the genuine 1/- green (SG 101).

When a London dealer bought a parcel of Edwardian £1 greens of 1911 attached to pieces of brown wrapping-paper from a certain Mr Lowden, he suspected nothing wrong until he examined them later and discovered that they were forgeries. They had been produced by photo-lithography and were much coarser than the genuine stamps – the 'Jersey' postmarks, too, were forged, to suggest that the clippings had come from tobacco parcels from the Channel Islands. Lowden was prosecuted and convicted, and a few stamps survived.

During World War II, forged banknotes and postage stamps were part of the 'propaganda war'. Forgeries of German stamps were made in England and in Switzerland, while the Germans made rather crude imitations of the King George VI definitives and the Coronation stamp of 1937. Examples of King George VI stamps show the Hammer and Sickle within the rose at the top left (to indicate Soviet domination), and the Jewish 'Star of David' in the thistle (top right) and above the Tudor crown at the top. Other wartime forgeries included the silver jubilee stamps of King George V inscribed 'This war is a Jewish war', while in both these stamps and the coronation stamps mentioned above Stalin's portrait replaced that of the monarch.

Reprints, like forgeries, can usually be distinguished by their colour, paper and gum. Unlike forgeries, they are printed from the original plate, block or stone, but *after* the issue of the original has ceased. This was often normal practice in the last century, when collectors seemed not to care whether they owned reprints or the original stamps. Sometimes the printing plates were disposed of with the remainder stamps so that the purchaser could print – and sell – as many more stamps as he wished, as in the case of the notorious Nicholas F. Seebeck who contracted to supply certain Latin-American states with stamps free of charge in the 1890s: in return he acquired the original plates and all unsold stamps at the end of a predetermined period, when the stamps were officially demonetized.

Seebeck was a New York stamp dealer and, later, an official of the Hamilton Bank Note Company – he was thus in an ideal position to print and supply the free stamps. The countries which succumbed to his blandishments were reputedly Ecuador (1892-6), Honduras (1890-5), Nicaragua (1890-9) and Salvador (1890-9). Eventually, bad publicity affected his stamp sales and the 'Seebeck' reprints fell into disrepute. Unused they are common; postally used, rare.

The 10s. 'Sea-horses' stamp showing Britannia in her chariot drawn by these noble beasts. These magnificent stamps (there are other high values in this design) were the work of master engraver J.A.C. Harrison, seen at top.

4
Stamp Design and Designers

'Stamp design is the motive power behind the specialist with his plating, errors and re-entries, the artistic collector who acquires what he thinks beautiful, and the historian or anthropologist who gleans facts from commemorative and pictorial issues.' John Easton, *British Postage Stamp Design*

In other words, the design of the stamp — its subject and the way it was printed — is the key to our enjoyment of collecting. Stamp design is a combination of art forms and craftsmanship represented, sometimes successfully, sometimes not, in miniature. It was the late Edmund Dulac, designer of several fine stamps for Britain and the French colonies, who said: *'The most difficult part of designing a postage stamp is planning the theme for all to understand and appreciate in so little space.'* David Gentleman, a Royal Designer for Industry and a fertile and inventive designer of modern British postage stamps, echoed this thought in his book, *Design in Miniature,* when he said: *'Designing is deciding — the problem is not what to include, but what to leave out.'*

While the basic purpose of the postage stamp — the prepayment of postal charges for the carriage and delivery of letters — has not changed perceptibly in 140 years, the fundamental precepts and principles of design and print have been continuously developed and improved to the present day, when the quality of design and the high standards of multicolour printing have become almost commonplace in our daily lives. But this process of development, which stems from the Penny Black and the gradual evolution of stamp design, was at first haphazard and fortuitous. The late 19th century was a period of experiment and trial and error for designers, engravers and printers, a period when many beautiful stamps began to emerge from the Victorian doldrums.

The Designer-Engravers

In early days the stamp designers were the engravers employed by the printing firms, either full-time or freelance, and they had unique responsibilities — engraving an exact replica of a sketch or watercolour, portrait or colony badge, in minuscule size on steel or copper. Scaled-down reductions were achieved by the use of the pantograph, a primitive device which nevertheless effectively reduced the design image while maintaining the exact proportions of the original, and they engraved in recess for the line-engraving (recess) process, or in relief (with a raised printing surface) for the second of the three main printing processes then in use — typography or letterpress. The lithographers drew their designs directly on to the 'stone'.

With a few notable exceptions — Charles and Frederick Heath, Humphrys, Jeens and others mentioned in Chapter 2 — the identities of the designer-engravers of stamps for Great Britain, the colonies and dominions remained in obscurity almost until the turn of the century. When, however, Thomas De La Rue and Company of London were appointed to produce typographed stamps for Britain in 1855, the name of Jean F. Joubert de la Ferté came into prominence. Joubert, a highly skilled engraver *en épargne* (in relief), came to England from France in 1840. De La Rue commissioned him to engrave the Queen's head (or 'diadem') for their first stamp, the 4d. carmine of 1855 which, incidentally, was required to prepay the cost of letters to France. (Embossed stamps had been issued in 1847-54.)

Closely modelled on the Wyon head, Joubert's design was an immediate success and set the pattern for British stamps to the end of the reign. Joubert stayed with De La Rue until 1866, and during that time he completed seven other diadems which were used for the stamps of Ceylon, India, Jamaica and many other countries. His classic design for Hong Kong in 1862 was continued, with the necessary changes of the monarch's head and inscriptions, through the reigns for 100 years — to 1961.

A feature of late-Victorian, Edwardian and early Georgian stamp design was the opportune use of the talents of the leading portrait painters, coin designers and medallists of the times. Heinrich von Angeli, the celebrated painter of emperors and archdukes who was born in Hungary in 1840, became court painter to Queen Victoria and was responsible for the popular 'Jubilee' portrait of Her Majesty which was the basis for numerous colonial stamp designs. Von Angeli painted his masterpiece, a full-length portrait of the

Canada SG 140 – Chalon and von Angeli heads.

Joubert de la Ferté, stamp engraver (1810-84).

Queen standing on the steps of her throne, holding a black fan in her hands, in 1885, just before her golden jubilee. The ageing Queen wore a coronet over a white veil.

Ten years later, on the eve of her diamond jubilee, India called for some new high-value stamps, and De La Rue used the von Angeli head as a model. In 1898 India reissued the three pie stamp with the same portrait, which was again used for British East Africa (1896) and Uganda (1898). The famous Canadian diamond jubilee issue of 1897, designed by L. Pereira and F. Brownell, displayed the finest version of the von Angeli head, paired with the earlier Chalon portrait, and superbly engraved and printed by the American Bank Note Company. The Southern Nigeria issue of 1901 gave De La Rue another – and final – opportunity of employing the von Angeli head. Von Angeli died in Vienna in 1925, aged 85.

Another portrait painter, who was also a distinguished sculptor, was an Austrian, Emil Fuchs, who came to England in 1896. Following a successful exhibition of his work at the Royal Academy, Fuchs was commissioned to design the coins, medals and stamps for the new reign of King Edward VII, and his sculptured profile of the new King became the 'standard' head for the stamps of Great Britain and the colonies. The British stamps were printed by De La Rue and, later, by Harrison & Sons and at Somerset House.

Great Britain – Fuchs's head of Edward VII.

The first stamp designers of British stamps named as such were Bertram Mackennal (later Sir Bertram) and G.W. Eve, responsible for the head and frames respectively of the first stamps for King George V in 1911. The head was based on a photograph by W. and D. Downey, the court photographers, and the stamps were typographed by Harrison & Sons. They were not entirely successful, despite being re-engraved and reissued in 1912, and in that year a new series of stamps was inaugurated by the Mackennal-Eve team.

Mackennal was a sculptor from Melbourne, Australia, who was best known for his memorial to Edward VII at Windsor, and as the author of the

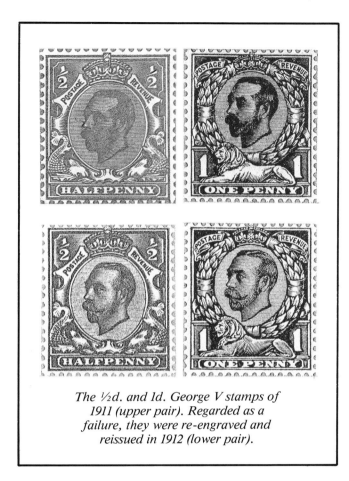

*The ½d. and 1d. George V stamps of
1911 (upper pair). Regarded as a
failure, they were re-engraved and
reissued in 1912 (lower pair).*

The First Commemoratives and Pictorials

While the formal royal portraits, heraldic devices and numerous versions of Britannia continued as the principal design motifs of Britain and some of her colonies and dominions well into the new century, other countries were more enterprising with their stamp designs. Canada's 'Beaver' (1851), the New South Wales 'Sydney Views' (1850) and Western Australia's 'Swan' (1857) were emblematic rather than pictorial, but it was in fact New South Wales which produced the British Empire's first pictorial stamps in 1888. The subjects depicted – all in the traditional

North Borneo pictorial stamp of 1894.

coinage and medals for the new reign. The new profile head of George V was based on Mackennal's own coins and medals, and, like the earlier work of Emil Fuchs, it remained the 'standard' head throughout the reign. Mackennal also designed the magnificent 'Sea-horses' (Britannia in her chariot drawn by three sea-horses), the line-engraved high-value stamps issued from 1913.

All these stamps were engraved by a master of his craft – J.A.C. Harrison (1872-1955). Harrison's long and distinguished career began when he joined Waterlow Brothers and Layton (later Waterlow and Sons Ltd.) as an ornamental engraver. Towards the end of the century he became a freelance engraver, specializing in the design and production of heraldic book-plates. Early in the 1920s he began to work exclusively for Waterlows and became their chief portrait engraver.

His work gained international repute and he engraved, both in recess and relief, many superb portraits and pictorial designs for the postage stamps and banknotes of countries all over the world. Most – if not all – of Waterlow's Georgian heads for the stamps of the British colonies and Commonwealth countries were engraved by Harrison, and there is a comprehensive collection of his die proofs of postage stamps in the British Library.

small format of the Penny Black – were an updated 'Sydney View', an Emu, Captain Cook, the Queen and the colony's coat-of-arms, a Lyre Bird and a friendly Kangaroo. Two larger high-value stamps issued at the same time showed a map of Australia and a portrait of Captain Arthur Phillip, the first governor, with Lord Carrington (inset), governor in 1888. All the stamps were inscribed 'One Hundred Years' and were thus also the first British commemoratives for the colonies.

The small pictorials continued in the Cook Islands with stamps picturing Queen Makea Takau and the Torea or Wry-bill Plover, a bird distinctive for its bent bill (1893); in Malta, where a view of Valletta Harbour appeared on a farthing stamp, the series including a Gozo fishing boat and an ancient Maltese galley (1899-1901); and in Bermuda where the emblematic 'ship in dry dock' (1902) was followed by a splendid picture of the three-masted cog, *Sea Venture,* in which Sir George Somers, who first settled the islands, was shipwrecked in 1609 (1910). Small designs were also adopted by the Maldive Islands, a minaret of the Juma Mosque, Malé (1909), and by the Turks and Caicos Islands with a coastal scene of salt-raking (1900) and another farthing stamp – the Turk's-head cactus (1910). The islands were a dependency of Jamaica and the salt-raking motif, with the fine sailing-ship in the background, was the dependency's badge.

Barbados Diamond Jubilee stamp, 1897.

The stamps probably most popular with collectors in the 1890s were the pictorials issued by North Borneo (1894) and Tonga (1897). The Borneo series – inscribed 'State of North Borneo' – showed a Dyak chief, a Sambar Stag, Sago Palm, Argus Pheasant, the arms of the British North Borneo Company, Malay *dhow,* Crocodile, Mount Kinabalu and the Company's arms with supporters. Neighbouring Brunei issued stamps showing a Brunei River scene in 1907, while Sarawak depicted her successive Rajahs – titled members of the Brooke family – from 1869 to 1947. The Tonga stamps showed the reigning King, George II of Tonga, and the arms, an Ovava Tree, a prehistoric Trilith or monument, Breadfruit, Coral, a Parrot and views of Haapai and Vavau Harbour.

For the Queen's diamond jubilee in 1897 Barbados issued nine stamps showing the colony's seal – Victoria standing in a chariot drawn across the ocean waves by two sea-horses – and followed this with a series for Nelson's centenary (1805-1905) showing his local monument (1906), and a pretty stamp showing Sir Oliph Leigh's ship, the *Olive Blossom,* marking the 300th anniversary of the island's annexation by the British in 1605 (1906). Jubilee stamps from British Guiana (1898) showed Mount Roraima and the Kaieteur Falls, the only clue to the commemoration being the date '1897'. Similar stamps showing the Llandovery Falls were issued by Jamaica in 1900, and Tasmania produced eight large pictorials in 1899.

Three West Indian Islands commemorated the 400th anniversary, in 1898, of their discovery by Columbus – Grenada, which he named 'La Concepcion', a picture of his flagship, the *Santa Maria*; St Lucia, a view of the Pitons (mountains which would have been his first sight of the island); and Trinidad, 'The Landing of Columbus'. Canada issued one of the first map stamps also in 1898 – it was designed by Postmaster-General Mulock and was a colourful map of the world representing the span of imperial penny postage. It was inscribed 'XMAS 1898'.

Canada followed this with a pictorial series in 1908 for the tercentenary of Quebec, and issued numerous commemoratives and pictorials, all attractively designed, in the 1920s and 1930s. The birth of the Australian Commonwealth was heralded in 1913 by a definitive series designed by B. Young – a kangaroo standing on an outline map of the country – and the first of the 'King's Head' definitives. New Zealand, having inaugurated pictorial stamps in 1898 – birds, lakes and mountain scenery – continued the theme with variations through the years to 1909. Newfoundland followed its 1897 commemoratives for

Great Britain's first commemorative stamps were for the Wembley Exhibitions of 1924 and 1925 (SG 430, 432).

Prince Edward   *Queen Victoria*   *Edward, Prince of Wales*

Alexandra, Princess of Wales   *Mary, Duchess of York*

*Members of the Royal Family were depicted on Newfoundland
stamps for the 1897 Diamond Jubilee (SG 83, 85, 87, 88, 89).*

the 400th anniversary of its discovery with a definitive issue picturing the Royal Family, and another pictorial series in 1910. H.S. Wilkinson designed the Union of South Africa's first stamp, a 2½d. commemorative for the opening of the union parliament, issued in 1910 – it was the first stamp of any country to portray the head of the new King, George V, and the design included the arms of the four South African provinces. Small pictorials were issued in 1926.

One of the most famous stamp designs of all time was the Sudan 'Camel Postman' of 1898. At that time, Kitchener (later awarded a peerage) was commander-in-chief of the Anglo-Egyptian forces engaged in ridding the Sudan of the Mahdi's fanatical dervishes. Stamps were scarce and one of his field officers, Colonel E.A. Stanton (later Governor of Khartoum), was instructed to produce a design for new stamps. Inspired by an advertisement for a carpet firm in the *Illustrated London News* – it showed a camel laden with rugs trotting up Ludgate Hill – Stanton produced his camel postman, carrying bags of mail optimistically inscribed 'Berber' and 'Khartoum' (which had yet to be captured). The design was approved and the stamps

were duly printed by De La Rue. They remained in use, with changes of size, watermark and inscription, for 50 years – until 1948.

Harold Nelson designed Britain's first commemorative stamps for the British Empire Exhibition at Wembley in 1924 – he featured the 'British Lion' (thereafter known as the 'Wembley Lion') in a bold, poster-style design which was repeated when the exhibition was reopened in 1925. Later, Mr Nelson adapted one of his Wembley essays very successfully for the superb £1 stamp – St George and the Dragon – engraved by J.A.C. Harrison and issued, with four low values, in 1929 for the ninth congress of the Universal Postal Union in London.

In Europe, the first commemorative issues came from Portugal – sets for Prince Henry the Navigator (1894), St Anthony (1895) and Vasco da Gama (1898). Greece was soon in the running with a set depicting the classic Olympic Games to mark the first games in 1896, and the Netherlands issued a portrait stamp for the coronation of Queen Wilhelmina in 1898, and three stamps honouring Admiral de Ruyter in 1907. Germany's definitives of 1899-1900 featured the crowned bust of 'Germania', from a portrait of the actress, Anna Führing, and four pictorial designs, while the popular French 'Sower' definitives first appeared in 1903. Switzerland's first commemorative – for the 25th anniversary of the UPU – was issued in 1900. The legendary Swiss hero, William Tell, was depicted on stamps issued in 1914 – his son, holding the crossbow, made an earlier appearance, in 1907. Czechoslovakia's first stamps (1918) were designed by Alfons Mucha, the painter who moved to Paris and became a famous exponent of *art nouveau*.

In the United States the first pictorial stamps appeared in 1869 – followed by numerous issues featuring the American presidents until 1893 when a magnificent set of 16 'Columbus' stamps was issued for the Columbian Exposition in Chicago. The designs, all from paintings or engravings, depicted Columbus's *Santa Maria* and fleet, and important events and scenes in his life.

Modern Stamp Designs

Every year the British Post Office markets six, seven or eight commemorative or 'special' issues of stamps embracing a variety of subjects, ranging from art and architecture to royal occasions and wildlife. Since the beginning of the present reign in 1952, over 100 artists have created about 750 designs for more than 200 special series of stamps, mostly conforming to the basic criteria established in 1964 which authorized stamps –

To celebrate events of national and international importance.
To commemorate important anniversaries.
To reflect the British contribution to world affairs, including the arts and sciences.
To extend public patronage to the arts by encouraging the development of minuscule art.

Commendably, during that time, there have been only two major series of definitives, those featuring the 'Wilding' portrait of the Queen, first issued in 1952 and including the 'Castles' high values of 1955-8, and the 'Machin' portrait issues which commenced in 1967. The Machin stamps have proved as popular as they are complicated. The first series were inscribed in shillings and pence, 14 basic values from ½d. to 1s. 9d. with the 4d. and 8d. values both printed in two different colours. Four 'high value' stamps, values 2s. 6d. to £1, were added in 1969. The second series of 'low values' began in 1971 when Britain 'went decimal'; the initial set ranged from ½p to 9p but over the years has extended to the 75p value. Several values have changed colour along the way and others have been printed in both photogravure and lithography, with one or two phosphor bands or on phosphorized paper. Even the simplest listing in the *Collect British Stamps* catalogue runs to nearly 150 items; for the specialist collector this

British definitives of the present reign –
Wilding and Machin head low values, 1955
and 1988 Castle high values.

could be increased many times over. High value decimal Machins first appeared in 1970 (ahead of decimalization), printed in recess; a further series, printed in photogravure, began in 1977. The use of the Machin head did not prove as satisfactory on the larger high values as on the small-sized low value stamps and in 1988 an entirely new series of high value stamps featuring Castles was introduced; the fine engravings were based on photographs taken by the Duke of York.

Postage stamps are a country's ambassadors, and the regular issues of special stamps have far-reaching significance, over and above the functional require-

The Machin head on high values – 2s.6d. (1969),
10p (1970) and £5 (1977).

Stuart Rose, stamp designer.

ments of postage. Post Office policy is that the 'stamp designs and printing should reflect the highest skills available in Britain', and that 'the subject and its design treatment should reflect something worthy from the history, culture, achievement or important current affairs of our nation'. It is a policy which brings the Post Office several million pounds in philatelic revenue each year.

For many years the Post Office ploughed a lonely furrow in the complex processes of stamp design and production – selecting subjects for commemoration, commissioning artists and ensuring that all aesthetic and postal requirements were observed, finally obtaining the Queen's approval, briefing the printers and agreeing production schedules with them. Then, in 1944, a Stamp Advisory Panel was established under the aegis of the newly-formed Council of Industrial Design. In 1968 the Post Office formed its own Stamp Advisory Committee to take over the design responsibilities of the Panel, and also appointed its first Design Adviser, Stuart Rose, to supervise all design aspects of the postal business, including stamps. Mr Rose retired at the end of 1976. The current Head of Stamp Design is Mr Barry Robinson.

The Post Office receives hundreds of suggestions for special stamps each year, some outlandish, others feasible, and all of them are fully considered, although a tentative schedule of commemorative events for new stamps will have been drawn up two or three years ahead of the proposed year of issue. Details of new stamps are announced well in advance, and they will have been designed, approved and perhaps printed in the year prior to issue. Hitches occur, seemingly more frequently these days, when postal rates are increased and the face values printed on forthcoming stamps have to be changed.

Once a special issue of stamps has been decided upon, the first task of the Design Adviser, in cooperation with the Stamp Advisory Committee (whose members include prominent designers and philatelists), is to select and invite an artist, or a number of artists, to submit proposed designs. Unless a certain design subject calls for specialist knowledge and artwork for which a particular artist is the obvious choice, it is usual to commission perhaps three or four artists or printers'

Great Britain – Dorothy Wilding photographs were the basis for elegant Silver Wedding designs in 1948.

studios to submit designs, including one or two 'old hands' as well as newcomers to stamp design.

'Rough-and-Ready'

The Post Office brief instructs the designer in all aspects of the proposed designs – precise size and format, horizontal or vertical (though this may be optional, the former for 'landscapes', the latter for 'portraits') of the stamps; the relative style and size of the sovereign's head (a 'standard' head may be provided); and details of the printing process to be employed – likely to be photogravure which admirably reproduces the soft, graduated tones of artwork based on photographs or watercolour. For recess-printing a line drawing would be more acceptable to the engraver.

Foremost in the artist's mind, of course, is the commemorative theme of the issue and how he can best interpret it in the form of miniature pictures which must 'communicate' and be readily understood and appreciated. Design has three broad divisions – naturalistic, forms taken from nature; conventional, the stylized picture – painting or photograph; and abstract, 'the material manifestation of a mental concept' which, like some of the works of Picasso and Braque, may be incomprehensible! Depending on the subject, the artist probably elects conventional designs, and he may be given an indication of acceptable and appropriate motifs for, perhaps, four designs – these will need to complement each other in style and presentation. Alternatively, the artist may be given a free hand to choose his own design subjects.

After making any necessary researches, the artist prepares his preliminary sketches or 'roughs', both as stamp-sized 'visuals' and in the size applicable to the finished artwork, usually 'four times up' or about 6 × 4 inches for a 'landscape' design. He (or she) may have several alternative designs and in due course the artist's portfolio is presented to the Design Adviser and the Stamp Advisory Committee for approval. The designs may be accepted, subject to slight alteration of lettering or layout.

Inscriptions and figures of value may be set in a recognised type-face or hand-drawn lettering, and the designer has to ensure that these, and other details of the designs in the larger sketches, will be clear and legible when reduced to stamp size. The choice of colour is also discussed at preliminary meetings – colours have to be harmonious and at the same time conform to the three colour primaries – magenta, cyan (blue) and yellow – required by the printer in the form of colour separations. The artist completes the finished artwork and prepares the transparent overlays bearing the captions and denominations for each design. Finally, the artist may be required to prepare 'presentation packs' – descriptive folders containing a set of the stamps – and first day covers for the Post Office.

'The Stamp of Royalty'

All British (and Commonwealth) stamp designs have to be approved by Her Majesty the Queen. Since 1935, stamps issued by the British Post Office for various royal events and anniversaries have featured the Queen herself, her husband, the Duke of Edinburgh, the Prince of Wales, the Duke of York, Princess Anne, as well as King George V, and King George VI and Queen Elizabeth (the Queen Mother). The theme of 'Royal

Four designers contributed differing treatments for the Great Britain 1953 Coronation set. The 1s. 6d. was the work of M.C. Farrar Bell, pictured at foot.

Occasions' on British stamps provides a gallery of royal portraits, a permanent and colourful record of historic events and a reflection of the centuries-old ritual and ceremonial pageantry of successive reigns, including two coronations and a 25th anniversary, two silver jubilees, two silver weddings, an investiture, three royal weddings and royal birthdays.

In 55 years 'the stamps of royalty' can be seen to have developed from the formal and traditional designs of the earlier issues to the informal and very personal portraits and settings of later stamps, although old traditions were revived for the Queen's silver jubilee stamps and those for the 25th anniversary of her coronation.

For the silver jubilee of King George V in 1935, four stamps – ½d., 1d., 1½d. and 2½d. – were designed by Barnett Freedman, a young and talented book illustrator, who featured the 'Mackennal' profile head of George V as used on the contemporary definitive stamps, flanked by the crown, a wreath of laurel and the dates, 1910-35. A single 1½d. stamp was issued for the coronation of King George VI and Queen Elizabeth in 1937 – the selected design was that of Edmund Dulac, who was born in Toulouse and painted portraits as well as illustrating books until 1935, when he first came into prominence with his successful design for the King's Poetry Medal. Dulac drew full-face portraits of the King and Queen based on photographs by Dorothy Wilding, embellished by the crown and the royal monogram, with orb and the ampulla, part of the coronation regalia, in the borders.

Two attractive, modern-style stamps for the silver wedding of King George VI and his consort, Queen Elizabeth, featured 'twin' profile portraits by Dorothy Wilding – the 2½d. 'landscape' stamp was designed by G.T. Knipe, one of Harrison & Sons' staff artists, and the handsome £1 stamp, with its 'picture-frame' border, was executed by Joan Hassall, daughter of John Hassall, the poster artist and contributor to *Punch*. Miss Hassall, who survived four unaccepted essays, a rejected bromide and three competitors, was the first woman to design a British stamp.

For the first commemoratives of the new reign – the coronation of Queen Elizabeth II in 1953 – three of the four stamps featured the familiar Wilding definitive portrait of the Queen: the 2½d. by E.G. Fuller, 4d. by Michael Goaman, and 1s.6d. by M.C. Farrar-Bell, all flanked by the appropriate symbols and emblems of the occasion. For the 1s.3d. stamp Edmund Dulac defied convention with a drawn full-face portrait of the Queen, wearing the St Edward's Crown and an ermine cloak, and holding the sceptre and the orb, against a magnificent tapestry background.

Amidst the most colourful royal pageantry within Caernarvon Castle, the Queen invested Prince Charles as Prince of Wales on 1 July 1969. The investiture stamps, issued on the same day, were designed by

Left: David Gentleman, a prolific stamp designer; with the commemorative set of his that marked the Prince of Wales's Investiture in 1969.

Above: Stamps for royal weddings – Princess Anne (1973), the Prince of Wales (1981) and the Duke of York (1986). Right: Professor Richard Guyatt, and one of the five stamps commemorating the Queen's Silver Jubilee of 1977 (SG 1035).

David Gentleman, the most prolific and successful British stamp designer, who has twice, in 1969 and 1979, been awarded the Reginald M. Phillips' gold medal award for postage stamp design. He was awarded the distinction of Royal Designer for Industry in 1970. His designs for this exclusively Welsh occasion were in keeping with its grandeur – the three 5d. stamps depicted the castle's most prominent edifices, the King's Gate, Queen Eleanor's Gate and the Eagle Tower, all key points in the investiture ceremony. The 9d. stamp showed a 12th-century Celtic cross, while the 1s. stamp featured a bold, full-face portrait of Prince Charles, from a photograph by G. Argent. The stamps were inscribed 'Prince of Wales' in Welsh (*Tywsog Cymru*) and English.

For the royal silver wedding – the 25th wedding anniversary of Her Majesty the Queen and HRH The Duke of Edinburgh – in 1972, Jeffery Matthews, a well-known and experienced stamp designer, was commissioned to design two stamps. He submitted a number of stamp-sized visuals of royal portraits and family groups, actual wedding-day scenes and views of Westminster Abbey, all in a variety of colours. From these, four potential designs were selected for further development and at this stage it was decided to commission new portraits of the royal couple.

For this purpose, Norman Parkinson, the society and *Vogue* photographer who had produced memorable and romantic portraits of Princess Anne, marking her 21st birthday, was invited to take photographs of the Queen and the Duke of Edinburgh. From these emerged Jeffery Matthews' striking profile designs, used on both the 3p and 20p denominations.

A uniform design was used for the special royal wedding 3½p and 20p stamps of 1973, showing bold, smiling portraits of Princess Anne and Captain Mark Phillips. The designers were Collis Clements and Edward Hughes, and the photographs were taken by

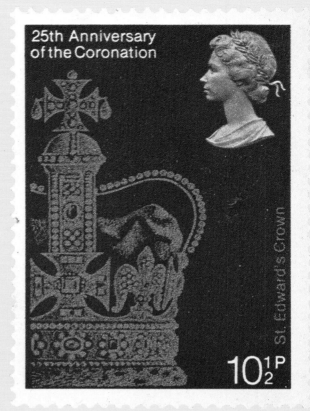

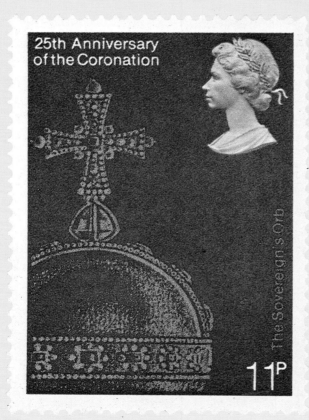

Jeffery Matthews's striking set for the
25th anniversary of the Coronation, 1978.

Lord Lichfield, cousin to the Queen. For the 25th anniversary of the Queen's accession in 1977, four stamps – 8½p, 10p, 11p and 13p, with the later addition of a 9p value – were issued in a uniform design by Richard Guyatt, Professor of Graphic Art at the Royal College of Art. His formal profile of the Queen was flanked by the large, decorative letters, 'ER'. For the 25th anniversary of the Queen's coronation, Jeffery Matthews designed four attractive stamps which recaptured its majesty and splendour – 9p 'The Coronation State Coach'; 10½p 'The St Edward's Crown'; 11p 'The Sovereign's Orb'; and 13p 'The Imperial State Crown'. The subjects were printed in gold on coloured backgrounds. Jeffery Matthews also designed the attractive 12p stamp commemorating the Queen Mother's 80th birthday, issued in 1980. The portrait was based on a photograph by Norman Parkinson.

The two stamps issued for the marriage of Prince Charles to the Lady Diana Spencer in 1981 featured a portrait of the couple by Lord Snowdon; the stamps were put on sale a week before the wedding. Although the wedding day was a public holiday, arrangements were made to provide collectors with a 29 July postmark.

There were two royal issues in 1986, in April to mark the 60th birthday of the Queen, and in July to commemorate the marriage of Prince Andrew, the Duke of York and Miss Sarah Ferguson. The stamps for the royal birthday were designed by Jeffery Matthews using photographs of the Queen taken in 1928, 1942, 1952, 1958, 1973 and 1982; the stamps were printed in se-tenant pairs with three portraits on each. The photographs were carefully selected so that the first portrait on each stamp showed a posed but happy monarch (or princess), on the second portrait an informal photograph was used and for the third a more formal, regal portrait. Mr Matthews was also responsible for the wedding stamps showing a smiling Prince Andrew and Miss Ferguson from a photograph taken by the Prince's photographer-friend Gene Nocon.

British Design Trends

The Elizabethan era has seen remarkable developments in the design and production of British postage stamps. In 1952-4, definitives bearing a three-quarter face portrait of the Queen replaced the former King George VI issues for which Edmund Dulac had provided the head of the King, and Eric Gill, famous sculptor, engraver and typographer, had drawn the frames and lettering (for the nine lower values). The 'Wilding' head was used on commemorative stamps until 1966 and on the 'Regional' stamps (for Northern Ireland, Scotland, Wales, Guernsey, Jersey and the Isle of Man) from 1958 to 1970. It was also extensively used on Commonwealth stamps.

Arnold Machin, Professor of Sculpture at the Royal College of Art, gave British definitive stamps a

Great Britain – the six regional 3d. stamps issued in 1958 for Jersey, Guernsey, Isle of Man, Northern Ireland, Scotland and Wales.

Shakespeare was the first non-royal person to appear on a British stamp. The 400th anniversary of his birth (1964) saw five stamps depicting characters from the plays; the 3d. featured Puck and Bottom.

'new look' when he modelled a plaster cast of the Queen's head in bas-relief, working from photographs of the Queen taken by Lord Snowdon. He prepared three casts, one of which was eventually selected for photography and the photogravure printing process. The stamps, which signified a return to the classic simplicity and dignity of the first stamps of Queen Victoria's reign (and to the short-lived definitives for King Edward VIII in 1936), were first issued in 1967. The decimal stamps appeared in 1971, as did new regional stamps (now known as 'Country' stamps) bearing the Machin head for the first time. Arnold Machin also designed the royal portrait for the decimal coinage of 1968-84.

Regular issues of commemorative stamps, year by year, started in the 1960s – the era of the 'long and narrow' commemorative shape (twice the width of the contemporary definitive), thought to provide the greatest scope to the designer. The horizontal, rather than the vertical, format was most generally used, notably for David Gentleman's 'Shakespeare' (1964), 3d. to 1s.6d., 'Churchill' (with Rosalind Dease) from a photograph by Karsh (1965), 'Battle of Britain' (with Miss Dease and Andrew Restall) (1965), 'Battle of

*Great Britain in 1965 recalled the Battle of Britain, fought
out in the skies 25 years before. The elaborate set of
eight stamps included designs by Andrew Restall (9d.);
also David Gentleman and Rosalind Dease (1s. 3d.).*

Hastings' (1966) and 'Ships' (1969) issues. Reynolds
Stone, the designer and engraver who was responsible
for Churchill's memorial in Westminster Abbey,
designed several stamps – the 3d. 'Victory' of 1946, the
3d. 'General Letter Office' and 'Europa' stamps of
1960, and the delightful 'Paris Conference' issue of 1963
among them. Mr Stone died in 1979.

Architecture and engineering were represented by
stamps for the 'Forth Road Bridge' (1964), 'Post Office
Tower' (1965), 'Westminster Abbey' (1966), 'British
Bridges' (1968), 'Cathedrals' and 'Post Office Technology' (1969). Michael and Sylvia Goaman designed
the 'Botanical Congress' flower stamps (1964), 'Chichester's World Voyage' – *Gipsy Moth IV* – (1967) and
one of the 'Concorde' issues (4d.) of 1969 – David
Gentleman designed the 9d. and 1s.6d. Numerous
famous paintings were reproduced in the 1960s.

Gradually, in the 1970s, commemorative stamps
acquired a new, broad shape, introduced in 1967 to
accommodate the 'Paintings' by Lawrence, Stubbs and

Top stamp: Great Britain, 1969 – Brunel's famous ship
Great Britain *on one of six ship stamps (SG 782).*
*Lower stamp: Great Britain, 1963 – 6d. stamp marking the
centenary of the Paris Postal Conference (SG 636).*

A superb engraving of the fan vaulting in the Henry VII Chapel of Westminster Abbey from the 900th anniversary set, 1966 (SG 688).

Lowry, and the Christmas stamps of that year. Designs generally became brighter, more colourful and less stereotyped, and there was a wider range of events commemorated and subjects depicted. The architectural theme continued with stamps for 'British Rural Architecture' (1970), 'Modern University Buildings' (1971), 'Village Churches' (1972), 'Inigo Jones' (1973), 'European Heritage Year', including London's National Theatre (1975), and 'Historic Buildings' (1978), the occasion for Britain's first miniature sheet – to publicise the London 1980 International Stamp Exhibition. It was sold with a premium of 10p for the benefit of exhibition funds.

David Gentleman designed the three stamps for the International Stamp Exhibition of 1970 – 'Philympia 70' – reproducing the Penny Black of 1840, the Embossed 1s. green of 1847 and the 4d. Carmine of 1855. Public interest in our national heritage was sustained by stamps depicting the paintings of Reynolds and Raeburn (1973) and J.M.W. Turner (1975); literature – the works of Dickens and Wordsworth (1970), Keats, Gray and Sir Walter Scott (1971), Jane Austen (1975), the Brontë Sisters, George Eliot and Mrs Gaskell (1980); and music by Vaughan Williams (1972). 'Scott of the Antarctic' was pictured in a set of 'Polar Explorers' (1972) and another series, 'British Explorers', portrayed Livingstone, Stanley, Drake, Raleigh and Sturt (1973).

Prominent amongst the many issues of the 1980s have been the bold stamps depicting 'British Theatre' (1982) by Adrian George, which earned the Post Office design awards, the 'Maritime Heritage' set, also of 1982, Eric Stemp's bold 'British Army Uniforms' set of 1983, the se-tenant strip of five 'Mail Coach' stamps of 1984 marking the bicentenary of the Bristol to London service, Terence Cuneo's 'Famous Trains' of 1985, Ralph Stedman's controversial designs for the 'Halley's Comet' issue of 1986, the recess and photogravure-printed 'Victorian Britain' quartet of 1987 and the popular 'Birds' and 'Industrial Archaeology' sets of

Cultural figures commemorated by Britain have included – 1968, Constable; 1973, Raeburn; 1972, Vaughan Williams; and 1973, Inigo Jones (SG 774, 934, 903, 936).

Below: Ronald Maddox's Industrial Archaeology miniature sheet of 1989.

The appealing strip of five 9p stamps for British Wildlife, 1977.

After 'Wildlife' (left), designer Patrick Oxenham drew horses for a 1978 set (SG 1066).

From Terence Cuneo in 1985, five Famous Trains including The Golden Arrow *(SG 1273).*

Many countries issued Halley's Comet stamps in 1986; Britain's set was highly controversial (SG 1312).

1989. The last-named set was designed by Ronald Maddox and issued both in vertical format from normal sheets of 100 and in horizontal format from a miniature sheet, one of three promoting the 'Stamp World London '90' international stamp exhibition.

In all the years since the Penny Black, British stamps have retained two unique features – the inclusion in all designs of the sovereign's portrait and the omission of the country name. The royal portrait on our stamps is universally accepted, both as a symbol of Her Majesty's realm and as a tribute to the nation which first issued postage stamps.

Guernsey, Jersey and the Isle of Man

The postal administrations of Guernsey and Jersey in the Channel Islands, and of the Isle of Man, now issue their own stamps, definitives and commemoratives, each in their individual styles.

Among the noted designers of Guernsey stamps are Richard Granger Barrett (the first definitives and the Silver Jubilee and Coronation 25th Anniversary issues), and the design studio of Courvoisier, the Swiss printers.

In Jersey regular artists such as Victor Whiteley, Gordon Drummond and Jennifer Toombs, are, or have been, prolific designers of Commonwealth stamps.

Guernsey has issued four sets of definitives featuring coats of arms and portraits (1969 and 1971), Army Uniforms (1974), Coins (1979) and Island Views (1984). Views, as shown on old postcards, were featured on the 1982 Postage Due stamps. Together with various commemorative issues, the 1984 definitives provide a delightful pictorial record of the beautiful scenery of the Bailiwick of Guernsey.

Jersey's first definitive set in 1969 featured views of the island; decimal stamps in similar designs followed in 1971 and lasted until 1976, when the second definitives showed views with the relevant parish crest as the central element of the design. The coat of arms theme

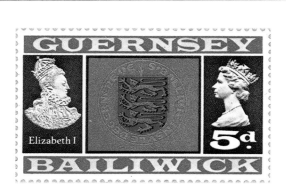

British monarchs are featured on
R. Granger Barrett's 1969 stamps
for postally independent Guernsey (SG 19).

Stamp designer Clive Abbott at work in his studio.

was followed for the third definitives in 1981; this time the stamps were reduced in size to that of conventional definitive issues. The latest definitive issue (1989) returns to the island views approach. Noteworthy amongst Jersey issues are the £2 and £5 definitives of 1977 and 1983 featuring fine portraits of the Queen by Alex Wilson and Norman Hepple.

J. H. Nicholson, the well-known Manx artist, designed many of the attractive Isle of Man stamps (he designed the first Manx 'Regionals' issued in 1958), definitives and commemoratives, while G.V.H. Kneale, former chairman of the Isle of Man Post Office Authority, himself a Manxman with a penchant for

Claude Debussy on Jennifer Toombs's
European Music Year stamp of 1985 (SG 359).
J.H. Nicholson's 1981 Folklore design
(SG 195).

H. Gerl's stylized stag on a
1969 Irish definitive (SG 256).

Manx history, inspired or designed several Isle of Man commemorative issues.

The Republic of Ireland has its own stamp designers and printers, regularly employed in producing commemorative stamps relating to Ireland's culture, art, celebrities, and historic anniversaries. Peter Wildbur has been designing Irish stamps since about 1963, and Louis le Brocquy, well-known in Irish and international art circles, designed the 'Flaming Sun' motif for the 1970 'Europa' stamps issued by numerous European countries, including Ireland. The Irish

J. E. Cooter designed beautiful 'Butterflies'
stamps for Jamaica, 1975 (SG 403, 401).

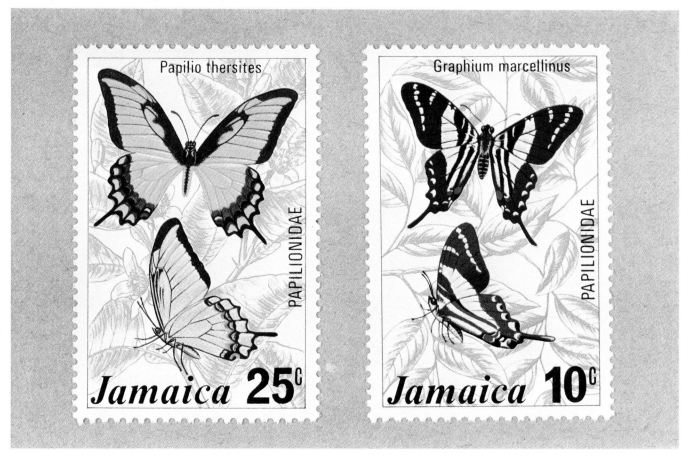

definitives of 1968-82 feature a stylized dog, stag, winged ox and eagle by H. Gerl.

Some Commonwealth Designs

About 75 Commonwealth territories currently issue their own stamps – designers and printers usually commissioned from Great Britain and Europe, directly, through CAPHCO Ltd (Crown Agents) or similar agencies, or from their own resources.

Excellent locally-designed and printed stamps are produced in Australia, Canada and India. New Zealand stamps are usually designed locally and printed overseas, as are those of Malaysia and Sri Lanka (Ceylon). Notable Australian issues in recent years have included the 'Birds and Fishes', 'Navigators' and 'Living Together' definitives of 1963-5, 1966-73 and 1988, 'Famous Australians', the high-value 'Australian Paintings' and the five stamps for the 'Centenary of Australia-England Test Cricket', forming a composite design of a cricket match. Noteworthy from Canada are the series of 'Canadian Indians', the portraits of the Queen by Annigoni (1959), Anthony Buckley (1973) and Peter Grugeon (Silver Jubilee, 1977). New Zealand, famous for her annual 'Health' stamps, contributed a miniature sheet of five contemporary portraits of the Queen by Warren Harrison for the silver jubilee.

In Cyprus, where there is now a separate Turkish

Famous Australians honoured in clean, uncluttered designs from 1970 (SG 479/82).

*Above: Gibbons's own designs to honour Sir Rowland Hill
– Anguilla, 1979 (SG MS364).*
*Right: Birds make excellent stamp designs. Nauru shows a
Wader (1979, SG 178) and Tristan da Cunha an Albatross
(1968, SG 113).*

Cypriot Post, many stamps recall a rich and ancient
culture – buildings, relics, monuments, paintings and
coins – such as the set of 'Treasures' (1976) designed by
A. Tassos. Gibraltar has a regular designer, A.G.
('Freddy') Ryman, who first designed the 'Sea Angling'
and 'Our Lady of Europa' stamps of 1966. His third
definitive series 'Birds, Butterflies and Fishes', was
issued in 1977, and he was commended by the Queen
for his 'Military Uniforms' series. Malta, too, has a
regular designer, Chevalier E.V. Cremona, whose
florid style is best depicted on the definitives of 1965-71
and on his numerous studies of the Grand Masters and
Knights of Malta.

   Innumerable commemoratives and pictorials high-
light the tropical attractions of the West Indian islands –
typical of them are the series of 'Butterflies' designed by
J.E. Cooter for Jamaica (1975–8) and Clive Abbott's
'Carnival' set for Trinidad and Tobago in 1979. The
John Waddington studio designed (and printed) a
splendid definitive series of 'Pirates and Smugglers' for
St Christopher, Nevis and Anguilla in 1970, while

Australian 'Living Together' definitive, Canadian Indian tribe commemorative and New Zealand's Parliament House.

One of the Cypriot Treasures set of 1976 – a terracotta statue (SG 459).

Handsome military uniforms from Gibraltar. Helpfully, short histories of the different regiments are printed on the reverse side (1969, SG 240; 1971, SG 292).

independent Anguilla's colourful stamps and miniature sheet for the Sir Rowland Hill centenary in 1979, reproducing famous and rare stamps of the past, were designed by Stanley Gibbons Ltd.

Two Cecil Beaton photographs of the Queen were used for the 1977 silver jubilee issues of the Cayman Islands and the Turks and Caicos Islands, also for Botswana (with Sir Seretse Khama), where the design honours were shared by M.F. Bryan and G.L. Vasarhelyi. Local folklore, traditions and wildlife are featured on the stamps of Papua New Guinea, local birds and scenes on the definitives of Nauru, the famous 'phosphate island' in the Pacific (1978), which were designed by David Gentleman.

The stamps of the Falkland Islands, British Antarctica and Tristan da Cunha recall the numerous sagas of exploration and discovery in the remotest parts of the world.

Falkland issues have been especially popular since the 1982 war, a £1 + £1 Rebuilding Fund stamp was issued a few months after hostilities ceased; this featured the map of the islands shown on the BBC news programmes during the war. The 15p stamp in the 1983 150th anniversary of British Administration set showed Government House which, with its occupier, Governor Rex Hunt, became one of the 'celebrities' of the nine-week conflict.

Likewise, the issues of tiny Tristan gained popularity after the evacuation of the island in 1961. Perhaps the best set is the 1954 definitives which depicted the peaceful way of life on this remote island. Wildlife has featured on many issues – such as the 1974 Rockhopper Penguin set and the Whales issue of 1975, by R. Granger Barrett and Gordon Drummond respectively.

Prologue

William Caxton 1476   8½P

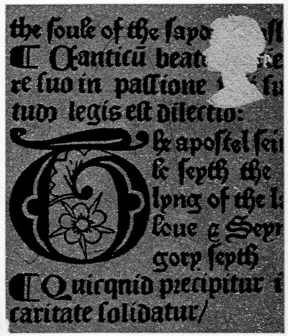

the foule of the fapo...
Of anticū beatī...
re fuo in paffione... fu
tuo legis eft dilectio:
he apoftel fei
le feyth the
lyng of the l.
loue g Sep
gory feyth
Quicquid precipitur i
caritate folidatur/

William Caxton 1476   10P

William Caxton 1476   11P

William Caxton 1476   13P

5
Stamp Printing and Printers

In September 1976, the British Post Office issued four stamps to mark the 500th anniversary of the introduction of printing to Britain by William Caxton. A wool merchant by trade, he spent most of his early life in Bruges, Belgium, where he became a man of eminence in the English community. While engaged in the laborious translation of a manuscript book, *The Histories of Troye*, for the Duchess of Burgundy, sister of the English King, Edward IV, a colleague, the calligrapher Colard Mansion, showed him copies of books printed in Germany, where, at Mainz, Johann Gutenberg had set up a printing press employing movable types in 1450.

Caxton visited Germany to learn more about the craft of printing and on his return to Bruges he set up a press with Mansion, and they produced their first book, the aforementioned *Histories of Troye*. In 1476 he moved to England with all his equipment, and established his press in the shadow of Westminster Abbey, at the 'Sign of the Red Pale', where he enjoyed a successful and prosperous career as writer, printer and publisher. Before he died in 1491, he printed between 80-100 books. The stamps illustrate a woodcut from the second edition of Chaucer's *Canterbury Tales*, printed in 1484, 'The Squire' (8½p); examples of Caxton's type-faces (Gothic characters were not replaced by Roman until 1518) and a decorated initial from the *Tretyse of Love*, printed around 1493 (10p); a woodcut from the second edition of *The Game and Playe of Chesse*, dated 1483 (11p); and an early 16th-century printing press (13p). The stamps were designed by Richard Gay.

From these primitive beginnings came the modern printing press and the technical skills of the present-day printer. Four printing processes have been involved in the manufacture of stamps – recess or line-engraving; typography or letterpress; lithography or photolithography ('offset'); and photogravure.

Johann Gutenberg on a West German stamp, 1961 (SG 1263).

The Caxton set came from 19-year-old Richard Gay, youngest-ever British stamp designer (SG 1014/17).

Recess or Line-Engraving

The best recommendation for recess printing (or direct plate printing as it is sometimes called by veteran printers) is that, even to this day, the finest stamps are still those printed in time-honoured fashion from line-engraved dies and plates in much the same way as the Penny Blacks were printed in 1840. That it is so little used these days – except notably in France, Sweden and the United States – is due to economical factors. Engraved stamps cost more to produce than other methods, engraving a single stamp die may take weeks of sustained effort and engravers with the necessary skills do not 'grow on trees'. While the old-established printing firms keep engravers on their staff, they can only do so when there is work for them, and more and more stamps are being made by faster and more economical methods.

The original design for a line-engraved stamp is usually a watercolour sketch with sharply-delineated highlights which the engraver can translate and reproduce in etched lines on the polished steel die. The full-size sketch is reduced to the size of the stamp – the prototype is perhaps eight times larger – and its outline transferred to the die by means of a pantograph or by tracing the miniature picture. Then, under a magnifying glass and studying the original in a mirror while he works (the die will have a reversed image), the engraver cuts with his burin or graver all the fine lines and detail of the design image. The deeper he cuts his lines, the more intense will be those parts of the design in the printed stamps – the deeper recesses hold more ink and thus print more solid colour tones. Shallow cuts have light tones, 'cross-hatching' produces medium textures and the raised portions print 'white' or blank in the finished article.

When the 'master die' is completed, and the engraver has checked his work with the original by 'proofing' – taking a series of progressive inked proofs – it is hardened and its image is transferred under high pressure to the curved surface of the transfer roller, a cylinder of softened steel, which now bears a positive

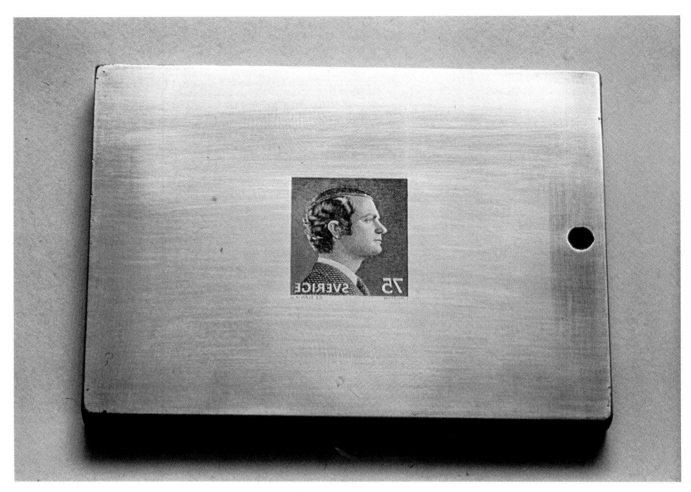

Above, top: The original, completed steel die. Above: The image is transferred to the curved surface of a transfer roller. Right: The hardened roller rocks in multiple images on to the printing cylinder.

The printed stamps leave the printing press.

impression (i.e. not reversed) of the design. The surface of the roller is then hardened and made ready for use in the manufacture of the printing plate or cylinder. A softened steel plate is placed in the transfer press and, under immense pressure, the design image is 'rocked in' on the plate as many times as required to form a printing plate of perhaps 50 or 100 stamps. Throughout the process the greatest accuracy and precision is required — one stamp image may comprise up to 30,000 lines, and a bad slip on the part of the engraver may necessitate the work having to be started all over again.

If some of the fine details appear faint or disappear in the process of 'rocking in', the transfer roller will once more be impressed on the plate in exactly the same position as before (and, if visible to collectors on the issued stamps, it is known as a 'fresh entry'). The metal displaced by the transferring process remains in the form of ridges and mounds between the engraved stamp images (now in reverse again on the plate), and these are removed by scraping and burnishing until the plate's surface is quite smooth and polished.

For 'flat-bed' printing, sheet by sheet, the printing plate is chromium-faced to withstand wear or, if intended for a rotary press, it is curved to fit the printing cylinder and then faced, prior to printing. The

rotary presses print stamps 'on the web' — on long reels of paper which are subsequently guillotined — and in some instances, as in Sweden, the transfer roller applies the stamp images directly on to the curved surface of the printing cylinder. The cylinder is of steel and covered with a thin layer of copper, which is more pliable and easier to print from than steel.

Printing monochrome engraved stamps in a rotary press is a comparatively simple, almost entirely mechanical, operation. In earlier days, bicoloured stamps were obtained by the use of two printing plates, one engraved with the 'vignette' or main design, the other with the frame, and the two sections were printed separately in their respective colours. For modern multicolour printing, special techniques have been evolved — the rubber ink rollers are cut to the shape of the parts of the printing cylinder which are to receive specific colours, and these are applied by inking rollers arranged 'in tandem', building up the multicoloured design. Modern French commemoratives are printed on a Serge Beaume rotary press which has two units — each printing in three colours. In one unit the printing is direct, cylinder to paper, in the other, printing is effected by offset cylinders, and in both units ink is applied successively by three plastic rollers.

The basic principle of recess or *intaglio* printing is that the ink remains in the recesses and lines after the surface of the plate has been wiped clean: in close contact with the plate, the paper picks up the ink in the recessed areas, resulting in the printed stamps. The stamp design stands out in relief (like the impression on the transfer roller) and the raised impression can be felt with the finger-tips. Perforation follows the printing process — for small print 'runs' this is usually performed on a separate machine, but modern rotary presses now incorporate perforating cylinders which operate immediately the stamps have been printed.

Occasionally recess printing is combined with another process, such as typography, lithography or photogravure. The Great Britain 'Commonwealth Parliamentary Conference' stamps of 1973 were printed by recess and typography, and the 'Sailing' stamps of 1975 by recess and photogravure.

Typography or Letterpress

Strictly, 'typography' is the art or style of printing, and a typographer is one who designs or sets type, or simply a printer, while 'letterpress', also known as 'surface printing', is a printer's term for printed matter. Both terms relate to the printing of stamps from raised type, which is basically the method, originated by Caxton, used for printing books in earlier days.

Using the same source of design — drawing or watercolour — as for recess printing, the master die, a steel plaque, is cut in relief (and reverse) by the engraver who cuts away the unwanted portions of the design, leaving the printing surface raised, just as in normal printing. Duplicate impressions are obtained by transfer under pressure to lead blocks corresponding to the size of the stamp, and the required number of blocks or moulds (to form a plate) is clamped in a frame and immersed in an electro-chemical bath ('electrotyping'), where a thin copper shell is formed over the embryo plate, then backed with a metal alloy, a mixture of type metal and lead, planed smooth and coated with steel or chromium, and the plate is then ready for printing.

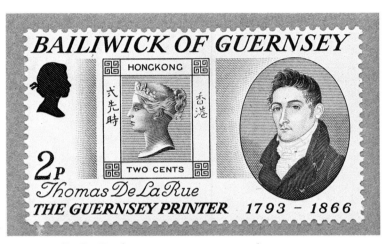

De La Rue's stamps commemorated.

De La Rue, who pioneered typographed stamps with their first issues for Great Britain, devised a system of preparing the moulds in which the original die was shaped to fit exactly inside a heavy metal 'ring' corresponding to the size and shape of the perforated stamp. The pieces of lead were forced down on to the original in a press, and the moulds thus obtained received perfect (reversed) impressions of the original die, the 'ring' ensuring that each mould was exactly the same shape and size as its fellows. Printing is from the raised portions of the plate which are inked and applied directly to the paper in the press. A similar reproduction process, stereotyping – employing plaster of Paris moulds – is sometimes used. Typographed stamps can be identified by 'splurges' of ink on the face and relief outlines on the back.

Typography in its simplest form – the setting of loose type within a locked chase, forme or frame and printing from it – is found among the numerous overprints and surcharges which appear on stamps. These may signify the change of a country's name, alter the purpose of a stamp or amend its original face value, and the need for 'provisionals' (as they are termed) usually arises in an emergency – when there is insufficient time for the preparation of new stamps, or supplies of the regular stamps are delayed. Time permitting, the larger printing firms are able to make a plate of stereotyped overprints and proceed with the printing, but often, in the past, the smaller countries and colonial territories entrusted the work to local printers and newspaper offices with inadequate quantities of type, and numerous errors resulted.

Lithography or Photo-Lithography

This is another surface process. Lithography was discovered by Alois Senefelder of Munich in 1798 – he found by chance that a greased impression on a wellwatered block of limestone could be inked and used for 'printing' on paper. The image or design could be drawn (in reverse) direct on the stone in greasy ink or applied by means of special transfers, the blank parts of the stone being neutralized by the water (grease and water being incompatible). Transfers were also taken *from* the stone – as many as required to form a plate for printing stamps – and this was the method used by the early printers of British colonial and foreign countries' stamps during the 19th century.

Lithography became an art form – an artist's work, drawn on the original stone, could be reproduced, inexpensively, any number of times and in the exact colours of the original. The process was adopted by several noted artists – Delacroix, Daumier, Géricault, Goya, Manet, and others – while Toulouse-Lautrec's famous posters of Paris 'night life' in the 1890s were mainly lithographs.

Photo-lithography or 'offset' has become the leading commercial printing process in the world today. It combines photography with economic plate-making and the fast, efficient rotary press; it involves the unique third ('offset') cylinder which relays the design image from plate cylinder to paper; and it provides an immaculate end-product which reflects the tonal qualities and brilliant colours of the original.

The initial photography is directed towards making a colour transparency of the original artwork, reduction and multiplication of the design to stamp size, processing the colour separations which form the separate printing plates, and the inclusion of the halftone screen to provide a range of tones for each colour. The transparencies and the overlays bearing the stamp's captions, country name and denomination, comprise the 'finished artwork' – the colour negatives are 'printed down' on to flexible aluminium or zinc plates, each of which is wrapped around a cylinder. The impression on the plate cylinder (which is equivalent to the printing cylinder in other processes) is a positive one – during the course of printing the impression is offset on to a rubber 'blanket' roller and then transferred (or 'printed') on to the paper. In keeping with the 'grease and water' principle, liberal sprays of water precede the inking process.

An average four-unit press will have the paired cylinders and blanket rollers operating in tandem, a pair for each colour (which represents part of the

Retouching blemishes on the printing cylinder of Great Britain 17p definitive stamps.

'Step-and-repeat' camera – used to produce a multipositive plate for the printing of stamps in photogravure.

design) – magenta, cyan (or blue), yellow and black – and the web of paper passing through the press will pick up each of the colour images in sequence and, providing all the units are in perfect register and synchronization, produce the sheets of printed stamps. Perforating and guillotining complete the operation. Litho-printed stamps from modern offset presses can be identified by the sharp edges to lettering and solid colour, and by the 'honeycomb' pattern of screened dots.

The Photogravure Process

The postage stamps of Great Britain and of many Commonwealth and foreign countries are today printed by photogravure which, as its name indicates, is a combination of photography and 'gravure' or recess printing. Harrison and Sons introduced photogravure in 1923 when they supplied a set of definitives picturing King Fuad I of Egypt. It is to their credit that, with few exceptions, Egyptian stamps have been photogravure-printed to the present day, first by the Survey Department, later by the Postal Authority Press, in Cairo. Harrisons first photogravure-printed British stamps, with the effigy of King George V modelled once again on Mackennal's coinage head, appeared in 1934. Bavaria pioneered photogravure stamps in 1914.

The key features of photogravure-printing are accurate and precise photography and etching. The artwork, which may comprise photographs or wash drawings, is photographed by a 'step-and-repeat' camera and the negative is processed to form a glass 'multipositive' plate which is approximately the size of

Completed sheets of Britain's 12p stamps pour from the Jumelle press.

Guillotining sheets of the panes of stamps for the British 1980 £3 Wedgwood book.

a sheet of stamps. The multipositive is then printed down on a paper coated with gelatine, called a 'carbon tissue'. The tissue has a 'screened' surface which is a form of grid patterned with tiny dots or 'cells' which vary in depth according to the tones of the original design. The tissue is then 'squeegeed' on to the curved surface of the copper cylinder – ultimately the printing cylinder – and etched, creating miniature reproductions of the original design in which the images are composed of tiny recessed dots, corresponding in depth (and in intensity of colour) to the 'bite' of the acid on the gelatine tissue.

For multicoloured designs, several cylinders will be required, each representing parts of the designs and their separate colours, and when these are completed and the numerous marginal sheet markings are added, the work is checked by proofing: the cylinders are chromium-plated and are then ready for printing.

Rotary presses may have four, five or more printing cylinders, but additional colours may be obtained by overprinting one on another. Each printing cylinder revolves in a trough of ink and, just before the fast revolving cylinder reaches the paper, a 'doctor blade' presses against it and scrapes off excess

ink, leaving ink only in the recesses. An impression cylinder holds the reel of paper hard against the printing cylinder, and an electronic 'eye' maintains the paper in the correct register for the next colour to be printed. Very fluid, but quick-drying inks contribute to long printing runs at high speed and low cost.

Photogravure-printed stamps have an attractive 'photographic' quality – soft gradations of colour and of light and shade are their distinguishing features. They can be identified by the overall pattern of microscopic dots on the printed surface, and by the coarse impression (as opposed to the sharp definition of photolithographed stamps) of the designs under a magnifying glass. The nature of the process, however, does not permit the satisfactory reproduction of very fine lines and cursive scripts.

A sheet of photogravure stamps 'hot from the press' (or from the post office counter) will be seen to have numerous marks in the margins. Sheets of commemorative or 'special' stamps are usually printed in double panes of 50 stamps in each pane, with the cylinder numbers – 1A, 2B etc. – recorded in vertical sequence in the left-hand margin, the right-hand pane identified by a dot or stop following the number.

Marginal arrows indicate the divisions of sheets for post office clerks, and the so-called 'traffic lights' – large coloured dots in a 'box' – are used to check sheets for missing colours. 'Autotron' scanner and various other registration check marks appear in the margins. Phosphor bands, used to activate automatic letter-facing machines and sort mail into first and second class, can be seen as semi-transparent vertical bars or lines.

The Stamp Printers

Harrison and Sons started as printers in the mid-18th century when, about 1750, James Harrison set up a press. From 1910, when the company was awarded a contract to print British stamps, Harrisons used the letterpress process, but in 1924 it was decided to install the special plant and equipment required for photogravure at their works at St Martin's Lane, London. (The long-established Hayes, Middlesex, printery is used mainly for lithograph printing.) In 1933, when the company again secured the contract to print British stamps, it became necessary to find another factory and suitable premises were acquired at High Wycombe in Buckinghamshire, now the firm's headquarters for postage stamp security printing and numerous other commercial printing activities. The development and improvement of photogravure printing was largely due to the ideas and innovations of one of the firm's directors, R.F. York, who was awarded the OBE in 1968.

In 1972, Harrisons installed a super rotary printing press – the 'Jumelle' – named from the French for 'twin'. This giant machine combines recess and gravure printing, and the two processes can be employed together on the same stamps, or independently on different issues with both units working simultaneously if needed. The recess image is impressed on the cylinder by an automatic transfer machine, and seven gravure colours combined with three *intaglio* colours can be printed in one pass through the machine. A rotary perforator is built-in, and the 'Jumelle' can also be used for printing stamps for coils (or rolls) and booklets from the same cylinders.

The 'Jumelle' press was first used to print some of the 3p 'Royal Silver Wedding' stamps of 1972, and Harrison and Sons were honoured by a visit of the Queen, the Duke of Edinburgh and the Princes Andrew and Edward to see the stamps being printed.

Thomas De La Rue was born in Guernsey in 1793, and at the age of ten he was apprenticed to his brother-in-law, a master printer. In 1818 he moved to London with his family; he set up shop as a paper manufacturer and produced his first playing-cards – he was granted Royal Letters Patent for printing them in 1832. Then, in 1840, he turned his attention to the printing of

Thomas De La Rue (1793-1866), pioneer printer of the Victorian era, an historic name for philatelists.

adhesive stamps, and in 1853 he won a contract for the printing of fiscal stamps for the department of Inland Revenue. Two years later, with the skilled help of Joubert de la Ferté, the engraver, he began the many years of printing stamps for Britain and the colonies. Until the death of Edward VII in 1910, De La Rue printed the entire postage stamp requirements of the United Kingdom.

Other countries, some 200 or more, have entrusted De La Rue with their print orders for stamps and banknotes in the past hundred years. Rival printers rallied round when the old De La Rue printing works at Bunhill Row in London were partly destroyed by air raids in 1940. The firm survived and the De La Rue Company (as it is now called) is now firmly established in Basingstoke, Hampshire, whence it moved in 1970.

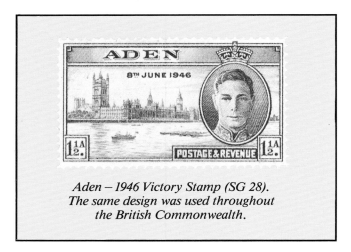

Aden – 1946 Victory Stamp (SG 28).
The same design was used throughout
the British Commonwealth.

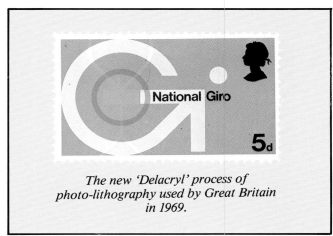

The new 'Delacryl' process of
photo-lithography used by Great Britain
in 1969.

Stamps are also printed at De La Rue's vast factory in Gateshead, which is largely concerned with banknote production. In 1946 De La Rue printed the Victory 'omnibus' issues for the Commonwealth, and shared the printing of the coronation 'omnibus' with Bradbury, Wilkinson in 1953. For the newly-formed United Nations Postal Administration, De La Rue had the great honour to supply the first stamps in 1951 with Enschedé of Holland.

De La Rue can offer stamps by all the known printing processes, including 'Delacryl', an advanced and refined photo-lithographic process which combines fine-line work and soft gradations of tone with multi-colour facilities. The first British stamps printed by 'Delacryl' were the 'Post Office Technology' issues of 1969, designed by David Gentleman.

Perkins Bacon, Bradbury Wilkinson and Waterlow are names long associated with the printing of postage stamps, both for Great Britain, the colonies and Commonwealth countries. Perkins, Bacon and Petch (Perkins, Bacon and Co. from 1852) printed the world's first stamps for Britain in 1840, and also printed the first engraved stamps for Natal, New Zealand, Newfoundland, South Australia, Tasmania and numerous other countries. With increased competition from the other printing firms, Perkins Bacon developed the printing of banknotes and cheques, becoming the leaders in that specialized field. In 1965, Perkins Bacon Ltd became a subsidiary of The Metal Box Company and they now print stamps on modern lithograph machines for the Commonwealth.

Bradbury and Evans set up business in 1824 and, as Bradbury, Wilkinson and Company, printed the first stamps for the Falkland Islands in 1878 and similar stamps for the Transvaal in the same year. As banknote printers they excelled in the engraved process and produced some classic designs for the British South Africa Company (Rhodesia) in 1890. They were involved in printing some of the British 'Seahorses' of 1918, the 'Postal Union Congress' £1 of 1929 and, in more recent times, the engraved 'Machin' high values of 1969 and

1970-2. Bradbury Wilkinson also now print modern litho stamps for Commonwealth territories.

Waterlow and Sons, formerly Waterlow Brothers and Layton, was founded by Sidney Hedley Waterlow, and the firm printed its first lithographed stamps for British Guiana in 1852 – rather primitive labels – and 1853, a classic 'Ship' stamp engraved by C.H. Jeens. Waterlows were best known for their British 'Seahorses', the 'Wembley' stamps, the engraved high values for King George VI in 1939 and 1951, and the first printing of the 'Castle' high values of 1955. In 1961 they

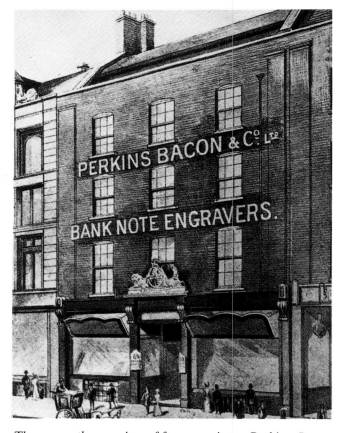

These were the premises of famous printers Perkins, Bacon
at 69 Fleet Street, London.

French 'Marianne' engraved and typographed (1945, SG 933, 915).

were taken over by De La Rue who continued the Waterlow contracts for printing definitives for Commonwealth countries, including British Guiana and the Falkland Islands.

John Waddington Ltd of Leeds, perhaps best known to the public for their games and playing cards, are a highly diversified group, with several factories in the area specializing in commercial printing – packaging, stationery, advertising, plastics, machinery and security printing. The design and printing of postage stamps is carried on by a subsidiary, The House of Questa Ltd, at premises in south-east London. The colourful St Christopher-Nevis-Anguilla definitives of 1970 were the first stamps produced by Waddingtons in their entirety.

The House of Questa specialize in photo-litho printing for numerous countries such as Anguilla, Antigua and Barbuda, Botswana, the Cayman Islands, Dominica, Grenada and the Grenadines, Nauru, the Solomon Islands, Tuvalu and many others. They have printed stamps for the British Post Office since 1980, principally the Country Issues for Northern Ireland,

Scotland and Wales.

Walsall Security Printers also prints photo-litho stamps – with a difference. They specialize in die-stamped or embossed cut-to-shape, self-adhesive stamps for certain countries such as Tonga, Sierra Leone and Norfolk Island. Their first stamps for Tonga in 1963, commemorating the First Polynesian Gold Coinage, were circular designs depicting the coins, embossed on gold foil (rather unkindly dubbed 'beer-mats' by collectors). Subsequent 'cut-to-shape' designs have included bananas, a water-melon, a parrot and a football for Tonga; map, cola and palm nuts, and a diamond for Sierra Leone; and an outline map for Norfolk Island.

Australian stamps are printed by the Note Printing Branch of the Reserve Bank of Australia, Canadian stamps by the British American Bank Note Co., the Canadian Bank Note Co. and a commercial printer, Ashton-Potter. South African stamps have been printed by the Government Printer, Pretoria, since 1929.

Printers Abroad

In Europe virtually every country has its 'State Printing Works' or similarly-named organization, devoted to security printing – postage stamps or banknotes, or both. The French Postage Stamp Printing Office has been located in Paris since 1895, and has always been noted for the quality of its stamps – for France and the French territories overseas – and for its large and versatile team of designers and designer-engravers, notably the ubiquitous Pierre Gandon who designed the 'Marianne' stamps of 1945-6, and engraved some of them. The first 'Marianne', designed by Edmund Dulac and printed by De La Rue, was the subject of stamps issued in France (following the liberation) in 1944-5. The most prolific designer of modern French stamps is Pierrette Lambert. In 1970 part of the Printing Works was transferred to Périgueux, and a special stamp printed there, was issued.

In 1979, two important anniversaries in the stamp-printing world were commemorated. West Berlin issued a stamp marking the centenary of the *Bundesdruckerei,* the State Printing Works in Berlin – the design showed the Prussian and German eagles. And Austria issued a stamp for the 175th anniversary of the

Above, top: A fine old steam-driven printing machine to mark the Austrian State Printing Works' anniversary in 1979 (SG 1850).
Above: Tonga has had many unusually shaped stamps using novel printing processes (SG 255).

The three Dutch princesses charmingly engraved for a 1946 Child Welfare set (SG 627, 628, 630). Beatrix is now Queen.

State Printing Office in Vienna, which has produced many fine engraved stamps, not only for Austria, but for numerous other countries.

Johannes Enschedé en Zonen of Haarlem, Holland, was founded in 1703 by Izaak Enschedé. Since 1866, Enschedé have printed almost all the issued stamps for the Netherlands and its overseas territories, and many stamps for the rest of the world, including British Commonwealth countries. Its destinies are guided by one of Europe's most famous and respected stamp designers and engravers, Sem Hartz, who joined the firm in 1934. Sem drew, from life, the sketches of the three Dutch Princesses – Irene, Margriet and Beatrix – for the 'Child Welfare' stamps of 1946. The lettering was the work of Jan van Krimpen, famous calligrapher and typographer.

'Stamps for the whole world' is the proud achievement of the Swiss photogravure printers, Hélio Courvoisier SA of La Chaux-de-Fonds, founded in 1880 by Alexandre Courvoisier, and formed as a company in 1926. A photogravure press was acquired in 1928 and their first stamps for Switzerland – a 'Pro Juventute' issue – were printed in 1931. They now print immaculate stamps for many countries besides Switzerland – a recent example was the Jersey issue for the Queen's coronation anniversary (1978) which showed the head of the Queen from the Jersey crown piece, and that of the Duke of Edinburgh from a commemorative medal.

For more than sixty years the Stamp Printing Works of the Royal Swedish Post Office has printed its stamps by the steel-engraving (recess) process. For many years, Sven Ewert was the principal engraver but today the studio team is headed by Polish-born Czeslaw Slania, one of the world's foremost stamp engravers, who also works for the Danish Post Office and other postal administrations. The Swedish team includes Majvor Franzén-Matthews, reputedly the only woman stamp engraver in the world at the present time. Other printers, all with worldwide interests, are the State Printing Works of Italy, Finland, Belgium and Japan, the Government Printers, Israel, with staff designers, M. and G. Shamir, also Aspioti-Elka of Athens, Heraclio Fournier of Vitoria, Spain, and Delrieu, So.Ge.Im. and Edila of France. De La Rue have a stamp printery at Bogota in Colombia, South America.

The French lithographers, Cartor S.A.; specialize in embossed or die-stamped issues on gold foil, a technique used by Harrison and Sons for the Queen's head on some British stamps and also on some Gambia commemoratives, while in 1966 Ajans-Turk Matbaasi of Ankara introduced 'thermography' – a form of plastic application – to provide a relief design on lithographed stamps. Bhutan issued stamps in 1967 with a laminated prismatic-ribbed plastic surface giving a three-dimensional effect.

6
Varieties and Printing Flaws

Stamp varieties form an unusual and interesting side-line for collectors whose enthusiasm is aroused and encouraged by the possibility of discovering distinctive flaws among current stamps – the stamps we use every day on our letters. New issues are minutely examined for flaws and, if found to be 'constant' – that is, recurring on every sheet or a number of sheets of stamps – their location is established and recorded for the benefit of other collectors and for eventual inclusion in the appropriate stamp catalogues.

Varieties are defined as stamps 'differing in some visible detail of their manufacture from the normal issues, due to faults in the process of printing'. Errors of design, printing, colour etc. originating *at source* (as described in Chapter 3) are often loosely termed 'varieties', but with the latter we are primarily concerned with machine faults arising during the actual printing of the stamps – the fortuitous blem-. ishes which are apparent on the printed designs, or in the perforations or watermark. Millions of postage stamps are printed and used every day, all over the world, and modern printing presses are as efficient and reliable as technology and innovation can make them. Nevertheless, imperfections do occur and their characteristics can be linked to the particular printing process involved.

A basic knowledge of the printing process is therefore helpful in tracking down specific types of varieties and flaws, and while many of them are com-paratively minor and have no especial interest or significance, the collector needs to be able to identify them if only to avoid a wild-goose chase. There is a lot of satisfaction to be gained in the discovery of an important and worthwhile flaw, or even in finding one that has already been noted and recorded in stamp magazines and catalogues.

The Classic 'Re-entry'

Each of the four main printing processes described in the previous chapter have produced their own varieties. Line-engraving or recess is the oldest and

most respected method of printing postage stamps, but flaws and re-entries (corrections of faulty impres-sions on the plate) also stem from the world's first stamps – the Penny Black and Twopence Blue issued by Great Britain in 1840.

First, a definition of 're-entry': 'A term used in philately to indicate a double impression, usually of a small portion of the design, which may be found on certain stamps printed by the line-engraved process. The duplication is the result of a second application of the transfer roller upon the printing plate, in a position which is "non-coincidental", ie not identical with the original entry, and causing impressions of both entries to appear on the printed stamp'. Strictly, the term 're-entry' applies only to instances where a plate has been used for printing and, through damage or wear, requires re-entering of the engraved lines by the transfer roller. If, during the initial preparation of the plate the return run of the transfer roller fails to coincide with the outward run, the correct term is a 'shift' or 'shifted transfer', but when a faint impression is superimposed or a faulty and incompletely erased image is entirely re-entered by the transfer roller, the term 'fresh entry' is used.

Though commonly accepted as re-entries, 'shifts' are generally caused by heavy pressure – undue pressure – on the plate which is seen as doubled or thickened lines on the stamp. If a new entry exactly matches the lines of the original impression – a 'coincident' re-entry – no doubling will be visible, only perhaps a deeper engraving on the issued stamp. However, most collectors are happy to accept doubled impressions as evidence of a 're-entry'.

Noteworthy re-entries on British stamps include the early line-engraved issues of Queen Victoria, the high-value 'Seahorses' first issued in 1913, the King George VI high values of 1939-48 and the Queen Elizabeth high value stamps – the 'Castles' – of 1955-8. Some clear re-entries are to be found on Australian stamps, notably the 1½d. 'Swan' (1929), 6d. 'Kings-ford Smith' (1931), 3½d. 'Royal Visit' (1954) and 3½d. 'Christmas' (1957). For Canada the catalogues record a major re-entry on the 3d. 'Beaver' stamp – Canada's first – of 1851, similarly on the 10d. 'Jacques Cartier' issue of 1855, and again on the five cent 'Beaver' of 1859. Canada's six cent 'Transport' defin-

---

Opposite: On the top stamp there is an extra flagstaff to the right of the Round Tower (SG 211a). This variety adds considerable value.

British Guiana retouched stamp – mountains shaded.

The 1931 airmail stamp illustrates a re-entry. The top stamp has FO of KINGSFORD and LD of WORLD partly doubled (SG 123a).

itive of 1970 was re-engraved in novel fashion – the original die was duplicated by transfer, and later the duplicate was re-engraved to make fresh printing plates (and stamps with much stronger impressions). Ireland's 3½p 'Rugger' stamp of 1974 showed clear re-entries – doubled frame-lines and inscriptions – on certain panes.

Retouches are minor corrections carried out by hand-engraving on the plate or cylinder and, though it is a term now commonly applied to flaws 'touched out' on photogravure-printed stamps, the early line-engraved stamps show evidence of numerous retouches on the plate – extraneous guidelines and dots were removed by the engraver, weak and shallow entries deepened, and other imperfections made good. Retouching on engraved stamps can usually be identified by comparison with the original (unretouched) stamps – seen as the strengthening of framelines, cross-hatching of clouds or an abnormal intensification of colour on parts of the stamp. Examples include Australia's ½d. 'Kangaroo' definitive of 1949 with shaded lines over the background hill, the British Guiana one cent 'Jubilee' stamp (1898) with mountains shaded, Brunei's pictorial series of 1907-16 with retouches in the sky and a distinctive '5c' retouch, the Kenya, Uganda and Tanganyika ten cent and 1s. 'shaded mountain' of 1949, and the New South Wales 2d. 'Sydney View' of 1851.

Printing flaws on engraved stamps usually appear as gashes, lines or blemishes in the designs, invariably caused by surface damage on the printing plate or cylinder. The G.B. 1d. black was printed from 11 plates – two of them were adapted to print the first 2d. blue stamps, and seven of them were used for the first printings of the 1d. reds. Each plate had its characteristic corner letters, re-entries and flaws which enabled the different plates to be identified. The 'stars' in the upper corners were all slightly different, and the well-known double star, known as the 'Union Jack' re-entry due to its resemblance to the flag, occurs on a 1d. red – plate 75. The normal star has 12 rays or points, often severely curtailed or missing altogether, and the location of faulty rays is indicated on the clock-face principle, perhaps '4 o'clock' or '8 o'clock' on the star. The hand-punched corner letters were frequently malformed or distorted, notably the square-footed 'J' caused by a defective punch which occurred on the earlier plates. The 1½d. of 1870 was lettered OP-PC for CP-PC.

Fortuitous indentations on engraved plates are, in effect, extra lines or recesses, and appear as extraneous coloured marks on the issued stamps; conversely, any dirt or foreign matter lodged in the grooves may well nullify parts of the stamp design – as the unrecessed portions of the plate are wiped clean of ink prior to printing – and will show as white streaks or blobs on the stamps. The well-known 'extra flagstaff' variety

Above: A very distinctive retouch to Brunei stamp. The '5c' at top left (left-hand stamp) appears much paler in consequence.

Left: Great Britain's first stamp printed by typography – the 4d. carmine of 1855.

one plate on to sheets of stamps which already bear impressions from the first – vignette or frame – plate, and they are apparent when the vignette picture impinges on one side of the frame, leaving a wide gap on the other side. Sometimes the two parts of a design overlap.

Varieties of Typography

Typographed stamps are printed from the raised portions of the plate, and defects in manufacture may occur at any stage in the course of electrotyping or plate-making, but most typo flaws – broken letters and frames, scratches and blobs etc – are caused by damage or wear on the plate. Raised type is especially vulnerable to accidental knocks which may occur through constant use. With a few exceptions, all British stamps were typographed by De La Rue from 1855 to Edwardian times, and some interesting varieties have been recorded.

The most common faults on these stamps are deformed corner letters or individual lettering in the inscriptions or face values, bent or broken frame-lines and fortuitous marks which may change a 'C' into a 'G' or an 'F' into an 'E'. Numerous frame breaks occurred in the very first surface-printed stamp, the 4d. carmine of 1855, while there is a rare variety of the

on numerous stamps of the King George V 'Silver Jubilee' omnibus series of 1935 – it appears alongside the main tower of Windsor Castle – was caused by a fortuitous scratch on the vignette plate. So-called 'colour shifts' were a common feature of stamps printed from separate vignette (main design) and frame plates. Strictly these are design shifts, due to the careless alignment or registration when printing from

1862 1s. (SG 89) with numerous typography flaws.

1862 3d. rose, the more usual 'no dots'.

1s. green of 1862 – the letter 'K' within a white circle (the stamp lettered 'KD' in the lower corners), apparently caused when a damaged letter was replaced by a 'plug' which formed a ring around the letter 'K'. Typo stamps include areas of solid colour and the 4d., 6d. and 9d. values of the 1862-4 series are known with fine hairlines across the lettered corners – the 9d. from plate 3 is the rare one. Also in 1862, plate 3 of the 3d. rose was distinguished by a small white dot at either end of the word 'Postage', almost level with the Queen's chin – the plate was never put to press, though a few stamps were printed, and while this is not a variety in the philatelic sense, the 'dotted 3d.' is an extremely rare stamp. Tiny 'ring' flaws are comparatively common on these issues.

The pretty little Penny Lilac stamp of 1881, first issued with 14 corner dots or pearls, but replaced by a 16-dot version after a few months, was in use until the turn of the century and had numerous misadventures during that time. It is known printed in error on the gummed side and also printed on both sides, and several broken frames are recorded – two major ones and a host of minor imperfections. 'Squashed dots' have been found and clogging of the raised type on the plate accounted for solid patches of colour instead of fine shaded lines.

Britain's first bicoloured stamps, the so-called

1881 1d. lilac (SG 170) – the rarer '14 dots'.

*Great Britain – Edward VII 6d. & 10d. stamps
showing 'no cross on crown' variety,
a desirable flaw.*

*The 4d. 'Jubilee' stamp (SG 205) with shading missing within
the figure 4.*

'Jubilee' issue which first appeared in 1887, the year of the Queen's celebration of the 50th anniversary of her accession, were printed from separate 'head' and 'duty' plates, except for the ½d. vermilion and 1s. green, the 2½d., 3d. and 6d. stamps printed on coloured papers, for which single plates were employed. In 1900 the ½d. was issued in blue-green and the 1s. in green and carmine. The numerous varieties on all values – frame breaks, deformed letters and emblems, and superfluous dots and dashes – were

due to flaws on the printing plates. Some plates, notably for the much-used ½d. vermilion, developed hairline cracks, visible on the stamps as irregular white lines, and this value is also known printed on the gummed side, on both sides and doubly printed. The 1½d. may be found with 'horns' on top of the two figures '1' in '1½d', the 2d. with a double frame-line, the 4d. with shading omitted within the figure '4' and the 4½d. with a dot between the '4' and '½', or as a full stop beneath the 'd'.

Some values of the Edwardian issues of 1901-10 repeated the 'Jubilee' designs and consequently similar flaws are to be found. The 10d. stamp and the 6d. and 10d. issues of later printings are recorded with 'no cross on crown'. Listed varieties of the first King George V

*The never-issued 2d. Tyrian Plum of 1910 (SG 266a)
remembered in 1979 by British Virgin Is. (SG 415).*

stamps of 1911-12 include the 'no cross on crown' flaw – it occurred on the 1d. stamp and, in later printings on three different watermarks, on both the ½d. and 1d. The cross on the crown projected above the frame at the top and was liable to damage, but the numerous faint impressions and incomplete crosses suggest weak engraving and consequent inking faults. A new range of King George V definitive stamps, 1912-22, the Mackennal 'coinage and medal heads', introduced two interesting and well-known varieties – the 'Q' for 'O' in 'ONE' of the 1d., also found with the 'Q' reversed or inverted, and the 'PENCF' (for 'PENCE') error on the 1½d. which was subsequently repaired. Broken frames and misshapen letters are numerous on these stamps.

The Australian Commonwealth's first stamps – 'Kangaroo' and King George V 'King's Head' designs – were typographed almost exclusively from 1913 to about 1936, and some distinctive varieties emerged, notably the 'Leg of kangaroo broken' on the 6d. ultramarine of 1915 which occurred again on the 6d. chestnut of 1923. Various printers were involved in

Great Britain – George V ld. stamps of 1912 can be found to have 'no cross on crown' (bottom row).

the manufacture of these stamps and they all contributed to the innumerable minor flaws, malformed letters and ornaments, spots and blemishes which may be found. Varieties of the early typo issues of Jamaica include the faulty printing of 'SER.ET' (for 'SERVIET') on the arms-type stamps of 1903-04 and 1905-11, and the 'dollar' variety of the one shilling stamp, '$' for 'S' in 'SHILLING' which originated in 1860 and was constantly repeated through various printings until 1910.

As mentioned in the previous chapter, typographed overprints and surcharges are a prolific source of errors and varieties – examples are figures and letters broken, misplaced, inverted, doubled or omitted, words – such as 'AFRLCA' for 'AFRICA' – spelt wrongly, mixed founts of typefaces, missing, misplaced or extra stops, fraction bars or rules – there's no end to them!

Lithographic Oddities

During the early days of colonial development, several countries elected to print their stamps (or have them printed) by the process of lithography, notably British Guiana, India (first issues), North Borneo, Victoria, Virgin Islands (first issues) and Western Australia. The first lithographed postage stamps were issued by Zurich, Switzerland, in 1843, and the method used by the printers, Orell, Fussli & Co., in preparing a printing 'plate', became a standard procedure and was adopted in principle by other printers. The designs for each value – the four and six rappen 'numerals' – were drawn by hand five times on a small stone, then paper transfers were taken of the strip of five images and laid down on the larger printing stone to form a sheet of 100 stamps. Thus any flaws in the original five units would likewise be repeated throughout the sheet and, coupled with faults, such as creases and cockles, would contribute to the numerous minor flaws and defects found on lithographed stamps.

Western Australia's celebrated 'Inverted Swan' (Chapter 3) was caused by the frame transfer being laid upside-down on the stone, and the *Gibbons Catalogue* records more than twenty other transfer varieties of the 4d. blue, including shortened, closed-up and squeezed-down letters, borders and lettering aslant,

The 1d. of 1912-22 can show Q for O in 'ONE' (SG 357a).

and other defects. Sometimes transfers of stamps of one denomination were included in error on the stone and eventually emerged as stamps with the wrong colour, as happened in Colombia, Peru and other South American countries. A classic example is the two schilling brown of the German city of Lubeck (1859) – two 2½s. transfers were included on the stone in error. The printers erased the '2½' from the four corners of each transfer and substituted the figure '2', apparently overlooking the fact that the face value was also expressed in words – 'ZWEI EIN HALB'!

Thomas Ham of Melbourne engraved the dies for the lithographed 1d., 2d. and 3d. Victoria 'Half Lengths' of 1850 on a single piece of steel. Impressions from the first printing were clear and fine, but the minor differences between one transfer and another, and the subsequent building up of transfer units to form a stone of 120 impressions, resulted in an enormous number of minor varieties during the various printings, some 600 for the One Penny alone. The Virgin Islands' first issues of 1866-70 were lithographed by Nissen & Parker from dies engraved by Waterlow & Sons, and transfer varieties included a large 'V' in 'VIRGIN' on the 6d. stamp and a long-tailed

'S' in 'ISLANDS' on the 1s. The 'Missing Virgin' was evidently an error of omission in making up the stone.

Modern photo-lithography or 'offset' and its inherent flaws and varieties are radically different to the old stone-and-transfer methods. Common faults are white flecks or streaks on the stamps caused by marks and scratches on the metal printing plates which escape the inking rollers. When these occur on a stamp which has white lettering, they may take the form of an extra serif on a letter or figure, or change a full stop into a comma. On the other hand, any impediment (such as accumulated grime) on the surface of the plate or cylinder will appear as a blob of colour on the stamp. Sometimes particles of dust and grit build up on the plate, forming a 'bump' of colour surrounded by a white ring – the ink is prevented from reaching the immediate vicinity of the protrusion, and a 'ring flaw' is formed.

Litho colours are inconsistent over long printing runs. The plate cylinders are first coated with water and then inked, and the ratio of water to ink has to be closely watched and controlled. In spite of this, coloured inks tend to become diluted and provide 'shades'. The apparent doubling of parts of a stamp design is caused by 'blanket stretch' – the rubber blanket of the offset roller expands when new and provides a duplicate impression.

Photogravure Flaws

Modern British and Commonwealth stamps are keenly collected by the present generation, not only for their attractive subjects, designs and colours, but also for their numerous varieties and flaws. Stamps these days are printed by the million and faults and blemishes are bound to occur. Nearly all British stamps – definitives and commemoratives or 'specials' – are now printed by the photogravure process, and the fact that they are readily available at post offices (and at the Post Office Philatelic Bureau in Edinburgh) is 'grist to the mill' for the variety hunter. Flaws – some significant, some not – may be found on the regular 'Machin' stamps, issued in sheets, booklets or coil strips from automatic vending machines, or in the new issues of special stamps as they appear.

Varieties should be constant (as previously explained), and if the position of a specific flaw is known, it should be relatively easy to find its equivalent on a comparable sheet of stamps, booklet or machine strip, if printed from identical cylinders. Odd faults and 'one-off' varieties which are not constant can only be regarded as freaks, and are of little interest unless they are particularly striking or unusual. The most common flaws – white or coloured blemishes, colour shifts and 'doctor-blade' (ink-wiping) lines (which will be explained) – are the least interesting because they are transient and are derived from minor faults of adjustment in the printing presses.

Retouches are probably the most interesting and intriguing photogravure varieties, mainly because they are evidence of handiwork on the printing cylinder before printing commences or at an early stage of the run. Cylinders are carefully inspected and any major flaws which would show on the stamps as white blobs or patches are made good. The retoucher uses his burin (engraving tool) to make pinpoint notches on the appropriate part of the cylinder – these are apparent on the printed stamps as clusters of coloured dots comparable to the area of the original flaws. Some retouches are small and not readily distinguishable, other larger retouches are easily seen as coarse patches of colour. The flaws which, at first, are put to press unnoticed and which, at a later stage, may be retouched on the cylinder, provide collectors with examples of the 'before and after' states of a retouch.

The random white dots, flecks, patches and scratches often seen on photogravure stamps may occur during the manufacture of the multipositive (or glass plate), through poor contact of the carbon tissue with the surface of the cylinder, or actually during printing when the ink tends to thicken in the trough and is stripped off the stamps – a form of 'dry printing'. Multipositive flaws may appear on more than one cylinder and possibly on other denominations. Photogravure is a recess process and, in theory, the only flaws which form a cell or recess on the cylinder will print in the colour of the stamp. However, foreign matter adhering to the cylinder (which fails to be removed in the ink-wiping process) will appear as coloured spots, blobs and dashes on the stamps.

The 'white' figures of value on the 'Machin' definitives (and figures and inscriptions on some commemoratives) are actually clear impressions of the stamp paper, created by the 'marriage' of two multipositives, one for the 'Machin' head of the Queen and the background, the other for the face value. Faulty registration sometimes results in the screened dots of

Great Britain – 1961 Post Office Savings Bank 2½d. stamp with retouch on Queen's forehead (SG 623).

the main design impinging on the white figures of value or in the sheet margins. Similarly, inexact registration of the multipositives explains the phenomenon of 'floating values' on the 'Machin' definitives – variations in the location of the face values in relation to the Queen's head on stamps of the same denomination.

The so-called 'colour shifts' are very common on photogravure issues and have little significance as varieties unless they are very extensive, possibly with parts of the design missing. They are caused by the printing cylinders (each reproducing a part of the design) not being in exact alignment – consequently certain colours are not accurately registered and may be seen to overlap or have conspicuous gaps in the design. One amusing example was the British 3p stamp of 1972 commemorating the polar explorer, Sir James Clark Ross, whose eyeballs rested on his cheeks. Regular checks and adjustments of the press in operation rectify these faults and such varieties are not constant, generally being confined to one or two sheets. Missing colours occur when the press is being slowed down and colours cease to register, and they occur fairly frequently on multicoloured stamps – a

Great Britain 1841 1d., correctly imperforate.

classic example is the missing Queen's head on the 3d. 'National Productivity Year' stamp of 1962.

Under a magnifying glass, a photogravure-printed stamp will be seen to be composed of tiny dots, and for this reason fine lines and letters do not always reproduce well. Cursive scripts are notably fickle – inscriptions may be faint and letters not joined. A missing dot will show as an apparent break in a letter, and the tiny imprints naming the designer and/or printer at the foot of some stamps have often been so weak that they have been reinforced by hand-engraving on the cylinder.

The 'doctor blade' is a fixed steel blade mounted on a heavy base close to the revolving cylinders in a rotary press. It scrapes off the superfluous ink as it moves slowly across the face of the cylinder, and if some tiny impediment lodges under the blade it leaves a 'trail' on the printed stamps, either a coloured or, more commonly, a white line which eventually peters out. These lines are known as doctor-blade flaws and may extend over several stamps in a sheet, but they are unimportant as varieties.

Perforation and Watermark Varieties

The first perforated British stamps appeared in 1854, following the experiments by Henry Archer, and the construction of perforating machines by David Napier

& Sons. The Napier machines operated on the principle of the 'comb' perforator which has continued to the present day – a horizontal row of steel pins with vertical 'flanks', mounted on a heavy base which could perforate the top and sides of a row of stamps in the sheet. Modern stamps are perforated by sheet-fed Grover machines, employing two or three-row combs, while the Kampf rotary perforator built into Harrison's Jumelle press perforates the stamps as they are printed.

Varieties of perforation range from the imperforate – without perforations – occurring in parts of a sheet or a whole sheet, to partially perforated and 'imperf between' stamps. Usually it is the stamps in the top or bottom rows of a sheet which miss being perforated due to careless operation – double or misplaced 'perfs' occur for the same reason. The single-line perforator, rarely used now, punches all the horizontal rows and all the vertical rows in consecutive operations, and if a row of perforations is missed, the adjacent stamps will be imperforate at top or bottom, or on one side, providing a number of 'imperf between' pairs. In earlier times, as for example in the classic issues of the Australian States and New Zealand, it was common practice to perforate the tops and bottoms of the stamps in a sheet in one gauge or measurement, and the sides in another – errors of perforation frequently occurred when the wrong perforator was used.

Minor varieties such as irregular lines of perforation holes, or stamps with 'blind' or imperfect perforations (holes not punched out) are caused by bent, blunt or missing pins. A shift of paper in the perforator can result in stamps being perforated down the centre, while a sheet which has been inadvertently folded back can emerge from the perforating machine bearing a criss-cross pattern of multiple perforations when unfolded. Misplaced perforations also cause a stamp design to be off-centre – close to the printed design on one side and leaving a wide gap on the other side, perhaps with similar discrepancies at top and bottom. Such lopsided stamps are ugly and are not popular with collectors. Some sheets of stamps are issued with the gutter (intervening) margins perforated like the stamps, and these blanks have no philatelic interest. Stamp booklets may also be found with imperforate panes and the other perforation varieties described above – it should be noted that some booklets, however, are closely guillotined so that the outer edges of the panes of stamps are imperforate. (The measurement of perforations is described in Chapter 10).

Watermark varieties originate in the course of manufacture of the paper or while the stamps are being printed. The watermark – no longer used on British stamps – is a device or pattern impressed in the paper by the dandy roll in the wet pulp stage during paper-

*Faulty colour registration – the black
printing has shifted to cause a confused
huddle of footballers (SG 694).*

making. The roll (roller or cylinder) has a wire-gauze surface to which are attached the 'bits' – usually ciphers or emblems in single or multiple form – which are seen as a thinning of the paper on issued stamps. A single emblem, such as the crown on the Penny Black or the crown over 'CA' (Crown Agents) used on early colonial stamps, is described as a 'single watermark' as opposed to a 'multiple watermark' which has an overall pattern of emblems.

Sometimes, when a 'bit' became detached, it was either replaced by an inverted emblem, by a slightly different device or not replaced at all, and these mishaps have provided some of the best-known watermark varieties. The distinctive St Edward's crown was found among the Tudor crowns on numerous Commonwealth stamps of the 1952-3 era – a missing crown 'bit' was replaced by the wrong type and the paper was used in printing the stamps of the numerous Commonwealth territories.

Classic errors of watermark include the 'three roses and a shamrock' in place of the normal emblems on British stamps of 1862-7, and the Transvaal 1d. Edwardian of 1905 with the 'cabled anchor' watermark instead of the normal multiple 'Crown CA' – the 'cabled anchor' was the normal watermark of contemporary Cape of Good Hope stamps. Stamps are usually printed with the obverse watermark viewed through the front of the stamp, but watermarks generally are best seen on the backs of stamps. Inverted watermarks

are usually due to single sheets being presented the wrong way round in the sheet-fed printing press. These, and reversed or 'back to front' varieties, are fairly common, as also are the various permutations such as inverted *and* reversed, sideways inverted etc. Some British stamps were normally printed with inverted watermarks in sheets intended to be folded for the manufacture of stamp booklets, and sideways watermarks appear on the stamps made up into coils or rolls for sideways delivery in vending machines.

Among the watermark devices in common use in the Commonwealth territories are the multiple 'Crown CA' in diagonal rows (Crown Agents' countries), multiple 'KC and Map' for Cyprus, multiple 'J and Pineapple' for Jamaica, multiple 'Basuto Hat' for Lesotho, multiple 'Maltese Cross' for Malta, and multiple 'WS and Kava Bowl' for Samoa. Many of these occur sideways according to the method of printing the stamps, as well as in the normal vertical arrangement. Many Commonwealth territories have discontinued the use of distinctive watermarks.

Stamp paper may be distinguished by the 'watermark' used in its manufacture. Wove paper, most used for stamps, has a plain, even texture created on a fine gauze mesh; laid paper is also impressed in the wet state with closely-set parallel lines, horizontally or vertically laid; and *quadrillé* (or 'squared') paper is a form of laid paper where crossed lines produce squares or rectangles.

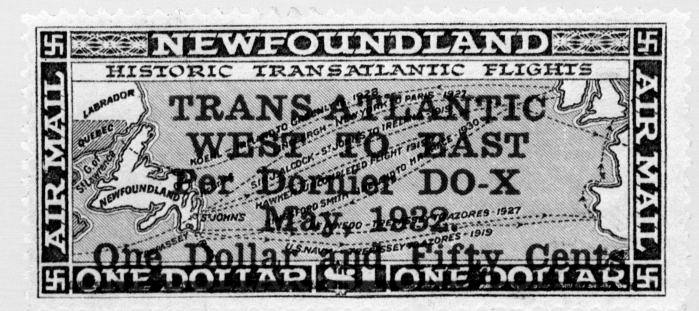

Newfoundland is noted for its airmail stamps.

*Above, left: The rare 1919 'Hawker' (SG 142). Only 200
stamps were overprinted; the plane was forced down but
the mail was later salvaged and delivered.*

*Above, right: For Boyd and Connor's flight to England
in the 'Columbia', 300 stamps were surcharged. About half
were actually used (SG 191).*

*Lower stamp: Historic flights detailed on an airmail
stamp of 1931, surcharged here for a later
transatlantic flight (SG 221).*

7
Many kinds of Stamps

The word 'stamp' is defined as 'an adhesive paper used as a substitute for stamping', also, in its original sense, as an 'impression, stamped device or imprint'. Henry Bishop spoke of a 'stamp' when he introduced the postmark in 1661, and the Stamp Act of 1765 enacted that all legal documents used in the colonies should bear government stamps. The Americans defied the taxation and riots broke out – in 1766 Pitt persuaded the government to repeal the act, nevertheless it was one of the grievances that led to the War of Independence. Rowland Hill's rotary printing press (Chapter 1), which could have revolutionized the printing of newspapers in the early 1830s, was thwarted by the Treasury's refusal to allow the printing of the newspaper tax stamp in the same operation. So we can see that the postage stamp was derived from a long ancestry of impressed and adhesive stamps.

While the great majority of the world's postage stamps serve no other purpose than to indicate that the postage fee or tax has been paid, most, if not all, of them have an alternative function for the collection of revenues, and there are stamps intended only for such purposes – documents, deeds, insurance and receipts etc – known as 'fiscal' or revenue stamps. The stamp family is a large one including many special kinds of issues for the various postal services.

Definitive Stamps

The ordinary every-day postage stamps are known as 'definitives' – being well-defined or determined for regular use – and most countries have their own definitive issues: complete ranges of stamps linked to the postal charges for inland and overseas, to various 'steps' in weight, special rates for printed matter, parcels and airmail fees. In Britain, for example, we have first- and second-class letter rates with basic fees for airmail services to three global zones – Middle East, North Africa, etc; Canada, USA and South

A 'Cinderella' stamp purportedly for local delivery of circulars, but actually made for philatelists.

Africa, etc; and Australasia and the Far East. By tradition, British stamps for definitive use bear the head of the reigning sovereign, and the current issues range from 1p to £5. The words 'Postage and Inland Revenue' were introduced with the Penny Lilac stamp in 1881, adapted to 'Postage and Revenue' in 1883 and continued with the definitives of successive reigns, except on the high values, to the end of the 'Wilding' portrait issues which were phased out in 1967 and 1968. Current stamps have an implied validity for revenue use.

Commemorative Stamps

Commemorative stamps are issued in honour of a celebrated person, or to record an anniversary or some other event of national or historical importance. British Post Office policy, the first commemoratives and 'royal occasions' have all been described in Chapter 4, 'Stamp Designs and Designers'. A striking feature of the commemorative scene is the issue by numerous Commonwealth (and foreign) countries of stamps for the same event or theme, known as 'omnibus' issues. For the first Commonwealth omnibus issue, the silver jubilee of King George V in 1935, some 60 countries issued 250 stamps, and for the 75th anniversary of the Universal Postal Union in 1949, 65 Commonwealth and many foreign countries issued special stamps – the Commonwealth total then was a record of 314. Recent omnibus sets have included the Queen's 60th birthday (1986), the centenary of J.J. Audubon, ornithological artist (1986), the 300th anniversary of Lloyd's of London (1988) and the 400th anniversary of the discovery of America by Columbus (issues from 1987 onwards, for 1992).

Since Great Britain and a few other countries commemorated the centenary of the 'First Adhesive Postage Stamps' in 1940, many countries have similarly honoured their first postage stamps. Stamp centenaries

1935 Silver Jubilee of King George V – two of the omnibus issue from the Empire countries – Kenya, Uganda, Tanganyika (SG 124) and Antigua (SG 91).

The 75th anniversary of the Universal Postal Union saw this Commonwealth 'omnibus' issue.

The Penny Black elegantly remembered: Great Britain commemorates its first postage stamps (SG 480).

and anniversaries are popular with collectors, mainly because they usually bear replicas of the original stamps, many of which are famous and rare, and lend themselves to the 'stamps on stamps' theme. Following Britain's lead with a £1 stamp for the royal silver wedding in 1948, the Crown Colonies also issued high-value stamps with a total face value of about £45 for the complete series. Collectors protested (in vain) about the high cost of these stamps, but subsequently they have proved to be a good investment – the catalogue value for the complete omnibus series of 138 stamps is now £1,400 unused or postally used. The Commonwealth issues for the Queen's coronation in 1953 had more moderate face values, corresponding to local letter rates.

Commemoratives are among the most attractive of postage stamps, not only for their qualities of design, but also for the story behind the stamps and their issue. An example of a commemorative issue, which, besides being pictorially attractive, has considerably appreciated in value since it first appeared in 1933, is that of the Falkland Islands' stamps marking the centenary of British occupation. The barren nature of the islands is revealed in views of Port Louis and desolate South Georgia (a dependency), and there is also an awesome iceberg, a leaping whale with the whale-catcher *Bransfield* in hot pursuit, a Romney Marsh ram representing the colony's wool industry, a map of the islands, views of Government House and the memorial to the Battle of the Falkland Islands in 1914, when the Royal Navy scored a decisive victory over the German fleet (also commemorated in 1964), a king penguin and a magnificent portrait of King George V in military uniform on the £1 stamp. The arms of the colony, also featured, show a sea-lion, the ship *Desire* (in which Captain John Davis discovered the islands in 1592) and the motto 'Desire the Right'.

Most Commonwealth definitives now have pictorial designs and are distinguishable from commemor-

*Australian definitive
1959 (SG 314).*

*New Zealand definitive,
1944 (SG 608).*

*Canadian definitive,
1950 (SG 424).*

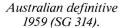

atives only by the omission of any special inscription. Such issues are usually changed every four or five years and relate to the flora and fauna, natural resources and produce, buildings, institutions and monuments of the country. Australia issues 'short-term' definitives which include the regular series of 'Famous Australians', occasional issues of Australian birds and flowers, and paintings by Australian artists on the high values. Canadian definitives currently feature animals, leaves and city streets, also a portrait of the Queen and the Canadian Houses of Parliament. The top values depict Vancouver and Quebec, and a supplementary series features the Canadian Indians. New Zealand's recent definitives picture garden roses, Maori artifacts and seashells, also a portrait of the Queen from a photograph by Warren Harrison.

In Europe and the rest of the world, the tendency is for the numerous commemorative issues to be widely used concurrently with the normal definitives while they are available. Austria's regular definitive stamps feature views, those of Belgium picture King Baudouin; Denmark (and Greenland), Queen Margrethe, as well as arms types; Norway has 'numerals' in a design which was first adopted in 1882 and various small pictorials; Swedish stamps depict King Carl XVI Gustav. French definitives, which traditionally show allegorical female figures such as 'Republique' and 'Marianne', now portray 'Sabine', who is regularly augmented by additions to the 'French Art' series and by 'Tourist' pictorials.

West Germany and West Berlin each have a series of 'Castles' and small pictorials for 'Industry and Technology'; the Netherlands' definitives share 'numerals' and the portrait of their Queen; Liechtenstein has landscapes; Luxembourg depicts Grand Duke Jean. Finnish stamps have a long-standing arms design; Italy shows castles; and Switzerland, 'The Post – Past and Present'.

Finnish definitives (SG 453, 651).

Danish definitives (SG 346, 569).

Luxembourg definitives (SG 513a, 765a).

EUROPEAN DEFINITIVES

Italy   Austria   Norway

Belgium: King Leopold III and King Baudouin   *West Germany: Presidents Heinemann and Heuss*

Netherlands   Sweden   France

France   Switzerland

Stamps for Charity

The so-called 'charity' stamps, which originated at the turn of the century, are perhaps one of the most contentious forms of obtaining donations for established charitable organizations. They are closely related to commemorative stamps, but they are distinguished by the imposition of a premium or surcharge over and above the normal postage rate or face value of the stamp. The premium is, in effect, a 'compulsory' contribution to the funds of a specific charity, and the stamps, which the Americans aptly call 'semi-postals', are sold mainly to collectors who are prepared to pay the extra cost of them. Charity stamps have been most successful in France, Germany, the Netherlands, New Zealand and Switzerland, due to attractive designs and small premiums.

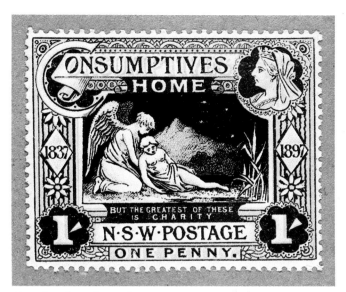

New South Wales – charity stamp, 1897 (SG 287c).

New Zealand – Health stamp, 1946 (SG 678).

*The Post Office experimental charity
stamp, issued in 1975.
Great Britain (SG 970).*

This was not the case with the charity stamps placed on sale by New South Wales in 1897 for the benefit of a consumptives' home. These were sold at 1s. and 2s.6d. respectively, but paid postage of only 1d. and 2½d. – they were censured by the philatelic press and boycotted by collectors. The furore was echoed later that year when Victoria issued stamps with similar premiums for a hospital fund and again in 1900 for a Boer War patriotic fund (incidentally the first appearance of the Victoria Cross on a stamp).

Spain – Red Cross stamp, 1926 (SG 412).

The International Red Cross has probably benefited the most from charity stamps. Belgian stamps of 1914 pictured King Albert, and France issued a 'Sower'-type Red Cross stamp in the same year, followed by another in 1918 which showed a sinking hospital ship and a bombed hospital. France now supports her Red Cross Fund with regular annual issues – a set of 'Celebrities' and two artistic stamps just before Christmas. Holland commemorated the 60th anniversary of the Dutch Red Cross in 1927, and Spain issued two Red Cross sets totalling 23 stamps in 1926 – one set featured the royal family, the other, pioneer flights by Spanish airmen.

Child welfare is one of the principal charitable causes. The Netherlands first issued a charity stamp in 1906 – three in fact for the Society for the Prevention of Tuberculosis – and started a series of children's stamps, inscribed 'Voor Het Kind', which has continued to the present day, in 1924. Switzerland is famous for her 'Pro Juventute' stamps, first issued in 1913, which appear regularly on 1 December each year. The stamps are in attractive, modern designs and the themes in recent years have included birds, roses, 'fruits of the forest' and the cantonal arms. Each year since 1929, New Zealand has issued the well-known 'Health' stamps which help to provide funds for the maintenance of children's health camps. The first stamp depicted a nurse and the design was repeated in the 50th anniversary issue of 1978. Miniature sheets were introduced in 1958.

Britain's first charity stamp was issued experimentally by the Post Office in 1975. The stamp, which showed a handicapped person in a wheel-chair and was inscribed '4½ + 1½p for health and handicap charities', was not a great success. Five and a half million of them were sold 'by request' over post office counters during the four weeks they were on general sale. Four of the five 1989 Christmas stamps were surcharged 1p for charitable purposes, resulting from public and press suggestions.

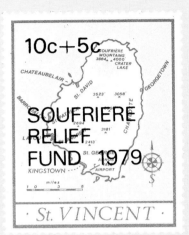

Three Relief Fund stamps: 1954, for Austrian avalanche victims; 1962, for 'Hurricane Hattie' victims; and 1979, for Soufrière Eruption relief.

Cultural, humanitarian, social and war victims relief typify the charity funds for which stamps are issued. Natural disasters such as earthquakes and volcanic eruptions are more spectacular causes. An Austrian stamp of 1954 was for the benefit of avalanche victims, and Barbados issued a stamp in 1907 for the relief of Kingston, Jamaica, after an earthquake. British Honduras (Belize) overprinted four stamps for 'Hurricane Hattie' in 1962; similarly, four stamps were issued by St Vincent for the Soufriére Relief Fund after the island's solitary volcano erupted in 1979.

Aviation and Airmail Stamps

During the siege of Paris in the Franco-Prussian War, 1870-1, letters and newspapers were carried out of the city by balloons. The letters were inscribed 'Par Ballon' and these hazardous flights have come to be regarded as the world's first 'air mail'. A French aviator, Henri Pequet, carried mail on a demonstration flight of about five miles at Allahabad, India, in February 1911, and later that year, in September, Gustav Hamel and his fellow pilots made regular flights between Hendon and Windsor, carrying souvenir letters and postcards in the historic coronation 'Aerial Post'. The first regular airmail and passenger service between London and Paris was established in 1919 by Aircraft Transport and Travel, using an Airco 'DH' type of plane. In 1920 the service was extended to Brussels and Amsterdam, and in 1924 four existing companies were amalgamated as Imperial Airways.

The aero-philatelist, who specializes in the collection and study of airmails – stamps and flown covers – recognizes two kinds of air stamps: those issued by governments through their postal administrations for official use, and the stamps issued by

Ireland – airmail stamp, 1954 (SG 143a).

private aviation companies such as SCADTA of Colombia. Many stamps, though inscribed 'Air Mail', or in the foreign equivalent – 'Poste Aerienne', 'Correo Aereo', 'Luftpost' etc – and generally bearing the appropriate rate of postage, can be used on ordinary mail. Conversely, ordinary stamps are accepted on airmail letters, and in many cases where mail is normally transported by air, such as the services between Great Britain and Europe, airmail stamps are superfluous.

Many airmail stamps are part of a definitive or commemorative issue bearing no relation to the theme of aviation; contrariwise, there are ordinary stamps (not inscribed for airmail use) which feature famous aircraft – such as 'Concorde' – and historic flights. These are points to be borne in mind by the thematic collector.

The world's first official airmail stamps were issued by Italy in May 1917, when the current 25 Centesimi express letter stamps (inscribed 'Espresso')

The pioneer days of airmail. (Top) The scene as London and Paris were first linked in 1919 on a regular basis.
(Stamp, left) The very first airmail stamp, issued by Italy in

1917 for experimental postal flights.
(Stamp, right) A Mercury airmail stamp essay, sold in Britain as an exhibition souvenir in 1923.

were overprinted 'Esperimento Posta Aerea – Maggio 1917 – Torino-Roma Roma-Torino' for experimental postal flights between Rome and Turin. In the following month, unissued 40 cent express stamps were overprinted 'Idrovolante – Napoli-Palermo-Napoli – 25 cent 25' for a successful experimental mail flight by seaplane from Naples to Palermo and back. Austria issued special 'Flugpost'-overprinted stamps in 1918 for regular mail flights by military aircraft between Lemberg, Cracow and Vienna, later (briefly) extended to Budapest. Also in 1918, the United States issued three stamps for the newly-inaugurated New York-Philadelphia-Washington airmail route – the stamps depicted the Curtiss 'Jenny' mailplane and included the rare 'Inverted Jenny' mentioned earlier.

Among the most rare airmail stamps were those issued for the various pioneer transatlantic flights, starting in 1919. In that year, Newfoundland issued

stamps inscribed 'First Transatlantic Air Post April 1919' for the flight by Harry Hawker – he 'ditched' in the Atlantic and was picked up by a Danish steamer. Similar stamps were issued for the abortive Morgan-Raynham flight, and for the first successful flight across the Atlantic by Alcock and Brown. Later, stamps were issued for the De Pinedo flight (1927), and the 'Columbia' (1930) and 'Dornier DO-X' (1932) flights.

Great Britain must be one of the few countries in the world which has never had airmail stamps. In 1922, Bradbury Wilkinson printed pictorial essays inscribed 'British Air Mail' for the Post Office, but the idea of official stamps was not proceeded with. 'Mercury' airmail essays were sold at the London International Stamp Exhibition in 1923 – again these failed to impress the GPO and now they are just souvenirs of 'what might have been'.

A rare cover from an historic flight. The red overprint 'Air Mail DE PINEDO 1927' was applied to 300 stamps.

Officials and Postage Dues

The first British 'official' stamp was a Penny Black with the letters 'VR' in the upper corners, but, as described in Chapter 2, there was a change of heart on the part of Rowland Hill and the stamps were never distributed. Instead, Government departments were encouraged to use 'O.H.M.S.'-printed envelopes and handstamps, and it was not until more than forty years later – in 1882 – that government 'departmental' stamps were introduced.

The first stamps, overprinted 'I.R. Official', were for the exclusive use of the Inland Revenue, whose countrywide network of revenue offices and officers probably handled more correspondence than all the other departments put together. Denominations of ½d., 1d. and 6d. were issued in September and October 1882; additional values followed in 1885, including a £1 stamp intended mainly for registered packages. Next, in 1883, came stamps overprinted 'Govt. Parcels' for the use of all government departments, followed in 1896 by similar stamps – 'O.W. Official' for the Office of Works, and

'Army Official' for War Office paymasters in the provinces. In 1902 there were stamps for the 'Board of Education' – these and the others previously described continued through the new reign, overprinted on Edwardian stamps – and for the Royal Household ('R.H. Official'), while in 1903 the last of the departmentals were issued, overprinted 'Admiralty Official'.

The 6d. 'I.R. Official' of Edward VII is a great rarity, probably the rarest British stamp. It was withdrawn (with the other officials) almost as soon as it had been printed in March 1904, and possibly no more than six, postally used, exist. Another famous rarity is the Edward VII 10s. 'I.R. Official', worth more than the £1 stamp and worth even more with the variety, raised stop after 'R'. The second rarest stamp among the British officials is the Edwardian 'Board of Education' 1s. which had little use before being withdrawn.

Among the first colonies and dominions to issue official stamps were India, Ceylon, the Australian states of South Australia and New South Wales, and New Zealand. The Indian stamps, from 1866, were definitive issues overprinted 'Service' and later, 'On H.M.S.'. In 1939 definitive-type 'Service' stamps appeared, bearing the head of King George VI, and in 1950 these were replaced by a new series depicting the Asokan Capital, an archaeological ornament, and similar 'Service' stamps are in current use. The Indian

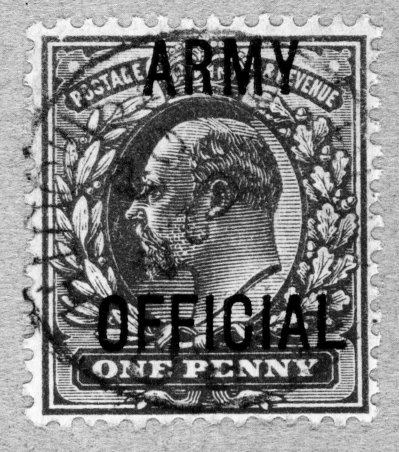
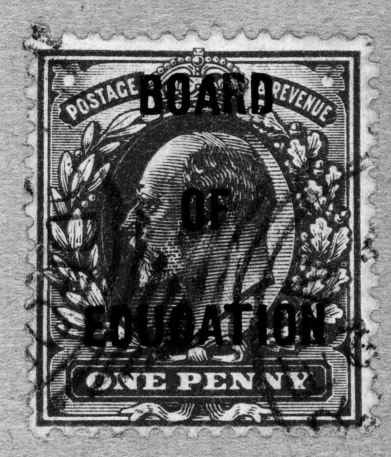
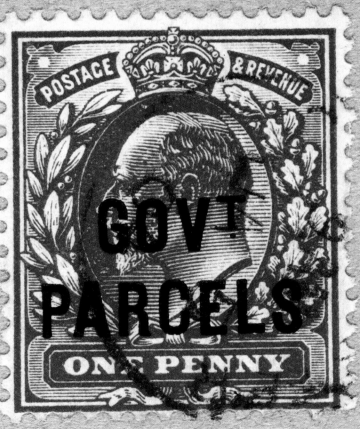
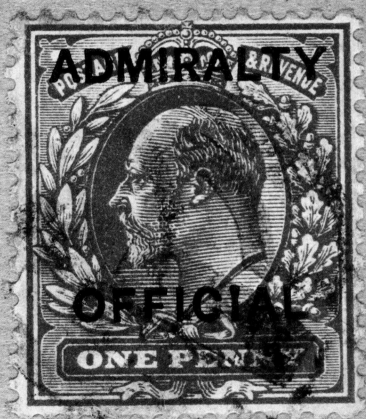

*Official stamps – King Edward VII definitives
overprinted for Government Department use.*

'On CGS' (Cochin Government Service) overprint for this Indian State.

State of Cochin overprinted its stamps 'On C.G.S.' ('On Cochin Government Service'), Sirmoor – 'On S.S.S.' ('On Sirmoor State Service') and Soruth – 'Sarkari' ('Service'). Other states had simple 'Service' overprints, as also did Ceylon.

South Australia issued an elaborate series of departmental stamps between 1868 and 1874, comprising numerous combinations of initials overprinted on current stamps, such as 'C.L.' Crown Lands, 'H.A.' House of Assembly and 'R.G.' Registrar-General. These were superseded by 'O.S.'-overprinted stamps. New South Wales used similar 'O.S.' stamps until the various states used stamps with perforated initials. Western Australia at one time used stamps with punched holes to indicate official usage. New Zealand's first officials were handstamped 'O.P.S.O.' ('On Public Service Only'), followed by 'Official' overprints. Queen Elizabeth definitive types were introduced in 1954 and continued until 1965 when official stamps were discontinued. However, attractive pictorials depicting New Zealand lighthouses continue to be issued by the Life Insurance Office.

Canada's first official stamps in 1949 made use of the current definitives, overprinted 'O.H.M.S.', then, from 1950, overprinted 'G' (for 'Government'). These, too, were discontinued in December 1963. The United States began issuing official stamps for the nine executive departments – portraits of presidents inscribed 'Navy', 'Interior', 'Post Office', 'Treasury' etc – in 1873.

Overprints showing official use began in Britain under Queen Victoria.

Indian official stamps inscribed 'Service'.

Left: New Zealand 'Official' overprint.
Right: Canada's simple 'O.H.M.S.' overprint.

In early days, before postage stamps were thought of, it was customary to collect the cost of postage on delivery. In fact, the prepayment of postage was offensive to some recipients who thought that their ability to pay on delivery was in question. These attitudes vanished with the introduction of stamps, but post offices everywhere have always had to contend with the un-

*Handstamped initials O P S O ('On Public Service 'Only'),
used in New Zealand 1892-1906.*

stamped or underpaid letter. To endorse such letters,
post offices have a wide range of rubber stamps and
'To Pay' markings, usually stating the amount due
(customarily double the deficiency) and the reason for
the charge – 'Insufficiently prepaid' or (for a postcard
in breach of a regulation) 'Liable to letter rate', or with
a 'T' for *taxe*.

Great Britain's postage due design for 56 years.

The British Post Office introduced postage due
'labels' (as they call them) in 1914 – these serve as
receipts for the payment of due sums on delivery and are
usually attached by the postman at the sorting office
prior to making his delivery rounds. British postage
dues have never been very attractive because, like those
of Commonwealth territories and foreign countries,
their main feature is the large figure of value with, until
recent times, a heavy ornamental setting. The stamps
are inscribed 'Postage Due' or, for the higher values
(often used in collecting customs' dues), 'To Pay', on

*Decimal re-design for Britain's postage dues
(1971 and 1982).*

**Both New Zealand and the Republic of South
Africa have issued postage due stamps.**

the 2s. 6d. to £1. All this changed in 1970 and 1982,
when the postage dues were completely restyled in
modern designs and retitled 'To Pay'. These now range
from 1p to £5.

Postage due stamps have been discontinued in
Australia, but continue in use in Canada, and in the
United States, where the engraved 'large numeral'
stamps issued in 1959 are still in current use. India has
never had them, New Zealand ceased using them in
1951, South Africa in 1975. Foreign postage dues can be
identified by the inscriptions upon them – France and
French-speaking territories, 'à percevoir', 'à payer' or
'timbre taxe'; Denmark, Hungary etc., 'porto'; Italy,
'segnatasse'; Germany, 'portomarke'; Portugal and
territories, 'porteado'; Sweden, 'lösen'; and the
Netherlands, 'te betalen'.

Other 'special purpose' stamps, though now
discontinued in most countries, are of interest to the
collector. 'Express' and 'Special Delivery' stamps
denoted the payment of extra fees for speedy transit of
letters – Canada at one time had a full range of these –
and there also you will find examples of 'Registration'
stamps intended for registered mail. Italian stamps were
inscribed 'Espresso', the Spanish ones, 'Correo (or
Correspondencia) Urgente'. Colombia first issued
registration stamps in 1865 ('Rejistro') and, later,
'Acknowledgment of Receipt' and 'Too Late'
('Retardo') stamps. Victoria had short-lived
'Registered' and 'Too Late' stamps (a 6d. fee for late
posting) in 1854-5, while the USA has issued high-value
express mail stamps since 1983. Czechoslovakia
introduced 'Personal Delivery' triangular stamps in
1937.

*Canada – 1942 special
delivery stamp (SG S12).*

The Bald Eagle on US express mail stamp (SG 2044).

*Canada – 1942 special
delivery stamp (SG S12).*

Registration stamp, State of Victoria, 1854 (SG 52).

Newspaper stamps, to prepay postage on newspapers, journals and magazines, were pioneered by Austria – the well-known 'Mercury' designs – in 1851, followed by the USA whose newspaper stamps of 1865 featured portraits of Washington and other American presidents. These looked like miniature banknotes, and were exceptionally large – about two inches by four. Smaller stamps depicting allegorical figures – Ceres, Clio and Minnehaha etc – were issued from 1875. The United States also issued a magnificent set of pictorial 'Parcel Post' stamps, depicting postal functions and mail transport, in 1912. The parcel post stamps of Italy and San Marino are in two parts, one half being held by the sender as a receipt, the other serving as the postage stamp. Belgium has many interesting parcel post and railway parcels' stamps picturing Belgian locomotives and stations. Danish parcel stamps are inscribed 'Postfaerge'.

Stamps have occasionally been used as money, enclosed in small transparent cases known as *jetons* or counters, but the currency stamps of Russia, 1915-17, were never intended for postal use though they were nevertheless used on letters. These 'stamps' were printed on thin card and bore some of the Romanov portraits from the normal stamp issue of 1913, inscribed on the back (in Russian): 'Having circulation on a par with silver subsidiary coins' or (later) '... with copper money'. 'Frank' (or 'free') stamps, usually without face value, are used to indicate that no postage is payable, such as the military frank stamps issued by Vietnam. 'Obligatory tax' stamps, however, represent

compulsory fees for charities such as the Costa Rica 'Christmas' and Dominican Republic 'Tuberculosis Relief' issues. Argentina issued special stamps in 1939 for the postage on gramophone records bearing recorded messages, while in Italy special 'Pneumatic Post' stamps were required for letters carried by underground pneumatic tubes between post offices in the larger cities.

'Cinderella' Stamps

The so-called 'Cinderellas of Philately' are Local stamps, Fiscals and Revenues, Railway and Telegraph stamps, Bogus and Phantom issues, Exhibition labels, Hotel stamps and Christmas seals – virtually everything other than postage stamps. The appellation 'Cinderella' ('the despised and neglected one') was

Chinese Treaty Port – Hankow, 1893.

Great Britain – Lundy 1929 ½ and 1 puffin (= penny) stamps and 1979 10p and 11½p stamps commemorating the 50th anniversary of the local postal service.

coined by enthusiasts at about the time of the founding of the Cinderella Stamp Club in 1959.

'Locals' are stamps valid for the prepayment of postage only in the country or region of issue as circumscribed by the issuing authority. Many countries have issued local stamps – often they have preceded regular stamp issues as forerunners and these are of great interest to the philatelist. Local posts were established in the various Chinese Treaty Ports, 1893-6, in Russia – the so-called 'Zemstvo' rural issues – from 1870, and in the USA. In Britain the Circular Delivery Companies issued their own stamps for local deliveries of circulars and printed matter in major Scottish towns and in London and Liverpool from 1865 to 1867, and 'College' stamps were issued in Oxford and Cambridge for local messenger services between 1870 and about 1885.

Britain's numerous offshore islands have often given their names to stamps which, privately sponsored, have no postal use even locally, and for these the designation 'local carriage labels' is ambiguous. Among the exceptions, however, are the local issues of Lundy Island in the Bristol Channel – the first stamps appeared in 1929 and subsequent issues have maintained a postal service between the island and the mainland operated by the owners, now the British National Trust. Numerous Channel Islands' stamps and services – Commodore Shipping Co. (Sark and Alderney), Herm, Jethou and Lihou among them – were suppressed by the Guernsey Postal Authority in 1969. In 1891, Julius Popper, the self-styled 'King' of Tierra del Fuego (Chile), issued his own stamps.

From 1891 British railway companies had stamps to pay for letters carried by passenger train.

Taxes have existed from time immemorial, and fiscal and revenue adhesive and embossed stamps have long existed, too, as receipts or acknowledgments of payment. They represent duties paid on bills, contracts, documents and on goods, and they are of little interest to the philatelist unless, as sometimes happened, they were authorized for postal use, when they are known as postal-fiscals. Examples are Hong Kong, 1874-97; India, 1866-7; New Zealand, from 1882; and Victoria, 1870 to about 1883.

Railway letter stamps were introduced by the various railway companies in Britain in 1891 – some are still used by the private 'tourist' companies – and in 1933-4 the Great Western Railway operated commercial air services using appropriate 3d. stamps. Telegraph stamps, normally issued for use on telegrams, were issued by numerous telegraph companies in the last century, also by many post offices abroad. Postally used, they are collectable items for the philatelist. Hotel stamps were used mainly in Switzerland during the 1860s to 1880s for publicity purposes and to frank visitors' mail to the nearest post office. In Britain the postal strike of 1971 resulted in numerous private services and stamps.

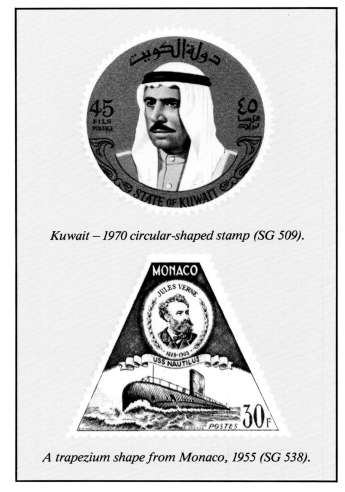

Kuwait – 1970 circular-shaped stamp (SG 509).

A trapezium shape from Monaco, 1955 (SG 538).

Great Britain – Two of many hundreds of stamps used by temporary postal service operators during the Post Office strike of January/March 1971.

All Shapes and Sizes

The traditional small rectangular shape of the Penny Black has remained constant for many countries' definitive stamps, including Great Britain, and the larger rectangles, in horizontal or vertical format, are usually employed for commemorative or special issues. But many – some quite extraordinary – shapes have been adopted from time to time. The list includes squares, triangulars, circles, ovals, diamonds, octagonals, and cut- or perforated-to-shape stamps.

Squares and diamond shapes are fairly common in modern issues, the diamond shape being either a square turned on its points or the 'squashed' type as

issued by Ecuador in 1959. Diamonds were used for the first stamps of New Brunswick (1851), squares and diamonds for Nova Scotia (1853), and a triangular – evidently inspired by the Cape of Good Hope triangulars of 1853 onwards – for Newfoundland (1857). The distinctive shape of the Cape stamps was intended to assist sorters in distinguishing local letters from overseas mail, but its subsequent use by numerous other countries was purely for decorative purposes. British Guiana issued the first circular stamps – the famous 'Cottonreels' of 1850-1 – and New South Wales used a circular 'coin' design for the 5s. stamp of 1861. Kuwait had circular stamps in 1970, and Thessaly used octagonal stamps in 1898. Malta and Monaco have issued trapezoidal stamps, and Pakistan, a rhomboidal design.

Very large stamps are often confused with miniature sheets, but *the* largest still seems to be the Chinese ten cent express letter stamp of 1913-14 which, though divisible into five parts, measures $9\frac{3}{4} \times 2\frac{3}{4}$ inches. A Russian one rouble 'Space' stamp issued in 1962 required much licking at approximately $6 \times 2\frac{3}{4}$ inches. The smallest postage stamps are the three issued by Bolivar (Colombia) in 1863-6; they measure 1×1.12 centimetres.

*Classic Nova Scotia using a diamond shape (1857, SG 6);
and one of the famous British Guiana stamps of 1850,
known to philatelists as 'cottonreels'.*

15½P SALMON (*Salmo salar*)

19½P PIKE (*Esox lucius*)

26P TROUT (*Salmo trutta*)

29P PERCH (*Perca fluviatilis*)

18p

Bull-rout *Myoxocephalus scorpius*
THE LINNEAN SOCIETY 1788/1988

26p

Yellow Waterlily *Nuphar lutea*
THE LINNEAN SOCIETY 1788/1988

31p

Bewick's Swan *Cygnus columbianus*
THE LINNEAN SOCIETY 1788/1988

34p

Morel *Morchella esculenta*
THE LINNEAN SOCIETY 1788/1988

8
Modern British and Commonwealth Stamps

The Post Office – the authority entrusted with the conveyance of mails and the collection of revenues – is a national corporation, having carte-blanche in its innumerable operations, but responsible to Parliament. 'Vesting day' for the corporation was 1 October 1969, and on that day four special stamps were issued marking Post Office achievements in the fields of postal and telecommunications technology – 5d. 'National Giro'; 9d. 'Telephones' – the development of international subscriber dialling; 1s. 'Pulse code modulation' – a system of combining telephone conversations over one circuit; and 1s. 6d. 'Postal mechanisation' – automatic sorting.

The Post Office, now divided into separate Letters, Parcels and Counters businesses, is controlled from various Headquarters buildings in London and elsewhere. Each business has its own Managing Director reporting to the Chairman of the Post Office. Here the various postal services are directed and managed, and here also new stamps are planned and evolved for distribution to some 20,000 post offices throughout the country. The main offices are called 'Crown Offices' and some are equipped with philatelic counters and 'first day cover' posting boxes for the convenience of collectors. Other services for the collector are the provision of presentation packs containing the stamps of special issues, with printed background information, and sets of picture postcards of new stamps reproduced in large format.

The Post Office's British Philatelic Bureau, 20 Brandon Street, Edinburgh EH3 5TT, provides a wide range of services by post for stamp collectors and dealers, at home and abroad. The bureau sells all current British definitive and commemorative stamps,

Opposite: Stamps depicting flora and fauna are always popular – the 1983 River Fishes and 1988 Linnean Society issues.

Inset: Stamps issued for 'Vesting day' (SG 808, 811).

first-day covers, presentation packs, stamped stationery and other items. The *British Philatelic Bulletin*, a monthly magazine in colour, is published together with a stock list of available stamps, and the *British Postmark Bulletin* is issued fortnightly for specialist collectors.

Stamps of the 1970s and 80s

In Chapter 4, in the section on 'Royal' stamps some of the commemoratives issued by the Post Office since the 1960s were mentioned. There is no shortage of worthy subjects for special stamp issues and, during the seventies, there were more than 60 such issues, many of them worth more than a cursory glance. These can be segregated into groups – anniversaries, special events, the way of British life – cultural and historical, and the regular Christmas issues.

The first stamps of 1970 featured 'British Rural Architecture' – 5d. Fife Harling; 9d. Cotswold Limestone; 1s. Welsh Stucco; and 1s. 6d. Ulster Thatch; representing all four regions of the kingdom. The architectural theme was continued in later years and the stamps combine, with previous issues, to form a comprehensive study of British architecture. 'Modern University Buildings' (1971) included 3p Physical Sciences Building, University College of Wales, Aberystwyth; 5p Faraday Building, Southampton University; 7½p Engineering Department, Leicester University; and the Hexagon Restaurant, Essex University, on the 9p. 'Village Churches' were pictured in 1972, and the stamps for 'European Architectural Heritage Year' in 1975 showed 7p Charlotte Square, Edinburgh; 7p The Rows, Chester; 8p Royal Observatory, Greenwich; 10p St George's Chapel, Windsor; and 12p London's National Theatre. 'Historic Buildings' were featured in 1978 – 9p Tower of London; 10½p Holyroodhouse; 11p Caernarvon Castle; and 13p Hampton Court Palace; and these were the occasion for Britain's first miniature sheet.

British culture and social reform have inspired

7p The Rows Chester

7p Charlotte Square Edinburgh

8p The Royal Observatory Greenwich

10p St George's Chapel Windsor

12p The National Theatre London

3p Greensted-juxta-Ongar Essex

4p Earls Barton Northants

5p Letheringsett Norfolk

7½p

9p Huish Episcopi Somerset

*Five stamps (opposite, above) as
Britain's contribution to
'European Architectural Heritage Year'
(1975); in 1972 an issue showed
village churches.*

Spectacular medieval warriors, 1974.

some unusual and attractive designs. Three stamps for the 'Ulster 71' Festival in Belfast (1971) showed paintings by contemporary artists in Northern Ireland – 3p 'A Mountain Road' (T.P. Flanagan); 7½p 'Deer's Meadow' (Tom Carr); and *Slieve na Brock* (C. Middleton). Medieval Warriors – 'Great Britons' – were portrayed in 1974 on four picturesque stamps – 4½p Robert the Bruce; 5½p Owain Glyndwr; 8p Henry the Fifth (victor of Agincourt); and 10p The Black Prince. Stark designs depicting labouring and despairing hands distinguished the 'Social Reformers' set of 1976, commemorating 8½p Thomas Hepburn (Hewing Coal); 10p Robert Owen (Cotton-mill machinery); 11p Lord Shaftesbury (Chimney-cleaning); and 13p Elizabeth Fry 'Women's prison reforms'. The 'Cultural Traditions' set of 1976 featured 8½p The Archdruid, and 13p Welsh harpist, both celebrating the 800th anniversary of the Royal National Eisteddfod; also 10p Morris dancing; and 11p a Scots piper at a Highland gathering.

Heroes of British exploration and discovery were pictured on two compatible issues – first, in 1972, the 'Polar Explorers': 3p Sir James Clark Ross, who established the North magnetic pole and discovered the sea named after him; 5p Sir Martin Frobisher, who first entered the Arctic Circle in 1576 in search of a North-West passage; 7½p Henry Hudson, who in 1610 discovered the bay named after him in Canada; and 9p Captain Robert F. Scott, who died with his companions returning from the South Pole in 1912. The 'British Explorers' set of 1973 included 3p David Livingstone, discoverer of the Victoria Falls, and 3p H.M. Stanley, who searched for Dr Livingstone and found him at Ujiji in 1871; 5p Sir Francis Drake, the first Englishman to circumnavigate the world; 7½p Sir Walter Raleigh, who explored the West Indies, North America and the Orinoco (and reputedly brought back the potato and tobacco); and 9p Charles Sturt, who led many expeditions in Australia.

Historical anniversaries have reflected some of Britain's past glories, and the notable achievements of her famous men and women. The 'Literary Anniversaries' set of 1971 commemorated and portrayed 3p John Keats (150th anniversary of his death), the poet; 5p Thomas Gray (death bicentenary), poet and Greek scholar; and 7½p Sir Walter Scott (birth bicentenary), the Scottish novelist. All the stamps bear their signatures. The 'Anniversaries' issue of 1971 marked, on the 3p, 50th anniversary of the British Legion (Servicemen and nurse of 1921); 7½p 1,900th of the City of York (Roman centurion); and, on the 9p, the centenary of the Rugby Football Union (players of 1871). A similar

Opposite, top two rows: Polar explorers honoured in 1972 and (others) more heroes of exploration the following year.

Below: The 50th anniversary of the discovery of Tutankhamun's tomb.

Above: American independence noted with a bust of Benjamin Franklin. Right: Three anniversaries celebrated with stamps in 1971.

series in 1972 was even more varied – 3p, 50th anniversary of the discovery of the tomb of Tutankhamun by Howard Carter and Lord Carnarvon, the Egyptologists, at Luxor in 1922 (Statuette of Head of Tutankhamun); 7½p, 150th of HM Coastguard (19th-century coastguard); and 9p, centenary of the birth of Ralph Vaughan Williams (composer conducting and part of score of the 'Sea Symphony').

Artistic anniversaries have included tributes to two famous painters, with reproductions of their paintings, in 1973 – Sir Joshua Reynolds, for the 250th anniversary of his birth: 3p 'Self-portrait', and 7½p 'Nelly O'Brien' (Reynolds was the founder and first president of the Royal Academy); and Sir Henry Raeburn, 150th anniversary of his death: 5p 'Self-portrait', and 9p 'The Skater' (the Reverend R. Walker). Four stamps in 1975 honoured the bicentenary of the birth of Joseph Mallord William Turner, one of the greatest landscape

painters – 4½p 'Peace – Burial at Sea' (a tribute to fellow artist, Sir David Wilkie, who died at sea in 1841); 5½p 'Snowstorm – Steamer off a Harbour's Mouth'; 8p 'The Arsenal, Venice'; and 10p 'Saint Laurent', a landscape.

Literature and music have not gone unrecorded, with sets in 1980 for both Famous Authoresses and British Conductors. The four authoresses chosen were all popular during Victorian times – Charlotte Brontë, author of *Jane Eyre*, George Eliot, *The Mill on the Foss*, Emily Brontë, *Wuthering Heights* and Mrs Gaskell, *North and South*. Scenes from their books were featured as background designs to their portraits. The eminent composers chosen for stamp recognition were all musical knights – Henry Wood, Thomas Beacham, Malcolm Sargent and John Barbirolli. The centenary of the death of Charles Darwin, one of the most influential writers of the 19th century, was marked by four stamps

12ᵖ Sir Henry Wood

13½ᵖ Sir Thomas Beecham

15ᵖ Sir Malcolm Sargent

17½ᵖ Sir John Barbirolli

Four of Britain's best-known and most-loved conductors.

PHOTOGRAPH BY BILL BRANDT — 17 PENCE

PHOTOGRAPH BY CORNEL LUCAS — 22 PENCE

PHOTOGRAPH BY SNOWDON — 29 PENCE

PHOTOGRAPH BY ANGUS McBEAN — 31 PENCE

PHOTOGRAPH BY HOWARD COSTER — 34 PENCE

British cinema stars, revered throughout the world.

*Medieval embroideries – the
Christmas theme for 1976; and
the sport of sailing, represented
in 1975.*

*Two of Britain's first Greetings Stamps, issued in books,
1989 (SG 1423, 1427).*

*One hundred years of the world-famous Wimbledon Lawn
Tennis Championship depicted in spirited style, from the
four 'racket sports' stamps of 1977.*

in 1982 showing a portrait of Darwin with birds and animals discovered during his voyages.

The work of the British Council in promoting music and reading was noted on the 22p and 34p stamps in a set marking the 50th anniversary of the Council in 1984. The subjects of the European Music Year set in 1985 were Handel, Holst, Delius and Elgar; the stamps did not feature the composers but an artist's impression of their works, respectively *Water Music*, *The Planets*, *The First Cuckoo* and *Sea Pictures*. The stamps were also noteworthy in having the values spelled out in full, i.e. 'SEVENTEEN PENCE' instead of '17p'. Arthurian Legends were the subjects of stamps later in the same year on the occasion of the 500th anniversary of the printing of Sir Thomas Malory's *Morte d'Arthur*. The designs featured the King, Merlin, the Lady of the Lake, Queen Guinevere, Sir Launcelot and Sir Galahad. Although of interesting design, the stamps

were rather dull in colour. Yet another 1985 issue – British Film Year – commemorated British genius, this time in the persons of Peter Sellers, David Niven, Charlie Chaplin, Vivien Leigh and Alfred Hitchcock. Shakespeare was depicted on one of four stamps issued in 1988 to mark the bicentenary of Australia, the playwright symbolizing the cultural links between the two countries. Also in 1988 the Post Office marked the bicentenary of the death of Edward Lear with stamps reproducing some of his comic drawings including, inevitably, the Owl and the Pussy-cat. The four stamps were also issued in miniature sheet format.

Sport has not been a main feature of British stamps although there have been a number of interesting issues beginning with the set for the Commonwealth Games in Edinburgh in 1970, featuring stylized runners, swimmers and cyclists. The set for the 1986 Games, also in Edinburgh, depicted Athletics, Rowing, Weight-lifting, Rifle-shooting and the fifth stamp in the set marked the World Men's Hockey Cup in London. Sailing was featured on four stamps in 1975 and the centenary of Wimbledon was marked by the 8½p stamp in a Racket Sport set in 1977. The centenary of the Lawn Tennis Association was commemorated by a second tennis stamp in 1988, again one of a set of four, the other three marking Football, Skiing and Gymnastics. Stamps featuring horse-racing were issued on Derby Day 1979.

The Christmas theme was well maintained through the seventies – the De Lisle Psalter (1970), Canterbury Cathedral's windows (1971), musical angels (1972), 'Good King Wenceslas' (1973), the Nativity – church roof bosses (1974), musical angels augmenting the heavenly orchestra (1975), the 'Opus Anglicanum' – medieval embroideries (1976), 'The Twelve Days of Christmas' (1977), 'Christmas Carols' (1978), and the Nativity (1979). The 1981 Christmas set was designed by children, ranging in age from five to 16. The pillar box design of the 1983 12½p stamp reminded us of the vast increase in the mail handled by the Post Office during the Christmas period. The 1986 set featured Christmas Folk Customs and the 1989 issue was linked to the 800th anniversary of Ely Cathedral.

Looking Around the Commonwealth

The main distributors of more than 40 Commonwealth territories' postage stamps in this country is CAPHCO Ltd of Sutton, Surrey, formerly part of the Crown Agents – the official financial and commercial agents for many overseas governments, public authorities and international bodies. The Crown Agents were established in 1833 and first produced stamps for Mauritius in 1847. CAPHCO became a private company in 1988 and continues the services previously offered – the negotiation of contracts for the design, security printing and supply of postage stamps, and their sale, through dealers, to collectors. New and current stamps of the countries they represent are distributed and news about them and their background stories is supplied to editors and journalists for publication in the philatelic press. A feature on new issues from CAPHCO countries – 'Stamping Around' – is published regularly in *Gibbons Stamp Monthly*. CAPHCO normally only sells stamps direct to collectors at the national stamp exhibitions, when CAPHCO staff are kept busy by collectors bringing their collections of Commonwealth stamps up to date.

The Australian Stamp Bureau in the United Kingdom is also established within the precincts of the CAPHCO building at Sutton, and carries stocks of current and recent Australian Commonwealth, Australian Antarctic Territory and Cocos (Keeling) Islands stamps. Guernsey, Jersey and the Isle of Man each have their own philatelic bureaux and services, publish regular stamp bulletins and supply official first-day covers, presentation packs and postal stationery. Many Commonwealth postal administrations overseas also have well-established philatelic bureaux – among them are Belize, the Cook Islands, Gibraltar, Kiribati and Tuvalu (the former Gilbert and Ellice Islands), Malta, Montserrat, Papua New Guinea, St Vincent and Seychelles. Stamps can usually be obtained direct from overseas bureaux, but their terms of sale vary and, in some cases, handling and postal charges are high.

British Commonwealth territories fall conveniently into geographical groups and are located on the continents and in the oceans of the world. The collector's choice is governed, not only by the attraction of the stamps themselves, but also by the historical, scenic, urban or even romantic background of a group or individual country. Most Commonwealth countries are established favourites with collectors so, for a newcomer, it is a matter of 'joining the club', or

Boosting tourism in 1977, the Cayman Islands had a striking evocation of scuba diving (SG 430).

branching out on some personal preference for one country or its stamps of a certain period or reign. This is the road to specialization and if one's energies are concentrated on the studies of particular issues of stamps, the methods by which they were printed, their varieties and postal use, then one becomes a philatelist in the true sense.

One of the largest Commonwealth groups, and one of the most popular with collectors, is the West Indies, a long-ranging string of palm-fringed islands, extending from the Florida Strait in the north almost to the coast of Venezuela (South America) in the south. The background stories of colonization, naval adventures, piracy and buccaneering in the 17th and 18th centuries have been graphically depicted on many West Indian stamps, while the modern issues show picturesque, travel-brochure scenes, cruise liners and tourist attractions. In Jamaica, we can go rafting on the Rio Grande, watch the pretty, long-tailed Doctor bird or pick pineapples and bananas, all on stamps. In the Cayman Islands we find turtles, source of the famous soup (which is exported), 'cat boats' (used for turtle fishing) and a Cayman schooner heading for the Turks and Caicos Islands, once famous for salt production, now best known for fishing and fishes, which are featured on the 1974 definitive stamps.

The Leeward and Windward Islands form a curving 'string of pearls' running north to south from east of Puerto Rico to north of Trinidad and Tobago in the eastern Caribbean. The Leewards comprise Antigua (with Barbuda), home of Nelson's Dockyard and English Harbour, St Christopher-Nevis and Anguilla (the latter under direct British control since 1971 and issues her own stamps), Montserrat, where the islanders speak with a strong Irish brogue and grow tomatoes, and the (British) Virgin Islands with many colourful stamps of fishes and ships. The Windward Islands include Grenada and the Grenadines, Dominica, famous for her bananas and citrus fruits, St Lucia, which Columbus discovered on the Saint's

Tristan da Cunha's popular stamps are a pictorial guide to island life; the lower stamp, a '4 potatoes' essay, was commemorated officially in 1979 (SG MS267).

The historic (and contentious) discovery of Lakes Tanganyika and Victoria by Burton and Speke was noted by Kenya, Uganda and Tanganyika in 1958 (SG 181).

festival day in 1502, and St Vincent, whose volcano, La Soufrière, erupted violently in 1979, also the St Vincent Grenadines.

East of the Windward Islands is Barbados – 'Los Barbados', the island of bearded fig trees – which now produces sugar, featured on the two cent stamp of 1950. Nelson and his fleet prevented enemy ships attacking Barbados in 1805, just before his ill-fated encounter at Trafalgar. The most southerly of the West Indies are Trinidad, where Sir Walter Raleigh discovered pitch or asphalt in 1595, and Tobago. Adjoining Venezuela on the mainland of South America is Guyana, formerly British Guiana, famous to philatelists as the issuing country of the world's rarest stamp, while away to the west in Central America is Belize, the former British Honduras, the land of an ancient Maya civilization, of butterflies and the armadillo. North of Cuba are the extensive Bahamas, a group of some 700 islands and cays (or keys) best known for holiday pleasures – tuna-fishing, water-skiing and yacht-racing. A special miniature sheet was issued to mark Tourist Year in 1972. Far to the north, a mere speck on the map, is Bermuda – the 'Bermudas' or 'Somers' Islands' – colonized by Sir George Somers in the *Sea Venture* in 1609, illustrated on the 2½d. definitive stamp of 1953.

Elsewhere in the Atlantic Ocean, north to south, it's a long voyage to reach the island of Ascension,

discovered on Ascension Day by a Portuguese mariner in the 16th century; St Helena, noted as the place of exile of Napoleon; and the group of islands known as Tristan da Cunha, whose stamps recall the volcanic eruption of 1961, and the evacuation and eventual return of the islanders. The Tristan councillors formally petitioned the Postmaster-General of South Africa for the provision of postage stamps in 1946 and submitted pictorial essays with face values based on the local currency, 1d equalling four potatoes etc. Tristan's first stamps were issued in 1952. The Falkland Islands lie away to the south-west, close to the tip of South

A pintailed whydah from The Gambia, 1966; a Bundu mask from Sierra Leone, 1961.

America – the centenary of their first stamps was celebrated with a special issue in 1978, while the Falkland Islands Dependencies are some hundreds of miles distant. Dependencies' stamps were withdrawn in 1963 and superseded by issues for the British Antarctic

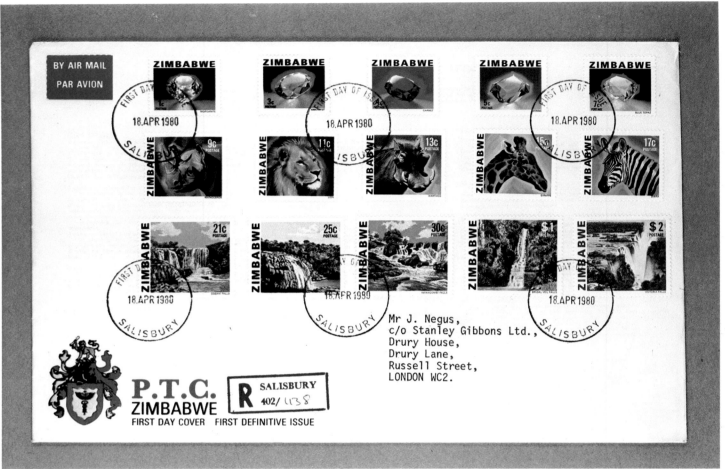

Zimbabwe independent: the first stamps on first day cover, 1980.

Territory and South Georgia – the designs feature Antarctic discovery, ships and fauna. Australian Antarctic Territory and New Zealand's Ross Dependency have and had their own stamps.

Africa has seen continual changes since the 'Empire' days and British rule has yielded to national aspirations and desires for independence. East Africa is a complex group for stamp collectors, starting in the 1890s with the issues of British East Africa and Uganda, and followed by the occupation and mandate of Tanganyika. Kenya and Uganda (and later Tanganyika, now Tanzania) formed a postal alliance which exists today only to the extent of occasional shared stamp designs and themes. Kenya, Uganda and Tanzania now have their own definitive series and commemoratives, too, many of them designed by Mrs R.M. Fennessy of Nairobi. Zanzibar once had its own stamps, but now uses Tanzanian issues.

West Africa includes four independent Commonwealth countries – The Gambia, Ghana, Nigeria and Sierra Leone. The Gambia's first 'Cameos' were commemorated by centenary stamps in 1969, and other

British South Africa Company territory became Northern and Southern Rhodesia in 1924.

A 1954 stamp (SG 11) from Rhodesia and Nyasaland, briefly united as the Central African Federation.

Issues from Malawi (formerly Nyasaland) include colourful birds (1968, SG 316).

Cecil Rhodes honoured in 1953 by former Northern Rhodesia (now Zambia).

The arms of the new Botswana (SG 243), known as Bechuanaland under the British.

Cecil Rhodes, and what used to be Nyasaland (now Malawi and formerly part of British Central Africa), reflect the numerous political and territorial changes. Rhodesian stamps, inscribed British South Africa Company, were first issued in 1890, followed by the famous 'Double Heads' of King George V and Queen Mary (1910) and the 'Admirals' (1913). Stamps for

The well-known Rock of Gibraltar is perforated in outline on the 1969 set (of four) marking the introduction of the new constitution (SG 236).

Malta's heroism in World War Two was recognized by the award of the George Cross (SG 284).

Northern and Southern Rhodesia were issued between 1924 and 1954, with the Federation 'Rhodesia and Nyasaland' stamps being used between 1954 and 1964. Then in October 1964 Northern Rhodesia became independent and was renamed 'Zambia', while Nyasaland also gained independence as 'Malawi'. Southern Rhodesia was renamed simply 'Rhodesia'. All these changes in title were necessarily reflected on the stamps; Botswana (formerly Bechuanaland), Lesotho (the former Basutoland) and Swaziland form a closely-related collecting group which can be linked with South African states – Bophuthatswana, Ciskei, Transkei and Venda.

The blue Mediterranean laps the shores of three places whose stamps are among the most popular with collectors – Gibraltar, Malta and Cyprus. The famous

stamps picture the steamers/travelling post offices which operate along the great River Gambia. Ghana, formerly the Gold Coast, and Nigeria, formed by the merger of Northern (Lagos and Niger Coast) and Southern Nigeria in 1914, issue picturesque stamps. Sierra Leone, famous for its diamonds and palm-oil, has issued many 'cut-to-shape', self-adhesive stamps.

Another interesting group is Central Africa, where the stamps of Rhodesia (now Zimbabwe), named after

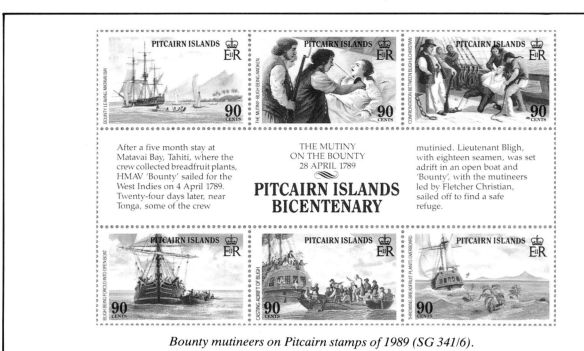

Bounty mutineers on Pitcairn stamps of 1989 (SG 341/6).

Rock, its aerial ropeway and cheeky Barbary apes, are all depicted on Gibraltar stamps – the Rock was additionally perforated in outline on normally-perforated stamps issued to mark the new constitution in 1969. Malta, a republic since 1974, has made stamps reflecting her history and culture, also commemoratives for the George Cross award and, in 1960, the centenary of Malta's first stamps. Cyprus, a republic since 1960, regularly issues colourful commemoratives.

The monsoons sweeping across the Indian Ocean caress – and sometimes lash – the islands of Sri Lanka (Ceylon), the Maldives and the Seychelles, Mauritius and – far to the east – Christmas Island and the Cocos (Keeling) Islands. The British Indian Ocean Territory, comprising the Chagos Archipelago, Aldabra, Farquhar and Desroches, was transferred to the Seychelles in 1976.

The South Pacific Ocean is liberally spattered with islands which owe allegiance to the British Crown, to Australia and to New Zealand. Fiji, independent since 1970, an island group virtually in the centre of them all, issues many colourful stamps depicting island life. Tonga, the only Polynesian kingdom, is a compulsive stamp-issuing country, while the New Hebrides islands (now Vanuatu) were under joint administration of Britain and France, with a single currency, but dual stamp issues. In the north and west are the island groups of Kiribati and Tuvalu (the former Gilbert and Ellice Islands), and the (formerly 'British') Solomon Islands. Joint Gilbert and Ellice Island stamps were issued in 1976, since then separate issues have been made. The far-flung Pitcairn Islands, nearly midway between Australia and America, have close connections with the *Bounty* mutiny – which has featured on their stamps.

*From a scenic set of 1955,
the Singapore River (SG51)*

The greater proportion of the island's revenues come from its sale of stamps.

The bicentenary of the mutiny on the *Bounty* was marked by stamps from several countries and of course by Pitcairn issues – three sets, each of six, issued in February and April 1989 and in January 1990 were particularly interesting – charting the sailing of the *Bounty*, the mutiny and the mutineers' arrival on Pitcairn.

Australian influence extends to the combined territory of Papua New Guinea, home of the famous Birds of Paradise, to Nauru, the 'Phosphate Island', and to Norfolk Island which is very picturesque and has a delightful climate. New Zealand keeps a watchful eye on the Cook Islands, including Niue, Aitutaki and Penrhyn which each have their own stamp issues, and on the remote Tokelau Islands – Atafu, Nukunonu and

First issued 1900, the well-loved Malay States' 'Tiger'.

Two fathers of modern India commemorated in 1973 (SG 693).

The Khyber Pass depicted on Pakistan definitive (1961, SG 128).

Bangladesh – 1978 flower stamp (SG 110).

Fakaofo. Samoa, once an independent kingdom, was under tripartite administration until 1899 when the eastern islands were assigned to the USA and the western to Germany. Western Samoa – 'Samoa i Sisifo' – was occupied by British forces in 1914, once administered by New Zealand and the United Nations, and is now an independent sovereign state.

Next stop, Malaysia – a complete change of scenery, historical background and stamps. The old Malayan Federation brought together the stamps of the Straits Settlements and the Federated Malay States – the famous 'Tigers' and the separate state issues for Johore ('Johor'), Kedah, Kelantan, Malacca ('Melaka'), Negri Sembilan ('Negeri Sembilan'), Pahang, Penang ('Pulau Pinang'), Perak, Perlis, Selangor and Trengganu. All, with Sabah (formerly North Borneo), Sarawak and Singapore, became part of the newly-formed Malaysian Federation in 1963. Federation issues continued with separate stamps in uniform designs for the states – Singapore became an independent republic within the Commonwealth in 1965, continuing to issue colourful pictorial stamps. The Sultanate of Brunei, located on the north coast of Borneo, did not join the Malaysian Federation – it is under British protection. Hong Kong, the Crown Colony at the mouth of the Canton River on the Chinese coast, comprises the island of Hong Kong and the mainland peninsula of Kowloon, and has issued its own Chinese-orientated stamps since 1862, through five reigns.

'Dominion' is an old-fashioned word, but it still applies to the great Commonwealth member nations of Australia, Canada (where Dominion Day is still observed) and New Zealand. India is now a republic, Pakistan withdrew from the Commonwealth in 1972 but happily rejoined in 1989. Bangladesh, Pakistan's former eastern province, remains a member nation and now issues its own stamps. Modern Indian stamps mainly comprise single-value issues of local and international interest, while Pakistan has a regular programme of large-size commemoratives and pictorials.

Australia, Canada and New Zealand all have attractive stamps as briefly described in Chapter 4. Picturesque scenery, historic events and anniversaries are commonly featured, and there are regular issues for the annual Christmas festival. New Zealand's definitives have pictured garden roses, Maori artifacts and seashells; Canada's modern stamps give emphasis to sport and the great outdoors – there were twelve issues for the Montreal Olympic Games in 1976.

Austria – 1972, Hofburg Palace (SG 1635).

Austria – 1970, Beethoven (SG 1632).

Netherlands – 1974, Benelux Customs Union (SG 1196).

Netherlands – 1964, Knights' Hall (SG 969).

Belgium – 1968, St. Laurent Abbey, Liège (SG 2088).

Belgium – 1964, Pand Abbey, Ghent (SG 1906).

Luxembourg – 1958, Moselle wine industry (SG 644).

Luxembourg – 1974, Differdange (SG 936).

9
Modern Foreign Stamps

To the uninitiated, 'foreign' stamps are those issued anywhere in the world except in Britain, but to the stamp collector – especially now that we are members of the European Communities – foreign stamps relate specifically to the countries of Europe or those in the rest of the world – in Africa and the Middle East, Asia and the Far East, and the Americas – other than those who are members of the British Commonwealth. Each country has its individual culture, history, language, natural produce and manufactures, urban development and way of life, all of which may be seen on stamps, contributing to their attractiveness and appeal.

The world's postal administrations comprise more than half-a-million post offices employing five million workers. The work of organizing, standardizing and developing the international postal services is undertaken by the Universal Postal Union, founded in 1874 as the 'General Postal Union', and an agency of the United Nations Organization since 1948. Montgomery Blair, Postmaster-General of the United States, started the postal ball rolling in 1863 when he convened the first international conference in Paris – it was attended by delegates from fifteen countries. In 1874, Heinrich von Stephan, Director of the North German Confederation's postal administration, presided over the postal congress in Berne at which the representatives of 22 member states reached agreement on the reciprocal exchange of letters, 'unimpeded transit' through their respective countries and uniformity of charges, whereupon they signed the Berne Treaty.

A second congress at Paris in 1878 revised the Treaty to admit 'any country, state or colony' to the union which was then renamed the Universal Postal Union. In practice, the UPU today mainly concerns itself with co-ordination of the postal services and the development of new techniques. The International Bureau at UPU headquarters in Berne records new stamps issued by its members, and there are more than 150 member countries. As with the Commonwealth territories, these are located in all parts of the world and can be grouped geographically according to region. The new range of Gibbons' Foreign Stamp Catalogues, in current publication, covers the 'foreign' world in 21 parts, and groups the various countries for the convenience of collectors. These groups correspond to the modern trends towards selective and more specialized collecting, and they are summarized briefly in the following pages, together with any distinctive features which may be attractive to collectors. Catalogue Part numbers are given in brackets.

The European Countries

Modern Europe is divided by the so-called 'Iron Curtain' which bisects Germany (and Berlin itself), and curves around the eastern borders of Austria and Italy to the Adriatic. Austria and Hungary (2), once a great empire, are thus divided and issue contrasting stamps – Austria excelling in finely-engraved portraits, Hungary providing thematic interest, such as the 'Science Fiction in Space Research' issue of 1978. The Balkans (3), mountainous setting for the wars of 1912 and 1913, embrace Albania and Bulgaria, both people's republics since 1946, and both good sources of art and cultural stamps; Greece, a republic since the monarchy was abolished in 1973, which issued stamps for the 150th anniversary of its postal service in 1978; Rumania, whose stamps regularly feature the Danube and tourist attractions; and Yugoslavia, where paintings, sculptures and museum treasures are frequent design subjects.

'Benelux' (4) was the name coined for the customs union – the (Benelux) Economic Union – between the neighbouring countries of Belgium, the Netherlands and Luxembourg, which came into force in 1948 and was consolidated in 1960. All three countries issue stamps of fine quality and exquisite design. The Belgian and Dutch colonies are included in this section of the catalogue.

Czechoslovakia and Poland (5) are republics east of Germany and west of Russia, with Austria and Hungary bounding Czechoslovakia (which was once part of Austria-Hungary) in the south, and the Baltic Sea providing a maritime outlet for Poland in the north. Czechoslovak stamps have long been stylishly designed and printed (from their own presses), and there are regular series for the 'Praga' international stamp exhibitions, and for Prague Castle, its paintings and other treasures. Poland celebrated its millennium

Czechoslovakia – 1973, Flower show (SG 2110).

Poland – 1964 stamp showing a lapwing (SG 1484) and a 1946 issue depicting Bedzin Castle (SG D573).

Albania – 1974, Greenfinch (SG 1685).

Rumania – 1972, Saligny Bridge (SG 3910).

in 1966 with special stamps, and numerous other issues honour Copernicus, Kosciuszko, Sienkiewicz, Mickiewicz, Chopin and other Polish celebrities. Popular thematic subjects include railways, aviation, birds and butterflies, and sport.

France (6), one of the first countries in the world to issue stamps (in 1849), has attracted many collectors by her numerous commemoratives and pictorials issued each year – stamps which add colour and variety to the French posts and to collectors' albums. Besides the French Art, Tourist and Red Cross stamps noted in Chapter 7, French stamps regularly feature the 'Regions of France', national and international events and anniversaries – flower shows, philatelic exhibitions, pioneer flights, nature conservation, film festivals and topical campaigns such as the economical use of energy. The catalogue includes French overseas territories prior to independence and those, such as Polynesia and the Southern and Antarctic Territories, which still belong to the French Group. Andorra (French Post Offices) and Monaco are included for ease of reference.

Germany (7) uniquely has three postal administrations – West Germany and West Berlin, which frequently share definitive and commemorative issues inscribed 'Bundespost' or 'Bundespost Berlin', and East Germany – the German Democratic Republic (DDR) – whose stamps are used in East Berlin and elsewhere in the republic. The 'Bundespost' stamps are exceptionally well-designed and printed, and with regular issues for youth welfare depicting railway locomotives, sport, ships, aircraft etc and humanitarian relief, an annual series of showing wildflowers. Occasional West Berlin stamps honour famous Berliners, depict Berlin views and record local events. East Germany issues stamps each year for the spring and autumn Leipzig fairs. The catalogue includes the former states, colonies and post offices abroad.

Above, left: France – 1968, Béziers Cathedral (SG 1802); and 1967, the Great Bridge, Bordeaux (SG 1751).
Above, right: West Germany – 1975, Diesel locomotive (SG 1729); and 1971, West Berlin steam train (SG B381).

1988 Pro Patria stamp (SG 1145) and two of 'Post – Past and Present' definitives (SG 1103, 1111).

Italy and Switzerland (8) is another popular section – modern Italian stamps include a pictorial series, 'Italian Fountains', another picturing 'Famous Italians' and a third publicising tourist attractions. Paintings and reproductions of classic sculptures are frequently featured, while the stamps of San Marino cater almost exclusively for the thematic collector. The Vatican City (Rome) has been under the independent sovereignty of the Pope since 1929, and issues its own stamps picturing religious art, St Peter's and the other famous buildings within its precincts. The death of Pope John Paul I was commemorated in 1978. Switzerland is famous among collectors for her immaculate 'Publicity', 'Pro Juventute' and 'Pro Patria' issues; Liechtenstein, the principality lying between Austria and Switzerland, tactfully has her attractive stamps printed in both countries. The Geneva UN stamps are also listed.

Portugal and Spain (9), the ancient Iberia, share a common heritage of postal history and are both industrious producers of postage stamps, locally designed and printed. Portugal has a series of 'Natural Resources' and of 'Tools and Implements', and has kept up-to-date with stamps for 'Energy', 'Road Safety' and the 'Introduction of the Post Code'.

Spain – 1977, Paintings by Madrazo (SG 2478, 2485).

Italy – Famous people: 1974, Puccini; 1973, Caruso; 1971, Grazia Deledda (SG 1410, 1384, 1294).

Vatican City – the Pope: 1979, John Paul II; 1978, John Paul I (SG 713, 711).

Vatican City – 1964, Paul VI; 1963, John XXIII (SG 419, 404).

*Greenland – 1950, Arctic ship (SG 35);
and 1946, Polar bear (SG 6a).*

Portugal – 1976, Hydro-electric power (SG 1636).

U.S.S.R. – 1961 Yuri Gagarin (SG 2576).

Spain, once again a monarchy – the King, Juan Carlos I is depicted on recent stamps – maintains numerous series of attractive stamps, including 'Celebrities', 'Monasteries', 'Stamp Day' (the works of famous artists), 'Fauna', 'Tourism' and 'Spanish Military Uniforms'. A series in 1978 depicted the 'Kings and Queens of Spain'. The Portuguese and Spanish colonies are also included, as well as the Spanish post offices in Andorra.

Russia (10), the Union of Soviet Socialist Republics (USSR) has issued over 6,000 different stamps since the Revolution and averages more than 100 commemoratives each year. As pioneers in space exploration, Russia has issued numerous stamps recording and illustrating achievements in space, from the early rocket flights and the first manned flight by Yuri Gagarin in 1961 to the 'Soyuz', 'Luna' and 'Salyut' (space station) projects. Russian art, ballet, aviation, railways and shipping are regularly featured, and a long series for the Moscow Olympic Games in 1980 began in 1977. The catalogue includes the Baltic States of Estonia, Latvia and Lithuania, also Mongolia.

Scandinavia (11), another popular collecting group, embraces Denmark, the Faroe Islands (a

Norway – 1965, Red Cross centenary (SG 580): and 1976, painting by Fearnley (SG 765).

Denmark – 1976, Viking longship (SG 618).

Faroe Islands – 1975, map and painting of islands.

*Iceland – 1940, Great Geyser (SG 230);
and 1963, Herring catch (SG 402).*

Iceland – 1972, Mount Herdubreid.

Europa stamps: 1989 Ireland (Hopscotch); 1960, Iceland.

King Olav V and King Carl XVI Gustav respectively – are depicted on their definitive stamps. Denmark has a regular series featuring the Danish provinces; Norway pictures her scenic attractions and winter sports; and Sweden favours tourism, 'Keep-fit' activities and the Nobel prizewinners of past years.

The 'Europa' concept originated in 1955 when six European countries formed a postal union and issued their first 'Europa' stamps in the following year. The six countries – Belgium, France, West Germany, Italy, Luxembourg and the Netherlands – formed the nucleus of the Conférence Européenne des Postes et des Télécommunications (CEPT), a permanent organization established at Montreux, Switzerland, in 1959 for the 'improvement of postal and telecommunications services'. A score of European countries now issue special stamps each year with a common design subject – the theme for 1989 was 'Children's Games, Toys and Activities'.

Overseas Countries

Africa today is a strange mixture of the primitive and the sophisticated. Its political character has undergone dramatic change since World War II – most of the countries are independent states and republics, though some maintain a token allegiance to their former Euro-

Danish possession in the North Atlantic), Finland (a former Russian grand duchy), Greenland (an integral part of the Danish Kingdom), Iceland (an independent republic, formerly under Danish rule), Norway and Sweden. Denmark, Norway and Sweden are independent kingdoms and their monarchs – Queen Margrethe,

*Algeria – 1969, Desert mail
coach of 1870 (SG 533).*

*Mozambique – 1954, the
country mapped (SG 496).*

*Central African Republic – 1965,
Team of oxen (SG 74).*

*Sudan – 1962,
Camel postman (SG 184).*

Somalia – 1963, Open-air theatre (SG 406).

*Somalia – 1954,
River Juba (SG 280).*

*Chad – 1974,
Insect (SG 368).*

*Sudan – 1967, Arab
Summit Conference (SG 222).*

*Ethiopia – 1955,
Haile Selassie (SG 458).*

*Niger – 1974,
Camel saddle (SG 538).*

*Congo – 1975,
Albert Schweitzer (SG 483).*

*Ivory Coast – 1974,
Cotton production (SG 437).*

*Morocco – 1966,
Rameses II (SG 187).*

*Tunisia – 1973,
Winged camel (SG 790).*

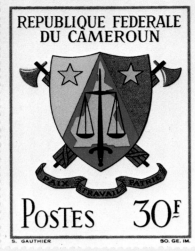

*Cameroun – 1972, Adamaoua
round house (SG 629).*

*Cameroun – 1968, Arms
of the Republic (SG 484).*

*Equatorial Guinea – 1971,
President Nguema (SG 14).*

*Dahomey (now Benin) –
1975, Flowers (SG 595).*

*Malagasy Republic – 1971,
Palm Beach Hotel (SG 198).*

*Mauritania – 1975,
Mining industry (SG 481).*

*Mali Republic – 1972,
Sarakolé dance (SG 336).*

*Togo – 1956,
Village school (SG 193).*

*Comoros – 1954, Tenth anniversary
of Liberation (SG 17).*

*Gabon – 1974,
Ogooué River (SG 521).*

*Liberia – 1976,
Leopard (SG 1294).*

Upper Volta – 1973, Hair-style (SG 399)

Bahrain – 1976, Concorde in service (SG 232/5).

Israel – 1952, Immigration (SG 75).

Jordan – 1967, Dromedary (SG 808).

pean masters, especially the French-speaking territories. 'Africa since Independence' takes up three
catalogue parts with the countries in alphabetical order
– A-E (12), F-M (13) and N-Z (14), and collectors may
prefer a regional grouping.

North Africa includes Algeria, Libya, Morocco,
the Sudan and Tunisia – a nice, compact group with
moderate issues of new stamps, mainly concerned with
Arab affairs and events. North-east Africa comprises
Ethiopia (Abyssinia), Somalia, a former Italian
colony, and Djibouti, formerly the French Territory of
the Afars and the Issas (the old French Somali Coast),
while in the heart of Africa are the Central African
Republic (formerly Ubangui-Chari), Zaire (ex-Belgian
Congo and Kinshasa), the Congo Republic (Brazza-
ville), Burundi and Rwanda (formerly Ruanda-
Urundi).

Many African stamps are brightly coloured,
designed to attract thematic collectors and often
motivated by national or political propaganda. Such
stamps may be found among the French-speaking West
African territories – Benin (formerly Dahomey),
Burkina Faso (formerly Upper Volta), Cameroun,
Chad, Gabon, Guinea, Ivory Coast, the Mali Republic
(formerly French Sudan), Mauritania, the Niger
Republic, Senegal and Togo. Still on the west coast,
Liberia, a negro republic founded in 1822 by American
philanthropists for freed slaves, has a lively and
consistent stamp programme; Guinea-Bissau, formerly

Egypt – 1972, Userkaf (SG 1139).

Kuwait – 1974, Shuaiba industrial area (SG 639).

Above: U.A.E. – 1975, Oil Conference (SG 32).

Right: Syria – 1970, Khaled Ben el-Walid (SG 1098).

Portuguese Guinea, was formed after an armed rebellion; and Equatorial Guinea comprises the former Spanish provinces of Fernando Po and Rio Muni. Angola and Mozambique, both former Portuguese possessions, are now independent. The Malagasy Republic (Madagascar) and the Comoro Islands are located in the Indian Ocean.

The Middle East (19) includes Egypt whose various stamps display some of her most famous antiquarian treasures; Jordan, an independent kingdom (formerly Transjordan); war-torn Lebanon which issues few stamps at present; the Syrian Arab Republic; and the 'oil states' of Bahrain, Iraq, Kuwait, Oman (formerly the sultanate of Muscat and Oman), Qatar, Saudi Arabia and the United Arab Emirates, which comprise seven states – Abu Dhabi, Ajman, Dubai, Fujeira, Ras al Khaima, Sharjah and Umm al Qiwain. The State of Israel has issued some 1,100 different stamps since it was founded in 1948 – the first issue depicted ancient Jewish coins – and there are regular issues for Memorial Day and the Jewish New

Year, Israeli art, architecture and culture, the Hapoel and the Maccabiah Games, historical personalities, views and landscapes. This section is completed by the Republic (and former kingdom) of the Yemen, and the Yemen People's Democratic Republic (formerly Aden and Protectorates, South Arabian Federation and Southern Yemen).

Asia and the Far East cover a vast area of the globe, and the catalogue parts are arranged by geographical region. Central Asia (16) conveniently groups Afghanistan, whose occasional 'home-made' stamps have a primitive charm; Iran (Persia); and Turkey. Iranian issues were, until 1979 and the revolution, largely devoted to the Shah and his 'White Revolution' of Western development and progress; Turkish stamps likewise featured Kemal Ataturk, who won the Turkish War of Independence in 1922 and founded modern Turkey.

South-East Asia (21) ranges from Burma and Bhutan, Nepal, the Philippines, Indonesia and Thailand (Siam) to Kampuchea (Cambodia), Laos and

Afghanistan – 1971, Pashtunistan Square, Kabul (SG 713).

Iran – 1967, Coronation of the Shah (SG 1518).

Bhutan – 1962, World Refugee Year (SG 9).

Turkey – 1952, Ataturk.

Iran – 1973, Bosphorus Bridge (SG 1805).

Burma – 1948, Aung San and map (SG 83).

Cambodia (now Kampuchea) – 1966, Preah Ko Temple (SG 191).

Khmer Republic (now Kampuchea) – 1973, Constitution (SG 362).

Philippines – 1955, Mayon Volcano (SG 774).

Laos – 1967, Harvesting (SG 219).

Japan – Philatelic weeks, 1956 and 1970 (SG 759, 1197).

China – 1968, Revolutionary opera (SG 2376).   *North Vietnam – 1965, Honouring Cuba (SG N342/3).*

Thailand – 1967, Royal barge
and palace (SG 582).   *Nepal – 1970, Lake*
Gosainkunda (SG 250).

South Korea – 1988 Olympic Games, Seoul (SG 1747/8)

Nicaragua – 1967, Poet Ruben Dario (SG 1571).

Panama – 1948, Cervantes commemoration (SG 485).

Costa Rica – 1948, National theatre (SG 462); and 1973, Tourist Year (SG 906).

Vietnam. The Philippines and Thailand issue the most attractive stamps – regular Thai series include birds, fishes and butterflies, Thai culture and dancing, and the Red Cross.

China (17) comprises the People's Republic, which was founded by Mao Tse-tung in 1949, and Taiwan (Formosa), the island ceded by China to Japan in 1895 and returned to China in 1945 after the defeat of Japan. The stamps of the People's Republic are generally large and ornate, almost exclusively devoted to the memory of Mao Tse-tung, revolutionary sites and activities, Communist Party anniversaries and the life of peasants and industrial workers. Taiwan stamps feature Chiang Kai-shek, folklore, coins, paintings, ceramics and lacquer-ware, fans and many other subjects.

Japan and Korea (18) face one another across the Sea of Japan, but their stamps have little in common. Japan, one of the few remaining empires, is a closely-knit, highly industrialized country whose people have inherited the artistry and culture of past centuries. Japanese stamps have an exquisite charm. Korea, once an empire, has become the independent republics of North and South Korea, and both issue stamps. Numerous issues were made by South Korea to commemorate the 1988 Olympic Games in Seoul.

Central America (15) includes seven mainland republics – Mexico, Guatemala, El Salvador,

Haiti – 1965, Cathedral; and 1967, Duvalier Airport, Port-au-Prince (SG 951, 1084).

Argentina – 1978, World Cup, Buenos Aires (SG 1582).

Peru – 1974, New Bridge (SG 1236).

Guatemala – 1967,
Yurrita Church (SG 791).

Mexico – 1973, Railway
centenary (SG 1273).

Chile – 1967, Forest (SG 584).

Paraguay – 1954, San
Roque Church (SG 731).

Brazil – 1956, Salto
Grande Dam (SG 936).

Uruguay – 1949, National
Airport (SG 942).

Dominican Republic – 1974,
Higuamo Bridge (SG 1192).

Venezuela – 1967,
Angostura Bridge (SG 1985).

El Salvador – 1969, Los
Chorros Baths (SG 1307).

Colombia – 1950,
Farming (SG 732).

Honduras – 1956,
Landscape (SG 556).

Cuba – 1955, Mariel
Bay (SG 738).

*United States history: Abraham Lincoln (1960, SG A1141)
and the White House (1950, SG 987).*

*U.S. space missions:
Landing of 'Viking 1'
on Mars (1978, SG 1730).*

Lunar landing (1969, SG A1367).

Honduras, Nicaragua, Costa Rica and Panama, whose stamps, with the exception of Mexico – these are excellent – are undistinguished and 'run-of-the-mill' – and three in the West Indies: Cuba, and the Dominican Republic and Haiti, the latter two forming the island of Hispaniola. South America has ten republics, many with interesting stamps – Argentina, Bolivia, Brazil, Chile, Colombia, Ecuador, Paraguay, Peru, Uruguay and Venezuela. Surinam, on the north coast, is allied to the Netherlands, though it is now independent.

The United States of America (22) comprise 50 states and one federal district, with several outlying territories. Recent stamps marked the bicentennial of the American Revolution, and numerous commemoratives are regularly issued. Subjects have included the 'Black Heritage' series, Wildlife Conservation, the Performing Arts, American Culture – Quilts and the Dance, Energy Conservation and historic anniversaries such as the 75th Anniversary of the first Powered Flight by Orville and Wilbur Wright. Continuing with the bicentennial theme, recent issues have marked the granting of statehood and the anniversaries of The Senate, the House of Representatives and the Executive Branch. The current definitives feature 'Great Americans' (sheet stamps) and 'Transport' (coil stamps).

*Bicentenary of the House of Representatives and The
Senate, 1989 (SG 2396/7).*

The United Nations Organization issues its own stamps for mail posted at its headquarters in New York, Geneva and Vienna.

NORFOLK ISLAND

1966 Provisional Decimal Definitives

1960-2 Definitives surcharged with Decimal Currency, in black on silver tablets obliterating the old sterling value.

Issued:- February 14th 1966. Ptg. Typograph.

1c Small tablet.
$1 Large tablet.

Reprints - May 1966

1c Large tablet.
$1 Small tablet.

10
Starting a Collection

Most people start collecting stamps by chance. Rarely is it a long-cherished ambition, although the prospect of collecting may have been in 'the back of the mind' for years. Sometimes an old schoolboy collection turns up and re-awakens a long-forgotten urge, or some attractive stamps on a letter from an overseas country may arouse the collecting instinct. Everyone should have a leisure pursuit – something to occupy one's spare time and provide the necessary relief to the pressures of work and the daily routine. Stamps, the longest-established collecting hobby, fulfil all the requirements of a worthwhile and rewarding pastime.

It is not difficult for the beginner to start a collection. Stamps are easily obtained from a variety of sources and there are medium-priced albums designed specifically for the novice. You have read in previous chapters how stamps came into use and of the many different kinds of stamps issued by the countries of the world. Your first stamps will be the common, 'every day' issues of these countries you and your friends may receive from abroad in the form of correspondence and business letters. The traditional way of starting a collection is to buy the largest packet of 'whole world' stamps you can afford from a reputable stamp dealer, together with a 'whole world' album and a packet of gummed 'hinges', and mount your stamps on the appropriate album pages. You will make mistakes – not too many, I hope – and place some stamps on the wrong pages – but you will be learning.

When you get to know your stamps and their inscriptions, you will be able to allocate them to the right album pages – beginners' albums usually have printed country headings and spaces or printed squares for the stamps, and often provide helpful information in the country headings. At this stage, keep all the stamps that come your way, unused or postally used. Many people collect either unused or used stamps, not both. Some may like their stamps to be in the original 'mint' condition as issued by the post office – others may prefer stamps with nice clear postmarks; it is a matter of personal choice. However, it is important not to mix used and unused when mounting sets and to choose stamps in good, clean condition, avoiding creased,

torn or heavily postmarked specimens. Unused stamps should have their original gum intact (although light hinge-marks are generally acceptable) – those which have been thinned or have lost their original gum in some other way are of little value and should be replaced at the first opportunity.

As you learn more about stamps (and you should read all the books, catalogues and magazines you can get hold of), and your collection grows, you may want to limit your collecting activities to a certain country or group of countries, or at least concentrate on those whose stamps attract you. In this way you will be able to build up complete sets or issues of stamps for display on the album page. Soon you will be wanting to buy more stamps for your album – many dealers run approval services and send regular selections of stamps for you to choose at your leisure. Of course you must return the unwanted stamps within a week or so, together with a remittance for the total value of the stamps you have kept. It helps the dealer very much if you can tell him which country's stamps you are most interested in, and roughly how much you are likely to spend, at a time. He will then make up a selection for you, but note that they will be better-class stamps (not common ones) and that a reasonable purchase these days would be £5 and upwards.

Some dealers sell 'one-country' packets of stamps – usually 50 or 100 different – and mixtures of assorted stamps of country groups or of the whole world. These come from business houses and charities, and have the original pieces of envelope attached. Unsorted mixtures and 'kiloware' – which is similar material often from official sources – are sometimes sold by weight. They are mostly common stamps with duplicates, but are generally good value with always the chance of a good 'find'. Before you clip a stamp from its envelope, be sure that the envelope itself – or the postmark – is not of special interest. Old postmarked letters may be more valuable as such than the stamps themselves, while modern stamped envelopes may have interesting commemorative, railway or shipping cancellations. If in doubt get an expert opinion!

The stamps you buy in mixtures are generally washed and cleaned *en masse* – individual stamps on pieces of the original envelope paper should be washed or 'floated' free of the paper, and never removed in

An album page 'written-up'. Simple, but effective, notes explain the stamps.

any other way as damage is sure to result. All you need is a large, shallow tray or bowl of water. Lay your 'bits' – stamps face upwards – on the surface of the water. After ten minutes or so, the backing paper will be adequately soaked, and the stamps may then be carefully separated and placed between sheets of clean blotting paper to dry them off. Stamps should *never* be totally immersed in water because some of them have fugitive colours which may 'run' or smudge when the stamps are wet. Similar care should be taken with coloured envelopes.

Loose stamps should be kept in one of the available 'slip-in' collecting books – pocket size – or, better still, in a 'stock' book such as dealers use. The small pocket books are convenient for carrying stamps about – 'swaps' or new purchases – and cost no more than a diary. Stock books are similar, with pages having eight or ten strips or 'pockets' for holding the stamps.

Countries within the Commonwealth – Gibraltar, Hong Kong, Jamaica, Malta etc – all have their names boldly printed on the stamps and can be sorted quite easily, so make a start with those you can identify. Place all the 'A' countries together in your collecting book, then the 'B' countries and so on. You may realize that 'Helvetia' is Switzerland, 'Norge' is Norway and 'Sverige', Sweden, but for the time being put aside any stamps you cannot identify – later we can look for these in the catalogue, or the 'Stamp Finder' (Chapter 16) may assist you. When the time comes for your stamps to be arranged in the album, each section can be dealt with in methodical fashion, one at a time.

Other sources of supply? Try your neighbourhood stamp shop. There are numerous dealers with shops in London and most provincial towns, and a personal call can establish cordial relations which can be to mutual advantage. Dealers not only sell stamps, albums and accessories, but also often buy collections of various kinds and one can buy second-hand or 'remainder' lots in most stamp shops. Remainders are collections from which the dealer has extracted the stamps he needs for stock, but which may still contain bargains for the average collector. Another good source of discarded collections and mixed lots of stamps is the auction-room. Stamp sales are held regularly in London and in other cities, and if you cannot attend in person most auctions accept postal bids.

The auction-room is a friendly, exciting place, not at all frightening as some people imagine. The lots are available for viewing on previous days and, in some cases, on the day of the sale – examine those that interest you, note the auctioneer's estimated valuation in the catalogue and how much you are prepared to pay and. . . bid! You may be lucky – at least you tried. Postal bidders have to rely on the

catalogued descriptions, but these are invariably carefully compiled and explicit about condition.

For the collector who is, or tends to be, a 'lone wolf', there are definite advantages in meeting other collectors and exchanging stamps as well as ideas – a very pleasant way of adding to your collection. The numerous philatelic societies and stamp clubs dotted around the country (there is a list of them in Chapter 19) are only too pleased to welcome visitors and new members, and many of them have special sections for juniors and beginners, where the exchange of stamps is encouraged. There are also stamp exchange clubs which circulate booklets of stamps individually priced to members who, as with 'approvals', take the stamps they require, and pass the 'box' on to the next person on the list, either by post or by hand in local areas. Remittances are forwarded to the club secretary or treasurer.

Stamp clubs have long been a feature of primary and secondary schools, where young children are encouraged to collect stamps, take part in competitions such as 'design a stamp', and write about stamps and their relation to the school syllabus – art, literature, geography and history, architecture, flowers and wildlife. With the encouragement of the Post Office, many teachers took advantage of the Rowland Hill centenary to introduce the subject of stamps and the early posts to their pupils. For some juniors, the stamp collecting hobby becomes a lifelong interest despite the many competitive hobbies and pastimes.

Stamp exhibitions have a twofold attraction for the stamp collector – selections of stamps from famous collections, as well as entries in the national competitions, are on display, and stamps can be purchased from the numerous dealers who attend these shows. The most popular exhibition is STAMPEX which is held in London twice every year – in the spring and autumn. Stamp fairs, where the dealers set up shop in large halls and you can visit each in turn or as you wish, are a phenomenon of recent years and are now held throughout the country at regular intervals.

The Stamp Catalogue

Edward Stanley Gibbons, stamp dealer of Plymouth, first published his penny price-list of stamps for sale in 1865. Today, Stanley Gibbons Postage Stamp Catalogues are world famous and cater for every type of collector from beginner to specialist. As described in Chapter 9, the main catalogue now comprises 22 parts – *Part 1 British Commonwealth*, which covers all British and Commonwealth stamps, and the foreign countries of the world, divided into regional groups.

Stamps of the World lists all the stamps issued everywhere in the world since the very first – Britain's famous Penny Black in 1840 – in three volumes, one

A London stamp auction in progress.

covering the issues of Britain and the Commonwealth, the other two the issues of foreign countries, arranged alphabetically A–J and K–Z. For the more advanced collectors there is the *Great Britain Specialised* in five volumes, and the *Channel Islands Specialised* catalogues. Handy check-lists are published in the 'Collect' series for Great Britain, the Channel Islands and the Isle of Man, at frequent intervals. The stamps are priced, unused and used.

The choice of catalogue depends very much on the intended scope of your collection, but for the beginner and the 'simple life' collector, *Stamps of the World* is an ideal catalogue. It is the successor to the popular *Simplified Catalogue* and records the world's stamps on a simplified basis, omitting details of paper, perforation, shade, watermark, designer and printer, errors and varieties. The current edition lists more than 275,000 different stamps and has thousands of illus-

trations to enable you to identify stamps by their inscriptions, emblems and face values, or to find suitable designs for a thematic collection. Browsing through the catalogue, you will get to know the 'look' of a stamp – most countries' stamps have a distinctive style of design which can be instantly recognized.

The countries are arranged in alphabetical order and the country headings indicate the appropriate section of the main catalogue which contains the more detailed listing. Stamp illustrations of Commonwealth countries are in actual size; those of foreign countries are reduced to three-quarters linear – usually only one illustration of a set is shown, but all the designs (if different) are described. Each illustration has its own 'type' number and this is repeated in the actual listing of the stamps to indicate which ones are shown. Brief descriptions of the illustrated designs appear as captions.

The main heading of an issue appears below the illustration – it gives the year of issue and, in the case of commemorative stamps, the nature of the event or person commemorated. If there is no such description, the stamps can be assumed to be definitive issues, while airmail stamps are simply described 'Air'. The list of stamps follows – each stamp has its own number, shown in the first (left-hand) column, and each country has its own set of numbers, which are uniform with other Gibbons catalogues. Next to the stamp number is the illustration type number, and then the face value of the stamp and its colour(s). To the right of this there are two columns of prices – the first column shows the unused price, and the second column, the used price of the stamp. The catalogue is basically the dealer's price-list, but it also provides a guide to market values.

The catalogue is used as a basis of exchange – or the 'swapping' of stamps – all over the world. Collectors quote 'S.G.' numbers and current prices when exchanging stamps, just as collectors and dealers use them when buying and selling them. *Stamps of the World* is an essential work of reference – it includes helpful notes for the collector, the historical and geographical backgrounds of each country, currencies, populations and an index.

As you progress in the hobby and begin to collect the stamps of certain countries in a more selective way, you will be looking for a stamp catalogue more suited to your requirements. If you are collecting British and Commonwealth stamps from the earliest issues, then you will certainly need the famous 'Red' catalogue – the *Part 1 British Commonwealth*. Besides Great Britain, it lists all the stamps issued by Commonwealth territories, past and present, from Abu Dhabi to Zululand, including the post-independence issues of Ireland, and South Africa – countries which are not members of the Commonwealth, but which interest many collectors. The listings include the details of designers and printers, differences of perforation and watermark, major varieties and shades.

The *Great Britain Concise Catalogue* is aimed at the collector who wants a more detailed listing than that given in the *Part 1* catalogue but not at the depth of the *G.B. Specialised Catalogue*. The *Concise* lists all issues from 1840 onwards, including the Country stamps of Northern Ireland, Scotland and Wales, the pre-postal independence issues of Guernsey, Jersey and the Isle of Man, Postage Due stamps and the short-lived 'Royal Mail Postage Labels' of 1984–5.

The five *G.B. Specialised Catalogues* are intended for the advanced collector and are virtual encyclopedias of British stamps through the reigns *1. Queen Victoria; 2. King Edward VII to King George VI; 3. Queen Elizabeth II, Pre-Decimal Issues; 4. Queen Elizabeth II, Decimal Definitive Issues* and *5. Queen Elizabeth II, Decimal Special Issues.*

A new departure for the *S.G. Catalogue* was the publication of the first thematic catalogue listing *Bird* stamps in 1983, this has been followed by volumes for *Mammals, Railways* and *Ships*, all of which have proved popular with the growing number of thematic collectors.

Albums Galore

Stamp albums are graded and priced according to quality, size and scope – there are many different kinds of album catering for the many different types of collection, and it is important to choose the right one for your stamps. A small collection will be 'lost' in a large album; a small album will 'burst at the seams' if stamps are crammed into it. Albums come in all shapes and sizes, fastbound (like a book) or loose-leaf, with various styles of binder. Stanley Gibbons produce a vast selection of stamp albums ranging from the popular illustrated kinds for the novice to the luxurious, leather-bound volumes intended for the finest collections.

For the beginner and junior collector, printed albums include the fastbound 'GB' and the whole world albums – 'Globemaster', 'Transworld' and 'Strand'. More capacious whole world loose-leaf albums are the 'International' and the 'Worldex'. These all have printed country headings and the advantage of the loose-leaf system is that the leaves can be re-arranged as required, and extra leaves can be added to augment any particular country. Collectors who prefer to arrange and 'write-up' their stamps on blank leaves have a wide choice – there are many splendid albums available for consideration, large, medium and small, with spring-back and ring-fitting or peg-fitting binders.

The spring-back types include the 'Tower', the 'Senator' medium and standard, the 'Simplex' medium and standard, the 'Utile', which has double linen-hinged leaves that lie flat when opened, and the 'Nubian' with black leaves. The standard leaves, about 11×10 inches, are slightly larger than the medium, and extra leaves can be obtained for all blank loose-leaf albums. The blank leaves have a feint quadrille background of tiny squares to assist in the arrangement of the stamps.

The multi-ring albums also lie flat when opened and many collectors find this convenient when adding stamps to the collection or when adding notes or 'writing-up'. Gibbons' general-purpose ring-fitting albums include the 'Avon' and the 'Universal System' which is available with a choice of leaves – white or black transparent-faced, or white without transparent interleaving, together with pockets for first-day covers and also stamp booklets. For the 'one-country' collector there is a popular range of fully illustrated, ring-fitting, loose-leaf albums – Great Britain, Channel Islands, Isle of Man, Australia, Canada and New Zealand. Supplements to bring the albums up-to-date are issued periodically and there is a universal one-country binder which can be used to augment any of the above albums.

Numerous publications and accessories exist for collectors.

The peg-fitting albums with a special release action are more expensive than other loose-leaf brands. The 'Devon' is a large-capacity album holding 200 leaves, while the 'Exeter' and the 'Plymouth' are each supplied with 40 transparent-faced leaves of superior quality. For the connoisseur there are two luxury albums – the 'Philatelic' and the 'Oriel', and for GB collectors there is the spring-back, loose-leaf 'Windsor' album with printed layout to accommodate your stamps, available in popular and presentation editions and with regular annual supplements.

For the 'sideline' collector there are albums for covers, including the popular first-day covers; stock albums and books; a stamp booklet album; and albums for picture postcards, including the Post Office PHQ cards which reproduce new stamps in large format. So, whatever your 'line' in stamp collecting, there is an album to suit you. With most albums there is a choice of colour of the binder – red or green, blue or black, and here again the choice is yours.

The foregoing albums are described in some detail to enable you to decide which type would be most suitable for the kind of collection you have in mind. There are numerous other brands of album on the market, and of course your choice may be governed by the cost and your personal taste. If you can decide on the type of album that is likely to suit you best and how much you are prepared to spend, your next step is to visit a stamp shop – your dealer will be pleased to show you all the different kinds of albums within your price range. If you purchase a 'one-country' album, the arrangement of your stamps is tailor-made – spaces are provided for all the stamps of your selected country broadly on the lines of the catalogue listings. With a loose-leaf album and blank leaves to fill, careful planning is required.

Layout and Arrangement

Get the tweezer habit! Stamps are easily creased or stained by careless handling – you will find the work of sorting, classifying and mounting stamps much easier with the help of stamp tweezers, an essential tool in the stamp collector's outfit. They are made especially for the purpose, light in weight and plated in nickel, chromium or gold, with broad 'spade' tips if required. Tweezers will give you an extra pair of fingers to handle stamps quickly and accurately.

Next you will want hinges – small rectangles of gummed paper – to mount your stamps in the album. These are usually sold in packets of 500 or 1,000, and are also available 'ready folded'. *Never* use paste or glue, for obvious reasons – your stamps will be spoilt beyond repair when you attempt to remove them! Fold down about a quarter of the hinge, gummed side outwards, moisten the narrow, folded portion lightly with the tongue and attach it to the back of the stamps, near the top, but not too close to the perforations – you need to be able to raise the mounted stamp to examine the back as required without bending the perforations. Now moisten the lower portion of the hinge – not too lavishly – and press the stamp gently and firmly into its allotted position on the album page. Repeat the process with your other stamps, keeping them in level rows. With practice the entire operation of mounting stamps can be done with your tweezers.

Hinges are cheap and probably best for beginners, juniors and the average collector, but there is an alternative method for the collector who wishes to preserve unused stamps in 'mint' condition – the popular 'Lighthouse' mount. This is a gummed paper 'envelope' which opens on three sides, with a black or clear background and transparent front, which is available in strips or in cut-style precisely sized for modern British stamps, and other popular issues, definitives and commemoratives, giving the stamps maximum protection in the album. The mounts are gummed on the back for attaching to the album page, and the strip form is useful for the in-between stamp sizes – a cutter and rule are available for made-to-measure trimming.

With a loose-leaf album and blank leaves to fill, mounting your stamps requires more preparation and planning than is necessary with a printed album, which has squares or outlined spaces for the stamps and a page or two for each country. Having selected an album, you probably have in mind some idea of how you intend to group your stamps and which countries or issues you are going to collect. The catalogue will indicate which stamps you are missing in a set, and you may wish to leave appropriate spaces for them to be filled later. Finding the stamps you need and filling the gaps in your collection can be a most rewarding and enjoyable pursuit, and there is great satisfaction in completing an album page. It is customary to arrange stamps in order of issue and if you have only a few stamps for a particular page, it may be best to keep them separately in your slip-in collecting book for a short while.

Planning a page is a matter of visualizing the finished work, creating a uniform style of headings or titles and writing-up (hand-written or typed captions or descriptions), and estimating the number of stamps the page will hold without overcrowding. If you are collecting the stamps of one country only – say Great Britain – there is no need to repeat the country name at the top of each page: a simple decorative frontispiece will suffice. For the British Commonwealth and Whole World collectors there are booklets of gummed country titles – printed labels which can be used as desired. Each country name is duplicated several times, providing

sufficient labels for the average general collection, or for certain groups of countries.

The average album page will accommodate five or six rows of five or six medium-sized stamps, and still leave room for the addition of notes about the stamps, their dates of issue and designs, perhaps also their perforation and watermark details. The collector who takes the time and trouble to work out a well-balanced page, avoiding monotonous rows of stamps with the same number in each row, will have the makings of an attractive collection. Much depends on the sizes of the stamps and whether they are uniform in shape – vertical or horizontal format – or mixed.

It is usual to arrange stamps in ascending order of value and this is a straightforward procedure if they are of uniform size. The current British 'Machin' definitives, for example, could be placed in alternating rows of 4. 5. 5. 4 or 4. 6. 6. 4., keeping to the favoured 'lozenge' layout, but varying according to the number of stamps and the size of the album leaf, rather than three rows of six or four rows of five. An acceptable alternative arrangement would be the 'hour-glass' – rows of 5. 4. 4. 5 or 6. 4. 4. 6 stamps which can be expanded or repeated to fill the page. The important thing to bear in mind is to avoid the imbalance of the top-heavy 'tree' and the bottom-heavy 'pyramid' arrangements.

Stamps with mixed designs – vertical ('portrait') or horizontal ('landscape') formats – in one set or series may have an unbalanced, lopsided appearance if arranged strictly in order of value, and the rows should be arranged as symmetrically as possible by changing the order, perhaps placing two vertical stamps in the centre of a row, flanked by horizontal designs, or having separate rows for vertical and horizontal stamps while maintaining the 'lozenge' or 'hour-glass' principles. Possible layouts can be roughly sketched beforehand in an exercise-book, and the stamps can be just laid on the album page to give you an idea of their appearance. The ideal formation is best found by trial and error – shifting the loose stamps around on the page until a pleasing arrangement transpires.

The quadrille pattern of the album leaf will assist you to mount your stamps in neat rows, leaving perhaps a ¼ inch or two of the tiny patterned squares between each and an equal space at the beginning and end of each row – never extend the rows to the edges or borders of the page. There are usually faint marks on the leaves to indicate the exact centre of the page, so the centre stamp in a row of five should fall plumb on the central mark, as also should the middle space in a row of four or six stamps. Use light pencil dots to mark the position of each stamp and place the middle stamps first, working outwards.

If the central mark on the album leaf is *not* the optical centre, place the middle row of stamps slightly above it with the remaining rows equally spaced – the general appearance will be more pleasing to the eye. And the requirement about level rows can be varied so that horizontal designs are in line with the *middle* of adjoining vertical stamps (the base-line of the latter falling below that of the former), again achieving a balanced pattern. Plan for stamps you have reasonable hopes of acquiring, but not for expensive items which may never come your way.

The Finishing Touches

Some form of written description is very necessary with blank leaves. Page headings should be uniform in style, whether drawn by hand or composed of gummed labels and, assuming that you have already 'titled' each page, you must consider how much space to allow for sub-headings and captions. Collecting the stamps of a certain country in chronological order, it is usual to show the year of issue and the event commemorated *above* the stamps, and to caption the design, very briefly, below each stamp – or set of stamps if the designs are closely related. A thematic collection requires a different approach and this will be described in the next chapter.

It is best to do the written work *before* you mount the stamps and to take the leaves out of the album binder in order to work on them. There are three basic methods of writing-up a stamp collection – one's own handwriting, stencil or transfer lettering such as the many forms of 'Letraset', or typewriting. Copperplate writing really belongs to the past or to those skilled in the cursive art. It is a dated style, hardly in keeping with modern lettering and the printed word – and it is difficult to condense. Keep your handwriting small and neat: practise first and try to maintain the size and style of lettering throughout. Avoid writing everything in block capitals – use them only when required at the beginning of a caption or for proper names.

Follow the examples of the printed word in any book – there you will see the correct use of capital letters and 'lower case' or small letters for sub-headings, a similar but smaller style for the captions below the stamps which comprise the names of people or places. Italic writing – sloping letters – does not look well and should be avoided or modified if you normally have a sloping hand. The backward slant is quite unacceptable and if you are a backhander, perhaps you should try one of the other methods!

Again it is preferable to rough out your headings and captions before you attempt any writing-up. Completed headings, dates etc, should occupy the middle of the album page in harmony with the top row of stamps – lines of words extending beyond the last stamp in the row (without a corresponding extension at the beginning) stick out like sore thumbs. Similarly, captions below the stamps should not impinge upon adjoining captions, but can be continued below – it is quite permissible for a caption to take up two or three lines underneath the stamp being described. The choice of pen is yours – use a normal fountain-pen if you can write easily and comfortably with it, and use black ink rather than blue or red. With a fairly broad nib you can produce the broad and narrow strokes which give style to your writing, and special pens for the different styles of penmanship are stocked by the art-materials shops. You will find books on the subject, too – a good guide is the Phillips–Rang *How to Arrange and Write-up a Stamp Collection*, published by Stanley Gibbons.

Stencilled letters and figures are stamped out on a special transparent plate which stands on raised guides, the appropriate letter being placed directly over the required position on the page and inked in with one of the special pens provided. With both stencils and 'Letraset' transfers, great care is needed to obtain regular and uniform spacing between letters and between words. Some outfits include a small drawing-board and a graduated rule, while the horizontal lines of the quadrille pattern on the album page can be used as a basis for level printing.

Typewriting is neat and quick, and the space occupied by any number of words is easily calculated. The modern small-typeface ('Elite') machines are most suitable, and the average portable typewriter will accept medium leaves. For standard leaves, you would need an office machine with a wider carriage.

All About Accessories

Philately has become a science and there are numerous 'scientific instruments' to assist the philatelist in the pursuit of his studies. As a beginner you will not be much concerned with the differences of perforation and watermark, but later you will want to know all about them – how perforations are measured and described, and how watermarks may be distinguished and identified. Many stamps which appear at first to be exactly similar in face-value and design may in fact differ in perforation or watermark or both. We have seen (Chapter 6) how errors of perforation occur and how, for various reasons, watermarks may differ from those of the normal stamps. To check these things and to separate different issues of stamps, you need a perforation gauge and a watermark 'detector'.

The yardstick of perforation measurement is that the number of holes in a measure of two centimetres shall indicate the *perforation* of a given side – or all sides – of a stamp. Perforation gauges of the printed card or engraved ivorine types have rows of dots inscribed on them – the dots correspond to the holes perforated on the stamp, and each row is numbered with the appropriate measurement, say '14'. One simply matches the black dots on the gauge with the stamp perforations and notes the figure quoted - there's no need to count the dots! If there are 14 holes recorded on

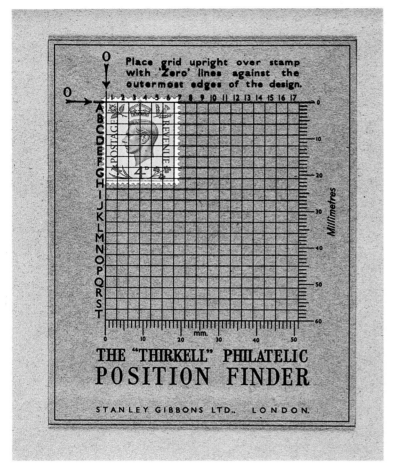

Exact positions are quoted with this gauge.

A widely used method of measuring perforations.

the gauge for a particular stamp – on all sides – then the stamp is said to be 'Perforation 14'.

The perforations at the top and bottom of a stamp may have a different measurement to those at the sides. The current British definitives measure '15' (top and bottom) and '14' (at the sides) – this is known as a compound perforation and is usually expressed in the catalogue as '15 × 14' (or 'P 15 × 14'), the horizontal measure being given first.

With the Gibbons' 'Instanta' gauge a stamp's perforations can be measured to the nearest decimal point – useful in cases where a measure appears to be midway between, say, '12' and '12½'. Simply lay the transparent gauge over the stamp, align the guideline with the left side of it and slide the gauge up or down until the converging lines (inscribed on the gauge) exactly correspond with the perforation holes – or 'teeth' if you prefer. The measure is indicated by figures on the left, with a more accurate decimal notation on the right. The row of perforations to be measured must be kept firmly at a right angle to the vertical guide-line during the sliding operation. Rouletting is a means of separation in which cuts are made in the paper by a roulette-wheel or toothed disk – the principle of

measurement is the same as for perforation, though perhaps a little more difficult with some variations such as the 'serpentine roulette' which has cuts in the form of wavy lines.

It is important to be able to identify watermarks because many issues of stamps have had two or three different ones in their lifetime, and often the earlier watermark is the most rare. The first Elizabethan stamps of Great Britain bore the flat-shaped 'Tudor' Crown and 'E 2 R' watermark, later changed to the 'St Edward's Crown' and 'E 2 R', both in multiple pattern. More recent stamps had an overall pattern of small 'St Edward's Crowns', until watermarks were discontinued on British stamps in 1967.

The earliest British colonial stamps usually had single-emblem watermarks – the 'Imperial' Crown with the letters 'CC' ('Crown Colony'), one emblem appearing on each stamp. Then the letters were changed to 'CA' ('Crown Agents'), and after some years came the multiple watermarks. The Multiple Script 'CA' appeared in 1921, and was followed by the Multiple St Edward's Crown 'CA' (in block capitals), introduced in 1957. Currently, the Multiple Crown 'CA' Diagonal watermark is used by some Crown Agents' territories.

Stamp watermarks are not always easily visible. Sometimes they show up well when held in front of a strong light, or placed face downwards on a dark surface. A time-honoured method of 'detection' is the use of a watermark tray or tile which is used in conjunction with a benzine-dropper. A few drops of benzine applied to the stamp reposing face down on the tray renders it momentarily transparent – and the watermark visible – before the benzine evaporates. But be warned that benzine (actually *petroleum* benzine, not 'benzene') is highly inflammable and is liable to stain photogravure-printed stamps. Use with care.

For the collector who regularly checks watermarks, the Morley Bright 'Inst-a-Tector' is recommended; this small, light, easy-to-use accessory is extremely effective, even on 'difficult' stamps. Unlike earlier watermark detectors, it requires no inflammable liquids, electric power or messy and time-consuming ink pads.

Many of the more advanced postal administrations now produce their stamps on phosphorescent or fluorescent papers – essential in highly developed postal mechanization programmes. British stamps have been overprinted with phosphor bands (or printed on phosphorized paper) since 1959 and for the advanced collector interested in telling apart differences in the phosphor the Stanley Gibbons Uvitec Micro Short Wave Ultra Violet Lamp is an essential tool. This enables the collector to differentiate between the 'green', 'blue' and 'violet' phosphors found on the Wilding stamps (1959–67) and the phosphor coated and advanced coated Machin stamps of more recent times. All these specialist variations are listed in the *G.B. Specialised Catalogue*, volumes 3 and 4. Some sheets of modern British stamps, also booklet panes, have tiny phosphor cylinder numbers printed in the margin. Whilst detection of phosphor bands is possible with the naked eye, these tiny numbers are almost impossible to see without the aid of a UV lamp. UV lamps can also be used to see if a stamp has been tampered with, for example, the removal of a manuscript cancellation or a repair. The Uvitec lamp can be carried around easily and is battery operated.

Stamps seen through the magnifying glass take on a new image. People and scenes, especially on engraved stamps, appear to come to life, and you will need a good glass to get real enjoyment from your stamps as well as looking for errors and varieties. Ideally you should have one for your pocket and a more powerful magnifier for your desk at home. They range from the simple watchmaker's eyeglass to folding magnifiers, stand models, reading glasses and the high-powered specialist's glass. The well-known Beck magnifiers are precision-made, scientific instruments including desk and measuring models with 8× magnification, a measuring stand magnifier with focusing lens and mm scale (10×), and two 30× types of pocket microscope, one complete with inbuilt light source.

Colour is perhaps the most important element of a postage stamp, other than the design. To most people, a stamp is either simply red, blue, green or brown, or a combination of those (and other) colours. To the philatelist the red may be carmine, rose or scarlet; the blue, royal blue, indigo or ultramarine; the green, emerald, yellow-green or blue-green; and the brown, purple-brown, chocolate or chestnut. A stamp may have varieties of shade which are quite rare and to complicate matters, some colours appear darker under artificial light than they do in normal daylight.

The Gibbons Colour Key will help to solve your problems of stamp colours and catalogue descriptions. It contains pivoting tabs, each bearing a selection of related colours (200 in all) which open out like a fan, enabling the appropriate tab to be selected. Remember that a stamp may have several tones of the same colour and that, when attempting to match colours with the Key, the patches of solid colour should be isolated on the stamp – this can be done by laying the punched colour panels (the hole about 3mm in diameter) on the face of the stamp.

Now, a useful gadget for the variety-hunter – the 'Thirkell' Position Finder. It is a plastic transparent type of gauge which bears an imprinted grid of small squares, quadrille pattern, with which one can chart the position of stamp flaws and varieties. The squares are numbered across the top and lettered down one side, and when the grid is placed over the stamp with the guide-lines at top and left just touching the outer edges of the stamp design, the location of the flaw can be recorded according to the square in which it falls. 'A 1' would indicate a variety in the top left of the stamp.

Flaws and varieties are popular with many collectors and new ones are being discovered all the time – often on stamps issued many years ago. The Gibbons magazine contains regular reports on new discoveries in articles entitled 'Through the Magnifying Glass' and 'G.B. Varieties'. The Thirkell position is normally quoted in these reports.

18p

Gaillardia

1987

22p

Echinops

1987

31p

Echeveria

1987

34p

Colchicum

1987

11
Thematic Collecting

Now that you have started collecting stamps, you may be content to jog along, adding new stamps to your collection and swapping duplicates with your fellow collectors. Your friends call you a 'philatelist', but there is a subtle difference between 'stamp collecting' and 'philately' – the first is basically no more than the accumulation of stamps and arranging them in the album, a pleasant enough pastime; the second involves the study of stamps, their origins, design and production in a limited field. Many collectors move beyond the elementary stage and restrict their collecting to one country or even one issue, and that is the first step from stamp collecting to philately – terms which are often used indiscriminately though there are no hard and fast rules.

One-country stamp collecting will take you into what is regarded as 'traditional' philately – the study of printing, shades, perforations, watermarks, varieties and possibly 'postal history' factors such as postmarks and the use of stamps on covers and cards at the correct rates of postage for ordinary, registered and other mail. This can be very rewarding, but for those interested mainly in the designs of stamps and the background to those designs, it can be rather tedious. Those more interested in design are perhaps more likely to develop their collections along thematic lines. Thematic collecting (or topical collecting as it is known in the USA) is now a respectable and growing branch of philately.

Theme with Variations

Postage stamps are miniature works of art – colourful, expertly designed and superbly printed. For many collectors the picture on the stamp is the main attraction, and collecting by subject or theme has become an important and popular branch of the stamp hobby, not only as a link with another hobby like bird-watching or music, but as a sideline to one's main collection. Almost any subject you can think of may be

found on stamps – some themes, such as animals, birds and flowers, run to hundreds, even thousands, of different designs providing a wide choice and an opportunity to 'specialize' within a particular theme.

The origins of thematic collecting can be traced back to Victorian times when people collected as many different portraits of the Queen as they could find on British and Colonial stamps. In the early 1920s, Stanley Gibbons offered a series of packets of stamps which were exclusively thematic – Royal Portraits, Foreign Portraits, Zoological, Maps, Engineering, Heraldry and History. As stamps gradually became more and more pictorial, more people began collecting them for their designs, and the range of subjects multiplied. With the development of mail transport, ships, trains and aircraft began to appear on stamps and became – as they are today – among the most popular subjects. Finding the stamps to illustrate your theme is the most enjoyable part of building up a collection.

In its simplest form the thematic collection is merely an assembly of butterflies, flags, paintings or whatever subject one fancies or is most interested in. The 'subject' collection needs no elaborate research or presentation, excepting perhaps that, for example, butterflies could be distinguished from moths and British species arranged separately from the tropical varieties; flags could be divided into national, military etc; and paintings arranged or grouped under painters.

There is another form of thematic collecting which has become something much more than the mere accumulation of like designs – the 'narrative' or story collection. This involves the development of a theme from its origins, using the appropriate stamps to illustrate a progressive story. The founding of the Red Cross by Henri Dunant (who witnessed the bloody battle of Solferino) is but one example – the growth of the organization, its services through two world wars and its worldwide present-day activities are fully represented on stamps. A third method of thematic collecting relates more to the 'purpose of issue' than to the designs of the stamps which may have abstract or symbolic motifs, linked by a common cause such as the numerous anniversary and commemorative issues of the United Nations Organization and its agencies.

Fauna and flora are among the most popular subjects for a thematic collection. These bold British stamps of 1987 were based on photographs by Alfred Lammer of the Royal College of Art.

For many years the thematic collector was scorned by the serious philatelist. Problems arose when thematic collections began to be submitted to society, national and even international competitions, and could not be judged fairly in relation to philatelic studies. Then, in 1967, the FIP (Fédération Internationale de Philatélie), philately's authoritative international body, introduced a set of 'international regulations for thematic, purpose of issue and subject collections' and established a place in the universal competitive field for thematic collections. The main stipulation was that stamps, philatelic items and postal documents should predominate – that includes, for example, special or commemorative postmarks relevant to the theme, though not necessarily on thematic stamps.

So, for the ambitious collector looking for medals, the rules laid down for national and international exhibitions now embrace the thematic collection – even the straightforward 'subject' collection is acknowledged and acceptable. But you need something more than the accumulation of stamp 'pictures' to catch the judge's eye. Your collection must have form as well as substance, and another FIP recommendation was that the collection should be preceded by an explanatory introduction, setting out its purpose and arrangement, and that the stamps themselves should be supported by a descriptive text. Every theme in a purely subject collection requires a different approach and arrangement according to its nature – theme with variations, in fact.

The Stamp Picture

Fauna and flora – these are among the most popular subjects for a thematic collection. All the creatures of the animal kingdom have 'family trees' of orders, families and species, and if your stamps can be grouped according to these various classifications, you will have a display which is attractively and scientifically arranged. You have a choice of 'creatures large and small' ranging from the elephant to the diminutive 3-inch humming-bird. Elephants belong to the order Proboscidea and extinct species are shown on Polish and Rumanian stamps – the stegodon on an Indian stamp. There are African and Indian elephants, Burmese elephants hauling teak, circus elephants and those in the world's zoos, all on stamps. You'll find delightful multicoloured humming-birds on the stamps of the West Indies and Latin-American countries. Alternatively, you could collect all the animals, birds, insects and fishes of a geographical area or zone in the world – say Malaysia and South East Asia or South Africa.

Flowers, too, can be grouped in families. Your introduction can explain the typical form of flower – the calyx or cup made of leaf-like bracts called sepals, and the enclosed petals which are usually the most colourful part of the flower; the (male) stamens within the petals, each tipped by the anther which contains the pollen, and which surround the female organ, the pistil.

With stamps you can have a more glorious array of roses than you will find in any garden. New Zealand issued 'rose' stamps for the first World Rose Convention in 1971 and also pictures roses on her low-value definitives, as well as on the cover of a stamp booklet. The United States produced a booklet of 15-cent rose stamps – 'Red Masterpiece' and 'Medallion' – in 1978, and South Africa issued 'Convention' stamps in 1979. The Royal National Rose Society (of Great Britain) celebrated its centenary in 1976, and the British Post Office issued four stamps for the event – 'Elizabeth of Glamis', 'Grandpa Dickson', 'Rosa Mundi' and 'Sweet Briar'. Many other roses may be found on the stamps of Europe and the rest of the world.

The most popular thematic subjects have been listed from time to time and include Space – astronauts, rockets, satellites and spaceships; Sport – athletics, team games such as football and cricket, the Olympic Games; Railways – locomotives, trains, railway systems, stations and signals; Ships – sailing ships, ocean liners, warships, native craft; Aviation – balloons and airships, fighters and bombers, early planes and modern airliners, helicopters, airports; or all three combined with motor vehicles under 'Transport'. Medicine and medical science are themes which appeal to doctors, nursing to nurses, and there are many famous names in the arts and literature which can be featured. Religion encompasses the Popes, churches, cathedrals and monasteries as well as the saints, religious festivals and Christmas.

Architecture, Engineering, the Sciences and Telecommunications are all 'big' subjects which have numerous sub-divisions, each of which can form a substantial collection. The various institutions and professions make interesting subjects – Parliament, Banks and Banking, the Law, Insurance, Journalism and Publishing, Printing, Drama and the Theatre. Industry includes Gas and Electricity, Factories, Mining, Oil, Chemicals and Manufacturing.

The Storyboard

That is an expression coined by the strip cartoonists and the graphic designers in advertising studios who literally plot their ideas and stories on boards, and make extravagant use of drawing-pins! But the basic idea is a sound one for anyone planning a thematic collection prepared to a definite plan which develops a theme, tells a progressive story and has a beginning and (unless it is a topical story) also a finale. 'Planning' is the key word – the proposed narrative collection needs to have a synopsis, an outline of the story just as novelists prepare their manuscripts. Research would involve appropriate sources of reference and, to find the stamps you need, a thorough search of the catalogue. You

Great Britain has had several sets illustrating the flowers and trees found in the countryside.

could have a series of short stories, all related to an overall theme, such as 'The Sea and Ships'.

The story of Bligh and the *Bounty* is a classic example of an exciting tale – a true story – of adventure and skulduggery on the high seas, with enough stamps to illustrate the celebrated mutiny and the events which followed. Briefly, Lieutenant William Bligh RN sailed from Portsmouth as captain of HM Armed Vessel *Bounty*, ex-*Bethia*, 220 tons, in December 1787 on a voyage to Tahiti to obtain breadfruit plants for transportation to the West Indies. Eventually, mission accomplished, the voyage continued, but Bligh's discipline antagonized his second-in-command, Fletcher Christian, and some others of the crew, who mutinied in the vicinity of the Friendly Islands (Tonga) and, on 28 April 1789, turned Bligh and some of his loyal officers and crew adrift in a longboat.

Christian and his men sailed the *Bounty* back to Tahiti and then on to the remote Pitcairn Islands where they scuttled the vessel and formed a settlement. Bligh

navigated his open boat through the Fiji Islands to reach Timor after 40 days at sea. He returned to England where he was given another command, and he later became Governor of New South Wales. He was promoted to Rear-Admiral of the Blue, a rank which he enjoyed for six years until his death in 1817. By 1808, when the American ship *Topaz* called at Pitcairn in search of seals, only one of the mutineers had survived – he was Alexander Smith who, as 'John Adams', had become 'chief' of the little community of Tahitian women and children. In 1856 the inhabitants were removed to distant Norfolk Island, but several families returned with John Adams to Pitcairn – their descendants now live there in comparative peace.

All the personalities and events described are reproduced on the stamps of the Pitcairn Islands – Bligh and the *Bounty*, Fletcher Christian, John Adams and the *Bounty* bible, the vessel's anchor and chronometer, and the ill-fated breadfruit. A Tonga stamp depicts the scene of the mutiny; Fiji stamps commemorate the 150th anniversary of Admiral Bligh's death; and Norfolk Island records the landing of the Pitcairners. The story (as described above) could be written or typed on the first album page, with the stamps following in chronological order of events – or it might be divided into short paragraphs and distributed, together with the relevant stamps, throughout the following pages. One or two illustrations would enhance the story – you can obtain a picture of the *Bounty*, and possibly reproductions of old prints, from the National Maritime Museum at Greenwich.

Numerous other story possibilities come to mind –

Flags make a particularly colourful theme and accurately mirror political and historical changes.

Butterflies (and moths) depicted on stamps are widely collected for their beauty and scientific interest.

William Tell, a fabulous story of defiance against oppression, of archery and the apple on his son's head (Switzerland); the Life of Napoleon Bonaparte, Emperor of the French – his battles and his eventual banishment to St Helena; Impressionism – the art form which revolutionized painting in the 1870s and 1880s, featured Manet, Monet, Degas, Cézanne, Renoir, Pissarro and Sisley among others, and greatly influenced modern art; or, for simplicity, the life of a great painter – Dürer, Goya or Rembrandt.

Thematic subjects already mentioned as 'stamp pictures' readily lend themselves to the storyboard treatment, particularly the three popular themes of Railways, Ships and Aviation – with so many stamp designs to choose from, the problem is not finding them, but selecting the most appropriate and attractive stamps to develop and illustrate your theme.

The story of railways begins with the dawn of steam power – George Stephenson's *Locomotion*, the Stockton and Darlington Railway and the numerous 'first railways' of European countries – and progresses through the years to the steam monsters of the 1920s and 1930s, the diesel, diesel-electric and electric trains, and culminating with the British, French and Japanese high-speed expresses.

The British Post Office has issued three popular sets featuring railways; the first, in 1975, marked the 150th anniversary of the Stockton and Darlington Railway. The set depicted Stephenson's *Locomotion* with locomotives of 1876, 1923 and 1975. The 150th anniversary of another pioneer railway – the Liverpool and Manchester – was commemorated five years later, this time with a se-tenant strip of five stamps designed by David Gentleman, showing the progress of the railway. The first stamp depicted the *Rocket* approaching Liverpool, the second, third and fourth stamps showed first-, second- and third-class carriages and horsebox and carriage truck passing, respectively, through Olive Mount cutting, crossing Chat Moss and near the Bridgewater Canal. The final stamp featured a goods truck and mail coach at Manchester with smoking factory chimneys in the background. The third set, in 1985, was entitled 'Famous Trains' and issued as part of the celebrations of the 150th anniversary of the Great Western Railway. The designs were based on paintings by Terence Cuneo and all included in the picture a tiny mouse – the artist's trademark. The trains featured were *The Flying Scotsman*, *The Golden Arrow*, *The Cheltenham Flyer*, *The Royal Scot* and *The Cornish Riviera*. Two of the five were GWR trains, the others were run by the other three big pre-nationalization railway companies, the Southern, London and North Eastern and London, Midland and Scottish.

Jersey no longer has any railways but there is considerable interest in them amongst the islanders and railway enthusiasts. A set of four stamps in 1973 marked the centenary of the Jersey Eastern Railway and a

Turner 1775-1851

Turner 1775-1851

Turner 1775-1851

Turner 1775-1851

ARTIST UNKNOWN *c.*1575   HARRISON

PIPER 1940 / HARRISON

LAWRENCE   HARRISON

Sir Joshua Reynolds
3P   *1723-1792*
Self Portrait

Sir Henry Raeburn
5P   *1756-1823*
Self Portrait

ASC. SCH. SEVILLE   HARRISON

The detailed progress of space exploration can be illustrated through highly popular stamps.

further set of five in 1985 featured scenes on the Jersey Railway. The Isle of Man is still rich in railways and tramways and these form the subject of the current (1988) definitives. The centenaries of both the Steam Railway and the Douglas Horse Trams were marked by stamps in 1973 and 1976 respectively. Across the Atlantic, railroads have featured on a good many US stamps including the current Transport stamps issued in coil form. Engineers such as the famous Casey Jones have also been commemorated on stamps. The Stanley Gibbons *Collect Railways on Stamps* thematic catalogue is essential for all those contemplating starting a collection of 'trains on stamps'.

In addition to the stamps issued by postal administrations, there are also numerous issues of the railway companies themselves. From at least the 1850s British companies issued stamps for the carriage of parcels of newspapers and other commodities. Most were of purely utilitarian design but a few featured the coat of arms of the company and could, therefore, be included in a thematic collection. One or two, such as the Eastern and Midlands and the Mersey Railway had stamps showing locomotives and rolling stock, clearly suitable for thematic collecting. After 1891 British railway companies were permitted to carry letters as agents for the Post Office and to issue railway letter stamps. Nowadays only the independent railways, such as the Welsh narrow-gauge Festiniog and Talyllyn railways, carry such mail and issue attractive pictorial stamps aimed at the thematic collector. These feature not only preserved steam locomotives but stations and scenes on the railways. Stamps are frequently issued to

Religious subjects can make an absorbing theme.

mark events in the railway's history.

The really keen collector of railway stamps can expand his collection to include mail carried on Travelling Post Offices and bearing TPO datestamps, or mail posted at post offices situated on railway stations. A number of companies have issued postage stamps perfined with their initials to prevent pilfering by

The romance of old sailing ships is often captured on postage stamps.

their staff; a collection of such stamps would make an interesting sideline collection to the main thematic collection. The scope of any thematic collection is almost endless and each collector will decide just how far he or she wishes to go. Whilst many may decide to stick primarily to officially-issued postage stamps, no collector should close his eyes entirely to 'fringe' material, which can often fill a gap in illustrating a person, place or artefact not yet depicted on a postage stamp.

Ships can be charted on stamps, from the primitive dugout canoe to the *QE2*. The subject is vast, as even a quick glance at the Gibbons *Collect Ships on Stamps* thematic catalogue will show. A possible line of demarcation would be between sailing and steam (or other powered) vessels. The first representation of a ship on a British stamp was a tiny drawing of the *Queen Elizabeth* on the Victory stamp of 1946. Sir Francis Chichester's *Gypsy Moth IV* was featured on a stamp in

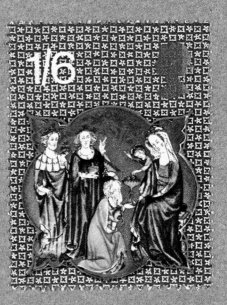

(Left) The special stamps for Christmas have become a popular topic; and (above) the religious theme can include cathedral architecture.

1967 but it was not until 1969 that a set was entirely devoted to Ships – showing the development from an Elizabethan galleon to the *QE2*. Three extremely well-known vessels were included in this set – the *Cutty Sark*, Brunel's *Great Britain* and the RMS *Mauretania*. A 1982 set for 'Maritime Heritage' included stamps showing Henry VIII's *Mary Rose* (raised from The Solent later that year) and Nelson's *Victory*. Not surprisingly, perhaps, it has been island postal authorities which have issued some of the most interesting Ship stamps. Various issues from Guernsey and Jersey have featured the ferries which have served those islands; both post offices issued sets to mark the centenary of the Great Western Railway steamers from Weymouth to the Channel Islands in September 1989. The designs recall days of more leisurely travelling – before long airport delays and hovercraft and jetfoil services.

Islands such as Ascension, St Helena and tiny and remote Tristan da Cunha rely almost entirely on ships for supplies and news from the outside world. All have issued Ship stamps and Tristan in particular is noted for such issues, for example the 1965–7 definitives and the 1979 set marking the visit of the *Queen Elizabeth 2*. Falkland Islands (and Dependencies) stamps are also a good hunting ground for the thematic collector. Amongst the most interesting issues have been those Mail Ship definitives of 1978–82 and the five stamps of 1970 marking the return from the Falklands to Bristol of Brunel's *Great Britain*. The Dependencies set of 1954 included such famous ships as the *Discovery* and the *Endurance*.

The story of the aeroplane begins with the Wright Brothers' historic flight of 1903 and continues with the development of civil aircraft, fighters and bombers to the jet age and Concorde. Oliver and Wilbur were featured on American stamps of 1978; Bleriot, another pioneer aviator, has been commemorated by France. Britain marked the 50th anniversary of the Alcock and

The story of the mutiny on the Bounty shown on Pitcairn stamps – the ship, Captain Bligh, breadfruit (the reason for the voyage), the mutiny, Fletcher Christian and Pitcairn Island.

Brown flight across the Atlantic in 1969 and military aircraft were depicted on a set entitled 'History of the RAF' issued in 1986. Many of the stamps depicting aircraft were specifically issued for use on airmail letters and postcards, the US Post Office has issued airmail stamps since the 1920s.

Sport is another fruitful area for the thematic collector, with numerous issues for Olympic and Commonwealth Games, World Cup football and regional, national and local games and tournaments of all kinds. Just about every sport has been commemorated, and in recent years there has been a marked increase in the number of stamps featuring individual sportsmen and women. In earlier days the designs were more symbolic or featured unidentifiable players or athletes. Greece issued a set to mark the first Olympic Games of the modern era in 1896 and issues have been made by the host nation for most subsequent Games. Nowadays these are joined with sets from other participating countries and often the issues are made long in advance of the opening ceremonies and sometimes long after the closing ceremony as well! Stamps are issued to commemorate the winners of various events, especially if they come from the stamp-issuing country. World Cup football stamps now exist from most of the major countries and the 1990 championship will no doubt yield a large crop of new issues.

British players such as Denis Law, Bobby Charlton and Bobby Moore, and teams such as Spurs, Manchester United and Everton have featured on stamps from countries such as Lesotho and Nevis. The England team in the 1986 World Cup was even shown on a stamp from Tuvalu!

Tennis stars such as Boris Becker, Steffi Graf, Stefan Edberg and Mats Wilander have been shown on stamps from as far afield as St Vincent, Sierra Leone and Niue; Swedish champion Bjorn Borg was featured on a stamp from his homeland in 1981. A tennis collection can be expanded to include mail posted from major tournaments; a special postmark is used on mail posted at the Wimbledon Tournament each year.

It is impossible in a book such as this to do more than scratch the surface of thematic collecting. Advice and guidance can now be obtained from a growing number of catalogues and books on thematic collecting and from the excellent publications of the British Thematic Association and the American Topical Association. The ATA has published a considerable number of catalogues and its magazine, *Topical Time*, is compelling reading for the thematic collector. The BTA is of much more recent establishment but is progressing well, and its journal *Themescene* contains much useful information.

There are a number of useful publications for thematic collectors, for example the Stanley Gibbons book *Stamp Collecting – Collecting by Theme* by James

Watson (published 1983) which includes a helpful A–Z of thematic subjects. In the same year the National Philatelic Society published *Introducing Thematic Collecting* by Alma Lee which is particularly useful for advice on writing up a collection and for preparing a display or competition entry. This aspect of thematic collecting is further discussed in Franceska Rapkin's *Guidelines for Thematic Judges and Exhibitors at Local and Federation Level*, published jointly by the British Philatelic Trust and the British Thematic Association in 1989. Most philatelic magazines contain at least one thematic article in each issue; *Gibbons Stamp Monthly* pioneered such articles many years ago. In 1905 H. R. Oldfield wrote a series of articles in the magazine under the title 'Bypaths of Philately' in which he suggested collecting stamps picturing scenery, historical events, coats of arms and maps.

A look through the *BPF Yearbook* will reveal a growing number of thematic societies. The oldest of these is the Glasgow Thematic Society, founded in 1948, and still the only one covering all themes. The Guild of St Gabriel, which caters for collectors of religious stamps, was formed in 1954 and other early societies include the Scout & Guide (1957), Railway (1966), United Nations (1968) and Music (1969). The Alba Stamp Group, founded in 1970, covers all things Scottish; there is also a Welsh Philatelic Society although this is less thematic in its approach. For collectors interested in sport, there are societies for Chess, Cricket, Football, Golf, Olympics and Rugby. Transport is covered by the Railway Group, Hovermail, Bicycles, Concorde, and Ships societies. There are specialist groups recording Captain Cook and Winston Churchill stamps; British Royal Portraits on stamps and Masonic and Methodist themes. The Bird Stamps Society, set up in 1986, has proved popular as has the Medical thematic society. Others cover Constabulary, Judaica, Maps and Salvation Army. The Letterbox Study Circle includes members interested in letterboxes on stamps as well as those studying the boxes themselves. Most of these societies publish interesting magazines and newsletters and hold meetings. They tend to be informal and many have female officers – thematic collecting seems to appeal strongly to the so-called weaker sex. The American Topical Association, already mentioned, has a considerable number of affiliated specialist groups, some of which produce journals and handbooks. The ATA has over 10,000 members – evidence of the popularity of thematic collecting in the USA.

Thematic displays are now regularly given to local philatelic clubs and societies and there is a thriving entry of thematic exhibits at national exhibitions. Amongst those shown at the British Philatelic Exhibition in 1989 were: History of Aviation and Airmail to 1914, An Account of Banking and Finance, The World of Birds, Conservation of Flora and Fauna, On Constabulary Duties and There's More than Fish in the Sea. The Link House Thematic Trophy was awarded to the Birds entry. At Spring Stampex 1989, Birds was chosen as the theme of the exhibition with fine invited displays by members of the Bird Stamp Society and live birds in the exhibition hall! The exhibition postmark featured birds and most of the mail posted was franked with the British Birds stamps issued earlier in the year. To mark the issue of the stamps, the Society put on a display at the National Postal Museum in London.

A fairly recent trend has been the staging of thematic exhibitions, for example Tembal (Basel, Switzerland) in 1983 and Olympic stamp exhibitions in Canada and South Korea in 1988. A thematic exhibition – Thematica – is now held annually in London.

Thematic collecting enables the collector 'to do his (or her) own thing'. Whilst there are rules to follow if you want to enter exhibitions, you are able to add to your collection anything you think relevant to develop the story. As well as postmarks and commemorative covers, many collectors find picture postcards useful, also booklet covers, pictorial postal stationery (in particular aerogrammes) and illustrations cut from books, magazines and newspapers. However one must be careful to ensure proper balance, after all a thematic collection is a stamp collection and should not be swamped by other material. Above all a thematic collection can be great fun and enjoyed and understood by the non-collector as well as the philatelist. To do the job properly you must be prepared to spend a fair amount of time reading up your chosen subject and many thematic collectors choose a subject closely allied to their academic studies or line of business. There is no doubt that thematic collecting is now one of, if not the most, popular branches of philately and the route by which many people now enter the hobby.

12
Stamp Exhibitions

The innovation of the international stamp exhibition was introduced in 1890 by the (Royal) Philatelic Society, London, who subsequently sponsored the London exhibitions of 1897 and 1906. The first post-war international show took place at Grosvenor House, London, under the patronage of King George VI, who made a personal visit, in May, 1950. That was the first of the great exhibitions planned to take place every ten years, and the London International of July, 1960, was held at the Royal Festival Hall, sponsored by the 'Royal' and by the (then) British Philatelic Association. The London International of September, 1970, was a much larger, more ambitious exhibition – it was held in the Empire Hall, Olympia, and was sponsored by three leading organizations – the Royal Philatelic Society, London; the British Philatelic Association; and the Philatelic Traders' Society. It was aptly named 'Philympia 1970' and three special stamps were issued by the Post Office.

'London 1980', the international stamp exhibition held at Earls Court, London in May, 1980, was organized by International Philatelic Exhibitions Ltd, under the sponsorship of the Royal Philatelic Society, London; the British Post Office; the British Philatelic Federation (formerly British Philatelic Association); the Philatelic Traders' Society; the Stamp Collecting Promotion Council of Great Britain; the National Philatelic Society; and the Great Britain Philatelic Society.

Every 10 years the international comes to London and the 1990 exhibition will be held at Alexandra Palace from 3 to 13 May. To be known as 'Stamp World London '90', the exhibition marks the 150th anniversary of the issue of the Penny Black and Twopence Blue. All the main philatelic organizations are involved in the staging of the exhibition, which is being guaranteed by the British Post Office through the issue of miniature sheets in 1988, 1989 and 1990. The

Stamps for international exhibitions in London in 1970 (above) and 1980, Melbourne 1984, Chicago and Stockholm 1986 and Paris 1989.

Chairman and Chief Executive of the organizing committee, Dr Alan Huggins and Leon Rapkin, are well-known figures in the philatelic world. It is expected that the exhibition will attract over 75,000 visitors.

Such is the worldwide attraction of stamps that many countries in Europe and the rest of the world regularly hold exhibitions of international and national status. Among the best known take place in Austria ('WIPA'), Czechoslovakia ('Praga'), Denmark ('Hafnia'), France ('Arphila' and 'Juvexniort' – for young collectors), West Germany ('IBRA Munich'), Italy ('Italia'), Netherlands ('Amphilex' – Amsterdam), Norway ('Norwex'), Spain ('Espana'), Sweden ('Stockholmia') and Switzerland ('NABA'). In recent years internationals have been held in Copenhagen and Toronto (1987), Helsinki, Luxembourg and Prague (1988), New Delhi, Paris and Washington (1989). In addition to the London exhibition, internationals will be held in 1990 in Brussels, Düsseldorf and Auckland, New Zealand.

For the beginner and the experienced philatelist, exhibitions and fairs are exciting places to visit. At the larger shows competitive entries are on display, providing countless examples of selections from many fine collections of every conceivable subject. Some of the most famous collections are displayed in the 'court of honour' by invitation, and the dealers' stands are an incentive to personal involvement. STAMPEX, London's national exhibition, is usually held at the Royal Horticultural New Hall, Westminster, in the spring, and again as British Philatelic Exhibition (BPE) in the late autumn.

Regular exhibitions are held at the National Postal Museum in the main building of the Chief Post Office in the City of London – other postal museums, such as the one at Bath, display stamps and postal history.

The Lure of a Medal

Many collectors, even those with very good collections, are reluctant to exhibit their stamps, perhaps because they are uncertain about procedures and conditions of

One printing process (embossing) carefully reproduced by another (photogravure) for the 1970 Exhibition.

entry. Preparing a display for your local society is one way of getting started on the rocky road to a bronze, silver or gold medal at one of the national or international exhibitions. You will be able to compare your exhibit with others and any friendly criticism from fellow members should be regarded as instructive and helpful. Ideally you should visit the national shows, and note how the competitors arrange their stamps – layout and writing-up. Decide which entries *you* think merit an award and then take a second look at the winning displays.

Exhibitions have conditions of entry and rules – entry forms, prospectuses and details of the different classes are obtainable from the exhibition authorities. Conditions vary according to the particular exhibition, but generally marks are allotted on the following lines: Philatelic knowledge – 30; Importance – 20; Rarity – 10; Condition – 20; and Presentation – 20. The criteria applied to thematic entries usually place more emphasis on: Originality (15), Development (25) and Extent of the theme (15), with 15 marks each for Philatelic Knowledge, Condition or Rarity, and Presentation.

Judges usually work by a process of elimination and marks can be lost for faults in presentation – poor or slipshod writing-up, overcrowding, unbalanced layout and spelling mistakes, mixing unused and used stamps, including damaged, inferior or heavily postmarked

specimens, and lack of continuity in the sequence of the pages or sheets. Specific faults may not lose marks if the 'general impression' is good, and 'rarity' does not imply the most rare and expensive stamps, but rather scarce and elusive ones.

If your entry in one of the national exhibitions is fortunate enough to gain at least a silver medal, then you are eligible to compete in an international show. Participation in the 'London 1980' exhibition was open to all collectors who were members of societies or federations affiliated to the member societies of the FIP, and a collector was permitted to enter more than one exhibit to a maximum of five. The following classification was applied to entries:

(a) Non-Competitive
1. Court of Honour: by invitation
2. Official Class: Postal administrations, museums, stamp designers, printers
3. Jury collections
4. Other exhibits

(b) Competitive
Class of Honour (FIP). Reserved for exhibits previously awarded three large gold medals or a 'grand prix' and two large golds at an international exhibition.

(c) General Competitive Classes
 1. National: United Kingdom
 2. British Commonwealth and former Possessions
 3. Europe and Possessions (excluding UK)
 4. Africa (excluding 2 and 3)
 5. Asia (excluding 2 and 3)
 6. Americas (excluding 2 and 3)
 7. Postal History
 8. Air Mails
 9. Thematic
10. Youth/Junior
11. Literature

Approximately 4,000 frames were available for competitive entries and each frame held 12 or 16 pages.

Some collectors maintain their collections in such a high standard that a selection from it can be submitted to competitions without any further preparation; others make up sheets especially for exhibition display, extracting choice items from their main collections for the purpose. Theoretically, your collection should be capable of segregation into a series of complete studies of the different issues or sections of a theme – you can then pick out the requisite number of sheets, adequately and logically written-up, then try your luck. But if you haven't this kind of collection-within-a-collection or you have some conspicuous gaps, you will have to select a particular phase or period which is reasonably complete from your main collection and prepare fresh sheets specially for the forthcoming event. Your display must have a clear objective, continuity page-to-page, and be attractively laid out.

Don't be discouraged by the fact that many of the premier awards go to highly specialized exhibits or those which contain expensive rarities. Your entry, along with the others, will be judged on the evidence of your knowledge and the study involved, on the condition of the stamps and other philatelic material, and on the manner of presentation – arrangement and writing-up. Most exhibitions have different categories and classes on the lines of 'London 1980', and your entry should have as good a chance as any. Originality and popular interest will attract good marks – pick some unusual and interesting aspect of your stamp collection and set it out in story form, supported by choice postmarks, blocks of four, varieties or whatever is applicable. Make it crystal clear to the judges exactly what your aims and objectives are – it's not enough to arrange ordinary stamps in catalogue order and write in the details of perforation and watermark. They are philatelists themselves and may have an excellent knowledge of your particular subject – they will be looking for some indication of *your* knowledge.

One of the two national exhibitions offers a range of handsome trophies for the best exhibits in the different classes. The AUTUMN STAMPEX/BPE Silver Mailcoach Trophy is the most outstanding and is awarded to the best entry in the show. Other trophies include the Stanley Gibbons Cup and the National Philatelic Society's Queen Elizabeth Silver Jubilee Trophy for the best presentation. Altogether nearly 200 medals are awarded including gold, silver-gilt and silver. Gold or silver-gilt medals are also given to the trophy winners. Bronze-silver and bronze medals, diplomas and certificates are also awarded.

Entries may be submitted in the following categories: International, Traditional (Great Britain, Commonwealth, Foreign and Locals sections), Postal History (Great Britain, Commonwealth and Foreign sections), Aerophilatelic, Thematic and Literature. The Melville National Youth Stamp Competition is now held as part of AUTUMN STAMPEX/BPE, named in honour of Frederick J. Melville, one of the greatest writers on stamps and publicist for the hobby. There are five classes in this competition, covering different age groups: 19–21 years, 16–18, 14–15, 12–13 and up to 11 years. A separate panel of judges assesses the Melville entries and there are separate trophies and medals awarded.

By far the most prestigious awards are those made at the international exhibitions. At LONDON 1980 1,400 philatelists entered exhibits, their displays filling some 4,000 frames. The highest award – the *Grand Prix d'Honneur* – a magnificent Wedgwood Jasperware vase provided by the British Post Office, was awarded to R.B. Pracchia of Brazil for his entry of the stamps of Imperial Brazil. The second and third highest awards, sponsored by the Philatelic Traders' Society and the Royal Philatelic Society of London respectively, were awarded for displays of the stamps of Queen Victoria and of Spanish stamps of 1850–1854. Over 570 medals were awarded – 48 large gold, 122 gold, 135 *vermeil* (silver-gilt), 141 silver, 86 silver-bronze and 40 bronze. The medals, produced by the Royal Mint, were seven-sided and depicted the Tower of London on one side and St George and the Dragon on the other. Awards were made for literature as well as stamps, some 177 medals being presented.

In addition to the competitive entries at LONDON 1980, there were some 27 invited displays in the Court of Honour, including material from the Royal Collection, the National Postal Museum, the British Library and the Royal Philatelic Society of London.

The great international stamp exhibitions have numerous attractions for the stamp collector. Her Majesty the Queen – and King George VI before her – have generously contributed exhibits from their respective sections of the Royal Philatelic Collection on loan for display, while the Royal Philatelic Society, London, also provides displays from its own collections. The Crown Agents and the British Post Office are regular exhibitors at national and international shows, as well as the smaller society promotions. Many philatelic societies hold regular exhibitions and fairs all over the country, and the Post Office provides philatelic counters, or kiosks, for the sale of stamps and the application of special postmarks to souvenir covers.

In 1956, Stanley Gibbons celebrated their centenary with a splendid exhibition at the Waldorf Hotel in London – it was opened by Sir John Wilson, then Keeper of the Royal Philatelic Collection. In 1965, they held a much larger exhibition at the Royal Festival Hall, London, for the centenary of the famous Gibbons Catalogue, which was first published by Edward Stanley Gibbons in 1865. On this occasion, the major attraction was the most valuable stamp in the world – the 1856 British Guiana 1c. black on magenta.

Stamp fairs are a popular development of recent years, and they are held – on the lines of the older-established antique fairs – not only in London, but throughout the provinces. Details of forthcoming fairs are published each month in *Gibbons Stamp Monthly* and other philatelic magazines. One of the most popular is the Strand Palace Hotel fair held in London about the middle of each month. An important fair in the north is the York Racecourse fair, organized by NNN Fairs, who have staged many hundreds of stamp fairs over the years. Postcard fairs also have material of interest to stamp collectors, a major postcard fair is held in London each month and there is the annual BIPEX (British International Postcard Exhibition) each Autumn.

13
Famous Collectors and Collections

'Those who now rise to the philatelic heights in the realm of general collecting, must have the purse of Croesus and the energy of Hercules.'

Stanley Phillips, *Stamp Collecting*

The late Mr Phillips, a former Managing Director and Chairman of Stanley Gibbons Ltd, was making the point that the great pioneer stamp collectors of the past had the instinctive talent of discernment and discrimination which enabled them to select the most choice pieces over a wide field of countries. They may not have had the purse of Croesus, though most of them were wealthy men, but they all had the touch of Midas. The great general collections of Ferrary, Tapling, Burrus, the Americans, Hind and Caspary, and others, included practically all the great rarities of those days, and today, forming a comparable collection would be a 'mission impossible'.

What happened to these wonderful old collections? Invariably they were sold by auction, enabling thousands of other collectors to acquire the many rare stamps and unique items, enhanced by the cachet, 'ex-Ferrary' or 'ex-Burrus' collections. The great majority of present-day collectors confine themselves to one country, or perhaps to small groups of countries, and the sales of the 'great' name collections enable them to add selected treasures to their own albums. In this way, more valuable and famous collections are built up until they, in turn, are sold and dispersed. Thus the hobby progresses — and the stamp auctioneers stay in business!

Occasionally, important collections are bequeathed or bestowed to museums – the famous 'Tapling' collection and the die-proofs of Waterlow's celebrated engraver, J.A.C. Harrison, repose in the British Library, and the late R.M. Phillips founded the National Postal Museum with his wonderful collection of British stamps.

Collectors Royal

For more than a hundred years, members of the Royal Family have been happily involved with the fascinating hobby of philately. The famous 'Royal' reprints of the

H.M. King George V – an ardent philatelist.

1d. black were ordered from the printers, Perkins Bacon, in 1864, ostensibly for the 'younger members' of the Royal Family. The most likely beneficiary was Prince Alfred, Duke of Edinburgh (later Duke of Saxe-Coburg-Gotha), who had started a modest general collection, and would not have been unduly perturbed by the fact that the 'reprints' had emanated from a 1d. red plate, no longer in use! Just before Alfred's death in 1900, the Prince of Wales (about to become King Edward VII) purchased the collection and presented it to his son, the Duke of York and future King George V, the real founder of the Royal Philatelic Collection.

Prince George of Wales entered the Royal Navy in 1877 and, encouraged by his uncle, Prince Alfred, used his numerous voyages to advantage in acquiring stamps for his general collection. In 1893, he joined the (Royal) Philatelic Society, London, and three years later, in 1896, he became President of the Society and continued in that office until his accession in 1910, when he became the Society's Patron. By this time he had decided to confine his collecting to the issues of the British colonies, dominions and protectorates, and these form the major part of the 'red' albums of King George V in the Royal Collection.

As Prince of Wales (from 1901), George pursued his hobby with ardent enthusiasm, and he devoted a great deal of time and personal attention to his stamps, assisted by J.A. Tilleard, Honorary Secretary of the (Royal) Philatelic Society and first Keeper of the Royal Collection; by E.D. (later Sir Edward) Bacon, who succeeded him; and by a personal friend, philatelist and bibliophile, the 26th Earl of Crawford and Balcarres.

With the help of his advisers, the Prince made extensive purchases of the stamps he needed at auction and from dealers who gave him first choice from the collections they bought. In 1904, he made a successful bid – through his agent — at auction for an unused 2d. 'Post Office' Mauritius, one of the rarest stamps in the world, which had been discovered by a Hampstead schoolboy. The price paid, £1,450, was a record for any postage stamp at that time, and the purchase aroused world interest, helping to establish stamp collecting as a serious and worthwhile hobby rather than, as many thought, a childish pursuit. Later, he was pleased to show the stamp to the Society's members, and was more amused than annoyed when an equerry enquired the name of the 'darned fool' who had paid so much money for 'just a little piece of paper'! He also displayed the 1d. 'Post Office' Mauritius stamp on an envelope which contained an invitation to Lady Gomm's ball at Government House in Mauritius – a unique item which had formerly belonged to the Earl of Kintore.

Through his friendship with Lord Crawford, the Prince began collecting original drawings of stamp designs, essays and proofs, and in 1906, when the Philatelic Society was favoured with the title of 'Royal' and held its third international exhibition in London, the Prince entered his GB Edwardian essays, Mauritius and Hong Kong collections for competition, being awarded a bronze medal for the former and silver medals for the colonial exhibits. After Lord Crawford's death in 1913, the King (as he had become) bought two sections of his British collection – stamps, proofs and essays, including the superb and valuable 'Treasury' essays. King George's accession on 6 May 1910 was the occasion for two remarkable coincidences. Firstly, it was the date of issue of the first postage stamps 70 years before; and it was also the proposed date of issue of the Edwardian 2d. Tyrian Plum which was officially never issued. Nevertheless one specimen is known, used on a cover addressed to the Prince of Wales at Marlborough House.

King George V became a prudent and experienced philatelist. He purchased many fine 'one-country' collections, and he received corner blocks of four (with plate numbers) of all new British and Commonwealth stamps – he also received back many original drawings and essays for stamps which he had previously approved. Gradually, he formed the finest British Commonwealth collection ever made, and he spent several afternoons a week with his treasures in the Stamp Room at Buckingham Palace where, during World War I, he found relaxation from the stresses of war. The King's stamps, known as the 'Red Collection', because it is contained in approximately 330 red morocco-bound volumes and has an estimated quarter-of-a-million stamps, are today a priceless tribute to the 'Philatelist King'.

The Royal Collection has been maintained to the present day. The collections of King George VI ('blue' albums) and of the Queen ('green' albums) are kept entirely separate, and while the 'Blue Collection' is virtually complete with all the British and Commonwealth stamps issued during his reign, including original drawings, essays and proofs, the Queen's collection is continually being augmented on similar lines with the addition of new issues of stamps. King George VI's interest in his father's collection and in his own stamps was kindled by Sir John Wilson, Keeper

H.R.H. Prince Alfred, Duke of Edinburgh, an early royal stamp collector.

The famous Post Office Mauritius 1d stamp of 1847, on a modern commemorative (SG 266).

of the Royal Collection from 1938, and eventually he took an active part in building up the collection with Sir John 'at his elbow'.

The Queen also takes a close personal interest in the progress of the Royal Collection and in the subjects and designs of all the new British and Commonwealth stamps which are submitted to her for approval. She has an eye for detail and artistic balance which, on occasion, enables her to authorize amendments and improvements to submitted designs. As patron of the Royal Philatelic Society in succession to King George VI, she visited the 'Royal's' Centenary Exhibition in April 1969 – earlier that year (February), she opened the National Postal Museum.

Keepers Royal

It was J.A. Tilleard the Honorary Secretary of the (Royal) Philatelic Society, who invited Prince George, then Duke of York, to become a member of the society. Tilleard was a man of great personal charm, popular with both collectors and dealers, and he was an able mentor for the Prince, for whom he acted as his adviser in buying stamps. He was a collector of the 'old school', always meticulous in his work for the society and in his choice of fine and desirable stamps for his protégé. When the Prince succeeded to the throne in May 1910 as King George V, Tilleard was immediately appointed 'Philatelist to the King' and was thus the first Keeper of the Royal Philatelic Collection. Sadly, the new responsibilities proved too much for him and he died from overwork in 1913.

After World War I, the 'Royal' instituted three medals to be awarded each year – the 'Crawford', for the best book on philately published in the preceding two years; the 'Tapling', for the best paper read at a meeting of the society; and the 'Tilleard' for the best display at a similar meeting. The King was awarded the first 'Tilleard' medal for his display – the 'India Four Annas of 1854'.

Edward D. Bacon was appointed in succession to Tilleard – 'to take the entire charge and arrangement of the King's fine collection of stamps'. Bacon was the leading philatelist of his time, a staunch member of the 'Royal' (which he served in various capacities from honorary assistant secretary to president), and a prolific writer. His services had always been in great demand prior to his Royal appointment – he acted as philatelic adviser to the British Museum from 1891 to his death – which came two years after that of King George V – in 1938, and he helped T.K.Tapling with his collection. When Tapling died in 1891, Bacon was given the task of arranging and mounting the collection for display in the museum. In the latter years of his life he was almost totally deaf and led a solitary existence in the Stamp Room at Buckingham Palace.

Bacon was recorded in the Royal Household lists as 'Curator' of the Royal Collection, but following the death of George V, the title was changed to 'Keeper' and it was as such that Sir John Wilson, second baronet, was appointed in succession to Sir Edward Bacon in 1938. Sir John was born in Carbeth, Killearn, Scotland, in 1898, and at the age of 17 he was head boy at Harrow School. Moving on to New College, Oxford, he subsequently served with the Coldstream Guards, but was invalided out of the army in 1918. At that time his father invited him to take over his very substantial stamp collection which was complete, except for the great rarities. He made special studies of Belgian line-engraved, early Rumania and Spain, and the Russian 'Zemstvos', and he joined the Royal Philatelic Society in 1921.

Sir John succeeded to the baronetcy on the death of his father in 1930, and was made KCVO in 1957. He served a double term as president of the 'Royal' from 1934 to 1940 and again in 1950, and he travelled abroad on many occasions as an accredited 'ambassador of British philately', often taking with him sections of the Royal Collection and acting as judge at international exhibitions, where he sometimes displayed his own stamps *hors concours*. He wrote many articles on stamps and literature, and is remembered for his sumptuous book, *The Royal Philatelic Collection*, published by the Dropmore Press in 1952. For more than 30 years he was philatelic adviser and mentor to King George VI and the Queen. He retired in 1969, when he was succeeded by J.B. Marriott, a housemaster at Charterhouse, distinguished philatelist and Fellow of the 'Royal'. Sir John Wilson died in 1975.

Among the highlights of the international stamp exhibition, 'London 1980', were approximately 4,500 frames of stamps, housing not only the competitive entries, but also an exhibit from Her Majesty the Queen, together with other invited exhibits, including displays from the National Postal Museum and the British Library.

Museum Treasures

With one notable exception, the great private stamp collections of the past no longer exist. The one exception is the famous 'Tapling' Collection which was bequeathed to the British Museum in 1891, and is still there (under the aegis of the British Library). Dr J.E. Gray, Keeper of Natural History, and William Vaux, Keeper of Coins and Medals, started the first museum stamp collection in 1864. Dr Gray was the indefatigable one – he built up a large personal collection and published one of the first stamp catalogues. The museum collection was merely tolerated by the authorities and faded into insignificance following the pioneers' deaths in the 1870s. The trustees, however, welcomed the Tapling bequest and, as described, commissioned Sir Edward Bacon to prepare the collection for display, a task which occupied him for 12 years.

Thomas Keay Tapling started collecting stamps as a schoolboy – he was educated at Harrow and at Trinity Hall, Cambridge, where he studied law and graduated with honours in 1878. Later he was called to the Bar, but gave up his promising career as a barrister to take over the family carpet business in 1882. He entered politics and became the Conservative Member of Parliament for Harborough (Leicestershire) in 1886. Meanwhile, in 1871, he had joined the (Royal) Philatelic Society and ten years later he was elected its vice-president. During the last years of his life – he died of pleurisy at the early age of 36 – he pursued his hobby with passionate fervour and acquired many rarities. His most fortunate deal was the result of an exchange with the exuberant Count Ferrary who, in 1886, parted with an unused 2d. 'Post Office' Mauritius stamp in exchange for an obscure Afghanistan issue. The 'Tapling' Collection is a treasure-trove of fine stamps including two other 'Post Office' Mauritius (1d. and 2d.) on cover, Cape triangulars (including 'woodblocks'), Hawaiian 'Missionaries' and many more.

Reginald M. Phillips of Brighton was the supreme philatelist and one of the greatest philanthropists of the 20th century. He built up one of the most comprehensive collections of British Victorian stamps ever formed and presented it to the nation. His unique collection, valued at the time at £275,000, was handed over to the then Postmaster-General, the Rt. Hon. Anthony Wedgwood Benn, together with a cash gift of £50,000 towards the cost of establishing and maintaining a National Postal Museum, in 1965. His numerous benefactions included large donations to the Royal Society of Medicine, and to Sussex University – for research into the education of deaf and handicapped children, and for work on the similar education of blind and partially-blind children. He founded the University's Philatelic Unit in 1971 and a Science Policy Research Unit in the same year.

Mr Phillips started his career as a real estate agent in 1910 and became a pioneer in property development – he began collecting stamps at about the same time, and it was the stamp centenary of 1940 which inspired him to specialize in the story of British stamps, their history and development. In his quest for fine material he spared neither time, energy nor expense, and he first came into prominence when he bid successfully for the famous block of 43 unused 1d. blacks – for £4,400. He won the Grand Prix at the London International in 1960, became a Fellow of the Royal Philatelic Society, and was awarded the CBE in 1970. Reginald M. Phillips died, aged 90, in 1977.

The 'R.M. Phillips' Collection comprises 46 volumes or some 2,500 album sheets with many unique items – 'Treasury' essays, Corbould's drawings, proofs, trials, official documents and superb stamps in choice condition, including the largest existing unused blocks of the 1d. black printed from five different plates. The numerous other acquisitions by the museum in recent years combined with Mr Phillips's stamps provide unique research facilities.

The Continentals

Philipp la Renotière von Ferrary was a cosmopolitan figure in the philatelic world – one with an extraordinary background of rank and wealth, charming in manner, flamboyant in dress, and reticent, even secretive, about his enormous and valuable stamp collection. He was born in 1848, the son of the Duchess of Galliera, of the Genoese banking family and, as a child, suffered from a form of nervous debility – at the age of 12, as a diversion, he started collecting stamps. With almost unlimited wealth at his disposal, his enthusiasm for stamps erupted, and from his home – a palatial mansion in the rue de Varenne, Paris – he travelled to London and the principal cities of Europe in search of stamps.

Ferrary purchased many famous collections – among the best of them were those of Judge F.A. Philbrick, vice-president of the (Royal) Philatelic Society; Baron de Rothschild, a refugee from the Siege of Paris; and Sir Daniel Cooper, who was the Society's first president and had formed a valuable collection of Australian stamps while Governor of New South Wales. Ferrary acquired the greatest rarities – the unique British Guiana 1 cent black on magenta (previously described), the Swedish 3 *skilling banco,* error of colour, and several 'Post Office' Mauritius stamps which, on two occasions, he used as 'swaps'. He befriended the best-known dealers including Charles J. Phillips of Stanley Gibbons (and Gibbons himself in the early days), Friedl of Vienna, Moens of Brussels and Pierre Mahé of Paris, who became Ferrary's close friend and adviser.

World War I brought a dramatic change in Ferrary's fortunes. His eccentricities had increased – he had declared himself the adopted son of an Austrian officer, Ritter von Kriegsfeld, when he was 50, and had eventually dropped the name 'Ferrary'. The war was a catastrophe for him, and his conflicting loyalties to England, France and his 'German Fatherland' (Austria) drove him to seek refuge in Switzerland where he died, in Lausanne, in May 1917. He had bequeathed his collection to the Reichpost Museum in Berlin, but it was seized by the French Government and confiscated as the property of an 'enemy alien'. The stamps were sold in a series of auction sales in Paris between 1921 and 1925 – the total sum realized was about five million francs or about £400,000. As recorded in Chapter 2, the famous 'One Cent Guiana' was sold to Arthur Hind for a record sum. The 'runner-up' was Maurice Burrus, the Alsatian tobacco magnate.

Burrus was born in Ste Croix-aux-Mines (Alsace) in 1882 and began collecting stamps when he was seven. He entered the family tobacco business and by his commercial acumen made a substantial fortune. During World War I he was imprisoned by the Germans, and later he became a member of the French Parliament for the district of Haut Rhin. He also collected antiques, porcelain, miniatures and rare books, but he was a philatelist of international repute and his vast collection of stamps, formed over a period of 60 years, was probably the most valuable in the world, exceeding in value and volume even that of the great Ferrary. After his death in 1959, his treasures – which included a cover bearing the 1d. and 2d. 'Post Office' Mauritius, numerous Mauritius 'Post Paid'

*Reginald M. Phillips's benefactions led
to a National Postal Museum for Britain.*

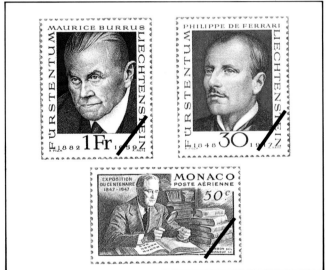

*Stamps honouring famous philatelists – Maurice Burrus,
Philipp la Renotière von Ferrary and President Franklin D.
Roosevelt.*

stamps, a unique 'Perot' provisional on cover (ex-
'Ferray') and a block of six 'Double Genevas' – were
sold through various auction houses for about
£2 million.

The Americans

Franklin D. Roosevelt, 1882-1945, is remembered as a
great President of the United States and as a keen stamp
collector. His collection included numerous gifts from
foreign heads of state, including Stalin who gave him
some rare items from the postal archives of Tzarist
Russia. Though basically a general collector, he built up
a rare collection of US stamps and specialized in one or

two Latin-American countries, notably Argentina. His
collections fetched almost $80,000 when sold by auction
in New York after his death. He is depicted on
numerous stamps as a collector.

Arthur Hind, born in Yorkshire, in 1856,
emigrated to the United States in 1890 and started a
successful business in the manufacture of plush. He
became interested in stamps and during his world
travels bought many fine collections and rarities, and in
1922 he purchased the famous H.J. Duveen collection.
In the same year, Hind made his memorable bid of
300,000 francs for the 'One Cent Guiana' at the Ferrary
sales; he acquired many other fine stamps – a Bermuda
'Perot', Hawaiian 'Missionaries' and the unique US
Boscawen Postmaster's stamp.

Hind was a collector and speculator, rather than a
philatelist; nevertheless he had become a celebrity, and
in 1923 he was invited by King George V to view
selections of the Royal Collection. It transpired that
'the brash American' was not exactly enamoured by the
King's stamps, and that His Majesty was left in some
doubt as to his guest's philatelic knowledge. In the same
year, Arthur Hind displayed the 'One Cent Guiana' at
the London International show and was elected to the
Royal Philatelic Society. After Hind's death in 1933, his
stamps were sold by auction in New York and London –
the superb Mauritius section attracted many buyers,
notably Alfred H. Caspary of the United States, but the
'Guiana' failed to reach the reserve figure and was
withdrawn. It was eventually sold privately in the
States, thence to an Australian collector, and in 1980
was again auctioned in New York when it was sold to an
undisclosed buyer for £400,000.

Caspary was a connoisseur of stamps and one of
the world's most eminent philatelists. He started life as a
Wall Street runner (messenger), 'played' the stock
markets and became a prominent member of the New
York Stock Exchange. His knowledge of the classics
was unsurpassed – 'nothing but the best' was his motto,
and he purchased only the most rare items in superb
condition. Among his principal interests were the
United States, the Confederate States, British North
America and Hawaii, but he also bought early
Europeans and Commonwealth classics, notably the
Mauritius 1d. 'Post Paid' in a mint block of four. Alfred
H. Caspary died in 1955, and his stamps were sold in a
series of auctions in New York and London between
1955 and 1958.

Many Americans have been invited to sign the Roll
of Distinguished Philatelists, created by the Philatelic
Congress of Great Britain in 1920, and now regarded as
philately's highest honour. King George V headed the
roll with his personal signature in a special ceremony
held at Buckingham Palace and there were 39
signatories at the Harrogate Congress in 1921. Congress
is held each year and usually from three to five
philatelists are invited to sign the roll.

*The 'Maltese Cross' cancellation
was introduced for use with the
first British postage stamps
issued in May 1840.*

14
Postmarks, Covers and Postal Stationery

A postmark is defined as 'the mark stamped upon a letter at a post office, defacing the postage stamp and/or showing the date and place of expedition or of arrival'. A 'cancellation' is *any* kind of defacing mark (including a postmark) applied to a stamp to prevent its re-use, and it embraces pen-marks, rubber-stamp impressions, printed words or even the word 'CANCELLED' seen on specimen stamps. To most collectors the words 'postmark' (or 'mark') and 'cancellation' are synonymous, while an 'obliteration' is a term generally applied to a heavy defacement such as the 'killer' bars of a duplex cancellation, cork impressions and other crude devices.

The history of the postmark goes back for hundreds of years and we have seen how Henry Bishop introduced his distinctive 'mark' in 1661, and how, through many variations (including Dockwra's triangular 'POST PAID' marks), the familiar circular datestamp (cds) was evolved. Some 1,500 Penny Posts were in operation at places throughout England and Wales, Scotland and Ireland when Rowland Hill introduced his postal reforms in 1840, and these were a prolific source of the 'straight line' town cancellations and other early marks. Then came the Maltese Crosses and, from 1844, the numeral (within bars) and duplex types, the large, bare 'skeleton', the Pearson Hill experimental machine marks of 1857-8, the squared circle, the scroll and the miniature circular datestamp, known especially to collectors of old picture postcards as the 'thimble'.

'Special purpose' cancellations were introduced for ship letters and 'paquebots', for the railways (at stations and on travelling post offices), military camps and field post offices, and for events such as exhibitions, fairs and local shows. The first slogan cancellations appeared in Britain in 1917 and these have now become a permanent feature of the world's postal systems. Underpaid or unpaid letters and postcards

A postmark reminder of the Boer War, 1901

have always required special attention by postal staffs, who have a range of appropriate 'To Pay' marks for the many different contingencies. The advent of electronic letter-sorting and the use of postal codes with their computer-style methods of handling have brought a completely new range of postal markings within the purview of the postmark collector. Postmarks provide a relief or 'escape' from the study of stamps – they are an essential part of postal history, and now play an important part in other fields of collecting, as we shall discover.

Postmarks from 1840

The so-called Maltese Cross cancellation, more closely resembling a four-petalled Tudor rose, was introduced in 1840 and remained in use for four years, during which time numerous local variations in design occurred. The handstamps were individually made and, for example, the style of the Manchester cross was entirely different to that employed by the Brighton post office. Identifying the different town crosses by their shapes and – in some instances – colours is a specialized study for the collector. Later (1843), the London Head Office used Maltese Crosses numbered from 1 to 12 in the centre, surmounted by a small cross to indicate the 'right way up' and to enable a '6' to be distinguished from a '9'.

While the Maltese Cross was effective as a cancellation, it gave no clue as to the source of a letter and it was customary to apply an additional handstamp, indicating the town of origin and date posted. It was this laborious double-stamping which brought about the change to numeral cancellations – the '1844 Type' – in that year, but although each main post office was allocated a specific number, there was still no apparent indication of the post town and date – the second handstamp continued in use.

The numeral cancellers took various forms – the number enclosed in a diamond (London Chief Office),

Upright oval postmark with District initials

or a circle (London District Offices), within a barred oval; the number – unframed – within a barred oval (English and Welsh towns), a barred rectangle (Scottish towns) or a barred diamond (Irish towns). In the 1850s, a time of continuous experiment and trial with different cancellers, the London postal district numbers – 'NE 3' etc – were used in the form of barred circles, and the Scottish numerals were adorned with large stars or asterisks at the sides.

At last, in 1853, came the duplex canceller – a dual device combining a circular 'town and date' stamp with the oval-barred numeral: designed to provide a legible postmark and at the same time obliterate the stamp (rather too effectively for the stamp collector!). The first duplex, in fact, had a square datestamp with cut-out corners and was used on 'Too Late' mail by London's chief office, and the first regular duplex types, still in the experimental stage, were the 'spoon'-shaped cancellers combined with the 'killer' barred numerals. Some 'spoons' were arranged sideways in relation to the adjoining numeral, other duplex marks had both sections sideways, and in 1857

Manually operated machine about 1865.

*Origin is marked by the Hull
handstamp additional to the (red) '1d'.*

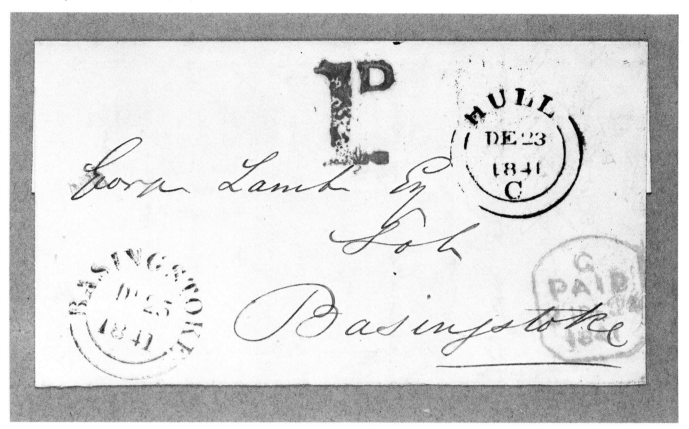

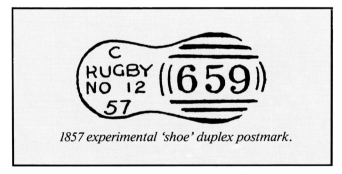

1857 experimental 'shoe' duplex postmark.

the unusual 'shoe' duplex was experimentally used.

Also, at about this time, British stamps and cancellers began to be used at post offices in the British colonies, prior to them issuing their own stamps, and at certain locations in foreign countries, mostly in Central and South America. Stamps 'used abroad' (as they are called) can only be identified as such by the numeral or duplex cancellations allocated to the different places, such as 'A25' or 'M' for Malta, 'A27' for Jamaica and 'C35' for Panama. Circular datestamps were also used in the British post offices in Beirut, Stamboul (Constantinople) and elsewhere. Postmarked British stamps of this period are thus well worth a second glance and are best collected 'on piece' or on cover.

Rowland Hill's son, Pearson Hill, designed a machine, worked by foot or steam, to postmark letters and even count them and stack them ready for sorting.

The use of machine cancellation had become a most necessary aid to handling the vastly increasing volume of mail in the 1850s and 1860s. Hill's first machine was given a trial in September 1857, an amended version later that year and a third in March 1858 – all were unsatisfactory, but examples of the trial cancellations exist and are now extremely rare, especially on cover. They were of the duplex type although the two sections were identical – the first without office name, but including the code letter 'M' and the date; the second, inscribed 'London' with codes 'A' or 'M'; and the third, also bearing the 'London' inscription, which is known as the 'opera glass' because of its design. Finally, Hill achieved success with his 'parallel motion' and 'pivot' machines which came into regular use.

The Post Office persevered with postmarking machines through the 1870s and 1880s – one, introduced by J.G. Azemar in 1869, stamped more than 49,000 letters per hour with a heavily-barred duplex-type datestamp, but it required seven operators and had a high average of 'misses': it was discontinued after a year. The first postcards were issued by Britain in 1870 and some intriguing cancelling experiments involved the cards being punched with round holes or clipped at the sides by a form of pliers. Joseph Sloper, who invented the 'perfin' method of perforating stamps with company initials, created a machine which punched small holes in the form of an arrowhead on the card – the 'Sloper Arrow' – but it required

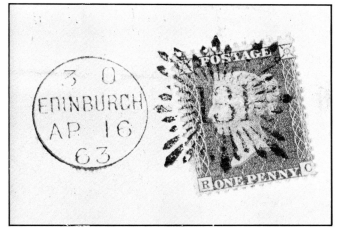

Examples of duplex postmarks. Opposite page, above: Irish diamond-shaped, 1856; below, Cambridge, 1878. Above, left: Welsh postmark, 1861; right, a 'Brunswick Star', Edinburgh, 1863. Note the great diversity of dispositions and styles for these marks.

constant maintenance and repair. Later cancellation machines – and postmarks – are known to collectors by the names of the manufacturers – 'Hoster', 'Hey Dolphin', 'Bickerdike', 'Krag' etc. They mostly comprised datestamp and bars in various forms, and are identifiable by their characteristics.

The duplex circular datestamp gradually became the 'maid of all work' from about the 1860s to the Edwardian era and beyond. Earlier types varied in style throughout the United Kingdom, and the distinction of enclosing the office numbers in a diamond within the barred circles or ovals for the London chief office, or within a circle for the district and suburban offices (as at first adopted for the numeral datestamps) continued with the duplex cancellations while those offices functioned. A scarce mark is the so-called

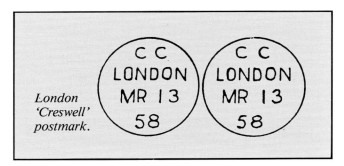

London 'Creswell' postmark.

'Creswell' which had a very small, 'thimble' size, datestamp adjoining the numeral 'killer'.

The early duplexes for Wales were of the sideways type – that is, the duplex was struck in the normal fashion, the town name and adjoining numeral appeared sideways: right way up, the cds surmounted the 'killer' numeral. The first Scottish types were also 'sideways on', but later came more elaborate versions

of the 'Brunswick Star' used originally in the numeral handstamps – an Edinburgh duplex with ornamented lines radiating from the number '131', and numerals between parallel bars of other places. A scarce Scottish duplex is one with a dotted circle adjoining the numeral – another is inscribed 'Posted since 7.20 last night' and explains late delivery. The Irish duplexes incorporated the numerals within barred diamonds of the earlier types and included some unusual patterns, especially one where the diamond enclosed the datestamp adjoining the normal barred numeral. Another unusual duplex, with a hexagonal datestamp, was used to signify 'late fee' charges paid.

An Irish duplex postmark, 1855.

The normal, everyday duplex emerged as a combined circular datestamp and 'killer' – the office number within an upright barred oval. As with the early numeral handstamps, each office was allocated a number or code letter and number when the maximum '999' number was reached (to avoid the use of four digits), and some cancellers were additionally numbered for identification.

The Circular Datestamp

As a basic 'shape' for the postmark handstamp, the ubiquitous circle continued in use throughout the nineteenth century and, indeed, has continued to the present day. Among the oldest established and most distinctive of the circular marks is the aptly-named 'skeleton' – it is the 'bare bones' of a postmark comprising a large, open single ring with the village or town name in crude, hand-set letters at the top (sometimes with the county name at the base), time (often omitted), date and year of posting in the centre. They were temporary handstamps, sometimes called 'travelling' handstamps, virtually 'home-made' and usually assembled by postmasters for use in emergency – for example, when the regular canceller was broken or lost.

Skeletons may be found in all sizes from the very large, some two inches in diameter, to the unusually small, sometimes hardly larger than the normal double-ring handstamp – an average size is approximately one-and-a-half inches across. Collectors look for good strikes – with the entire cancellation on the letter or card. Picture postcards of the Edwardian era are a good source of skeletons, and of most of the other types of postmark in use at the turn of the century. Another form of temporary datestamp which was used well into the 1920s (and resembles the present-day 'PAID' stamp used on packets) was the 'rubber' – an average-sized single-ring canceller showing village and/or town names with the date across the centre. Being a rubber stamp, impressions were generally blurred in a muddy blue or purple colour. Again, collectors seek sharp and clear strikes.

The 'scroll' (also 'hooded' or 'crested' circle) originated in Victorian times and is also found on Edwardian mail. It was a circular single-ring datestamp with a curved band or scroll around the upper circumference, bearing the name of the post town with the usual time, date and code details within the circle. The scroll was used almost exclusively in the London EC postal district (the Chief Post Office, St Martin's-le-Grand), and was more commonly employed to stamp the arrival of mail from abroad prior to delivery in the London area. Similar handstamps were issued to the Liverpool office and to some Irish post towns with main offices – these are regarded as 'treasure trove' by the postmark collector.

Another ubiquitous postmark of late-Victorian and Edwardian times was the 'squared circle' – it originated in its early experimental period as a single circle or octagon set within a number of concentric circles and, with one exception where the octagon was preserved, squared off on the outside – a circle within a square. The squared circle effectively combined the informative datestamp with the 'killer' element of the duplex (in one unit instead of two), and it came into regular use in the 1890s. Again it is a comparatively common postmark on picture postcards of the early

Above, middle: A rubber handstamp for parcels.
Above: 'Scroll' handstamp from pre-stamp days.

1900s, but those of the smaller towns and villages are harder to find. They are graded according to the number of arcs in the corners (one, two or three) or number of complete circles (three, with one arc, or four), and each type can be found in several sizes, some including index numbers.

Contemporary with the duplex, squared circle and the single- or double-ring cancellers were the delightful

*The 'squared circle' postmark,
used here from Jersey.*

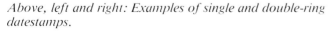

*Above, left and right: Examples of single and double-ring
datestamps.*

'thimbles' – very small circular datestamps no wider in
diameter than the stamps, used primarily as 'arrival'
backstamps, but later extensively as town and village
cancellations on postcards. Town names were inscribed within the perimeter of the circle – scarcer
types, across the centre – and ingenious abbreviations
were sometimes used for the longer names. On postcards it was the practice for sub-offices to avoid the

stamp, and to apply their thimbles alongside, the main
cancellation being applied at the receiving office.

The most common 'general purpose' handstamps
in use over the past 100 years have been the single- and
double-ring circular datestamps, the latter still
occasionally used in sub-offices or offices not
equipped with machine cancellers. The double-ring
types bear the town name within the rings at the top,
county or location at the foot and the usual details of
time and date of posting within the circle. The upper
and lower inscriptions are usually separated by curved

arcs which vary in length and thickness. Early Scottish double-ring types employed two pairs of double arcs, a style also used experimentally by the Birmingham office from about 1883. Sometimes the arcs are broken at the foot by the insertion of a 'Maltese Cross', a code number or a star. 'Paid' handstamps (in red) are similar, as also is the 'Hammer' – a Continental-type double circle which has the date in a single line across the centre.

Christmas 'X' postmark.

Between 1902 and 1909, the Post Office operated a scheme whereby greetings' letters and postcards, handed-in some days prior to delivery, were held for actual delivery on Christmas Day. The special cancellations used were either oval – single- or double-ring – inscribed 'POSTED IN ADVANCE FOR DELIVERY ON CHRISTMAS DAY' with the post town or code letters, circular single-ring types with a large letter 'X' or with the 'X' employed as part of a machine cancellation. Today there is no delivery on Christmas Day, but it was a joyous event in Victorian and Edwardian Britain. These cancellations are now extremely rare, the scarce ones fetching hundreds of pounds on cover or postcard. Ordinary items with the 'December 25th' postmark are more easily found.

Example of oval handstamp used to cancel stamps on registered letters.

Distinctive oval cancellations have long been in use for registered letters – registration was inaugurated in 1837 – and postmarks of the royal household, especially of the late Victorian and Edwardian eras, are keenly sought by collectors.

A modern travelling post office.

The Railway Post Offices

'On the night of April 1st, 1864, the Macclesfield mail-bag, which included two registered letters, was stolen from the standard of the apparatus for exchanging bags at Chelford railway station.' Just a contemporary news item and probably not unique, but it illustrates how, in the comparatively short span of 25 years since the first lineside mail-exchange apparatus was first installed, the country-wide travelling post office services had developed. This novel 'collection and delivery' system continued for more than 100 years – until it was finally taken out of service in October, 1971.

Generally the most common railway cancellations are those inscribed with the names of stations, for example 'RUGBY STATION' or 'CREWE STATION', or the railway sub-offices ('R.S.O.') such as 'BURNHAM R.S.O. SOMERSET' or 'GILLINGHAM R.S.O. KENT'. Other variations included 'Station Office', 'Station B.O.' or 'Station S.O.' (Branch or Sub-Office), and the station name with the initials of the railway company, as 'PADDINGTON G.W.Ry. Stan.'. The first recorded railway station postmark was that of Gloucester Station, dated 25 March 1840 – it was a large, un-framed circular datestamp with short double-arcs between 'GLOUCESTER' and 'STATION'. Similar cancellations are known, used at Berwick and Swindon stations with the distinctive serif letters. Subsequent station cancellations may be found in all the types of handstamp previously described, not only the fairly common single and double ring cds, but also in the form of squared circles, duplex and the rare early skeletons.

Travelling post offices are specially-adapted railway coaches attached to trains – or comprising whole mail trains – in which letters are sorted *en route*. Letters thus sorted were (and are) given distinctive handstamp cancellations, and these are eagerly sought by collectors, especially examples of the more remote and least used routes. Sorting carriages ('S.C.') or tenders ('S.T.') supplemented the TPO services in earlier days, and some of the best-known handstamps include

*A postmark used to cancel
mail posted at Broadstairs
Railway Station, Kent, 1909.*

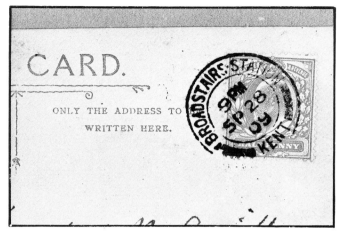

'HULL SORTING CARRIAGE' (or 'S.C.'), 'LINCOLN SORTING TENDER' (or 'S.T.') and 'SHREWSBURY & HEREFORD (or ABERYSTWYTH) S.C.'. TPO marks invariably designated the railway, route or location of the service, such as the 'GREAT WESTERN UP' (or 'DOWN'), still serving Devon and Cornwall to and from Paddington, 'LONDON – YORK – EDINBURGH T.P.O.' and 'NORTH EASTERN T.P.O.' or 'SOUTH WALES T.P.O.'. There are also numerous 'missent' marks and 'late fee paid' stamps used in conjunction with the TPO cancellations. Today, the streamlined 'Royal Mail' TPO services cover the entire United Kingdom.

A Post Office Packet of the type which sailed from the Falmouth Packet Station in the early 19th century. Mails were carried to the Americas, the West Indies and to the Mediterranean.

Ship Letters and Paquebots

For centuries letters have been carried across the oceans and around the world. The vessels – sail and steam – transporting letters, packets and passengers became known as 'packets', the most famous of them being the Falmouth Packets, founded in 1689 to operate postal services between this country and Spain. From 'packet-boat' came the familiar 'paquebot' postal mark (French being the official language of the Universal

Postal Union) which was brought into use internationally in 1894. Prior to this, letters posted at sea and subsequently handled by the postal staff at British 'ports of arrival' received 'Ship Letter', 'Ship Lre' or 'Packet Letter' cancellations, coupled with the name of the port of arrival – examples: 'DOVER SHIP LRE', 'HULL SHIP LETTER' or 'SHIP LETTER LIVERPOOL' – around the country.

1848 Ship Letter and 1911 Paquebot cancellations.

The London and provincial port marks, and those inscribed 'INDIA LETTER', on the original envelopes or entires are the most desirable 'ship' items for the collector, as also are the 'Packet Letters' from overseas. Local steamship companies operating in home waters also had mail contracts and used individual postmarks. They included (with postmark inscriptions in brackets) the Glasgow and Campbelton Steamer Service ('CAMPBELTON STEAM BOAT' in straight line), now Campbeltown, Argyll; the City of Dublin Steam Packet Company – Holyhead and Kingston (now Kingstown or Dun Laoghaire) Service ('H & K PACKET' cds); and David Macbrayne Ltd – Firth of Clyde Steamer Service ('GREENOCK – or GK – & ARDRISHAIG PACKET'; sometimes combined with 'IONA STEAMER', 'COLUMBA STEAMER' etc). The *Columba* and other Clyde paddlers had post office mail-boxes aboard and were virtually travelling post offices. Coastal steam-boats, such as *La Marguerite* on the Liverpool-Llandudno run, and the vessels of the Isle of Man Steam Packet Company, used coloured rubber cachets on letters and postcards posted aboard.

'Paquebot' marks – of which there are innumerable variations – are applied at ports of arrival to mail posted on board ship, either as postmarks cancelling the stamps or as cachets. Letters and postcards mailed at sea usually bear stamps corresponding to the nationality of the ship or its owners who supply the stamps. Thus a 'SOUTHAMPTON PAQUEBOT' arrival mark may be applied to a missive bearing a British stamp (from a Cunarder), a US stamp (from an American liner) or a South African stamp (passenger from Cape Town). An item with a British stamp posted on the Gibraltar-Marseilles run, forwarded by rail and cross-Channel steamer to a British destination, would bear the 'Marseilles Paquebot' mark.

There are two main types of 'Paquebot' cancellation – those in the form of circular datestamps incorporating the name of the port and the word 'Paquebot' (also sometimes additionally inscribed 'Posted at Sea'); and the port's normal datestamp with a separate straight-line 'PAQUEBOT' mark. The word takes various forms such as 'PAQUETE' (Portuguese) or 'PAKETBOOT' (Dutch), and in modern times the ever-increasing volume of mail handled at British ports is serviced by machine cancellations.

Many shipping lines had their own sea-post cancellations, notably the Woermann Steamship Company of Hamburg which, in 1921, amalgamated with Norddeutscher Lloyd SS Co. This, eventually, became the Hamburg-Amerika Line. The Woermann vessels used an oval postmark inscribed 'Deutsche Seepost Line Hamburg-Westafrika' with the date and figures in Roman numerals representing a specific ship, or its postal code. Some postmarks named the vessel, making these more interesting to the collector. The large companies also used rubber-stamped cachets – the Royal Mail Steam Packet Company applied a large oval cachet with 'Posted on the High Seas' across the centre. Sometimes just the name of the ship was shown, such as 'ANDES', in large block letters.

Maritime Mail postmarks – used on mail received from Royal Navy ships.

The cross-Channel ships especially merit attention – they carried 'Boîtes Mobiles' or 'Movable Letter Boxes', usually lashed to the ship's rail and taken ashore on arrival at the port for the contents to be postmarked with one of the special cancellations. They began about 1844 between the French ports and Southampton with a simple 'M.B.' handstamp, then in 1857 the boxed 'milestone' postmark, inscribed 'Southampton-France M.B.' and the date, was introduced, a similar mark being used on French mail to Jersey from 1858. Later, these marks were replaced by circular datestamps, similarly inscribed, while French arrival marks bore the letters 'ANG BM' ('Angleterre Boîte Mobile'). These services ceased in 1939.

The Post Office now uses machine cancellations or rubber stamps – 'POST OFFICE/MARITIME MAIL' – on mail received from British warships. Naval vessels in wartime were always at risk and postmarks had to

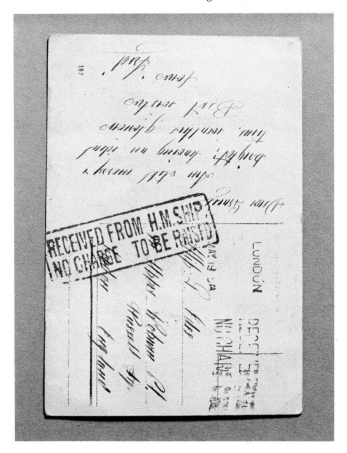

'Received from H.M. Ship' marking, remaining dumb about location.

preserve complete anonymity, ship and location. Typical of these precautions was the so-called 'dumb' cancel – a circle containing parallel lines applied to mail received from naval ships during World War I, and the two-line rubber handstamp, 'RECEIVED FROM H.M. SHIP – NO CHARGE TO BE RAISED', which was used on mail received from naval personnel, *circa* 1939.

Military and Camp Postmarks

Campaign letters are known from the Napoleonic and Peninsular Wars of 1805-15, and soldiers' letters from the Crimea, 1854-6, but these are of greater interest to the postal historian than to the postmark collector. Field Post Offices were established in South Africa during the Boer War, 1899-1902, thus contemporary letters and postcards may be found bearing the basic double-ring circular datestamp – 'FIELD POST OFFICE (B.O.) – BRITISH ARMY S. AFRICA', the scarcer octagonal 'ARMY POST OFFICE – NATAL FIELD FORCE V.R.', and others of the many existing types, including 'Mafeking' and the POW camps. Some 2,500 British Army and Field Post Offices have been recorded as operating during the two World Wars – they mostly used double-ring cds with code letters and/or numbers instead of place names for obvious security reasons.

The British Army established peacetime camps in this country during the 19th century on an unprecedented scale, holding regular manoeuvres and reviews.

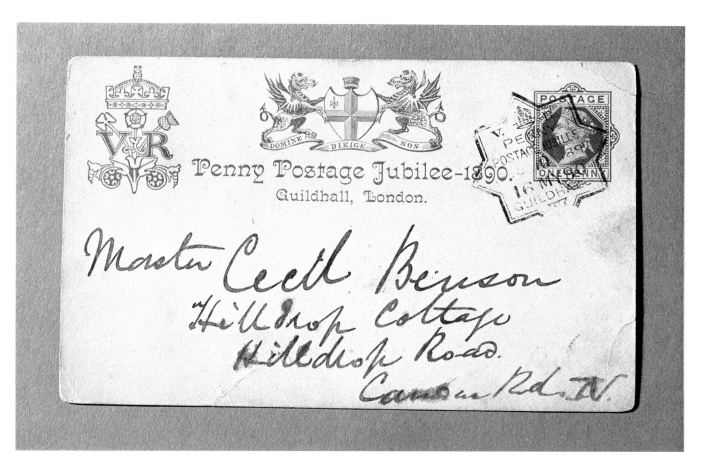

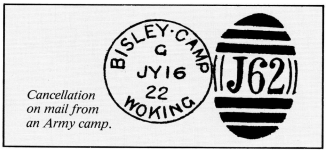

Cancellation on mail from an Army camp.

The largest of them all, Aldershot, in Hampshire, was founded in 1855, and the former village became a large town with numerous barracks, some having their own postal cancellations. Many more camps were established during World War I, and the great majority of the postmarks are in the various forms previously described – unframed circle with double arc at foot, duplex, skeleton, single and double circle (the most common), registration ovals and machine cancellations. Some of the best-known camps and cancels include Bisley (famous for its rifle ranges), Bordon, Catterick, Devizes, Lark Hill (Salisbury), Longmoor (Liss), Pirbright (Woking), Shorncliffe, Sutton Veny (Wilts) and Curragh in County Kildare.

Also of interest are the wartime censor markings, usually rubber stamps in black, violet or red ink, and in various shapes, inscribed 'Passed by Censor' and initialled by the censor.

The Great Exhibitions

The first great international exhibition was the famous one held in the Crystal Palace, Hyde Park, London, and opened by Queen Victoria in 1851. No special postmark has ever been recorded for this event, but it was followed by many other exhibitions, among them the Penny Post Jubilee of 1890 when there were two – one at the Guildhall, London, the other at the South Kensington Museum. Jubilee postcards and covers were published and used with a variety of decorative handstamps at both events. In 1891, commemorative cards showing the Eddystone Lighthouse were issued for the Royal Naval Exhibition in London, and special postmarks were applied in blue and violet. Paris was the setting for the International Exhibition of 1900 – the postmarks were inscribed *'Exposition Universelle – Paris 1900',* but often one finds only the normal city cancellations of Paris itself.

The Edwardian era was a prolific period for exhibitions – London's principal ones were those at Earl's Court, 1903, 1904 and 1905, and the Franco-British and Japan-British at the White City, Shepherd's Bush, in 1908 and 1910 respectively. Also familiar to collectors will be the special postcards used at the

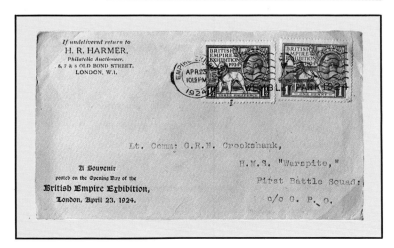

Glasgow (1901), Bradford (1904), Scottish National (1908), Coronation and Festival of Empire (1911) shows, but again the normal city cancellers were used, more often than the special postmarks.

The Franco-British Exhibition at the White City in 1908 stemmed from King Edward VII's visit to Paris in 1903. Features of this mammoth show were the complex of extremely decorative buildings and the fact that many events in the Fourth Olympic Games took place in the White City stadium which was a part of the elaborate complex. The postmarks, usually single-ring, circular datestamps, were inscribed 'FRANCO-BRITISH EXHIBITION – LONDON', and these are commonly found on the exhibition postcards.

Other Franco-British cards featured the Irish village of 'Ballymaclinton', sponsored by McLinton the Irish soap-makers, and mail posted there received a special cancellation, again a single-ring cds – 'BALLY-MACLINTON' – SHEPHERDS BUSH EXHIBITION W'.

The British Empire Exhibition at Wembley was probably the most ambitious of its kind since 1851. The exhibition, with its many ornamental buildings and pavilions covering more than 200 acres, was opened by King George V on 23 April 1924, and two special commemorative stamps – 1d. scarlet and 1½d. brown – were issued (and again in 1925). Numerous picture postcards, also special envelopes and letter-cards, were issued and there was a wide range of postal cancellations to adorn them. Besides the 'EMPIRE EXHIBITION – WEMBLEY PARK' slogan, there were special postmarks for some of the main pavilions – Government, Engineering and Industry – used as handstamps. The exhibition post office handled registered letters, airmails letters, packets and parcels, as well as ordinary cards and letters, each with their own cancellations.

STAMPEX handstamp.

A popular feature of stamp exhibitions and shows is the now customary use of special postmarks applied to mail posted, usually on souvenir covers. Many other

Special cancellations for mail posted at Exhibitions:
Top, left: From 'Ballymaclinton Village' at the Shepherds Bush Exhibition, London, 1908.
Middle, left: From the 1938 Chelsea Flower Show, London.
Lower, left: From the Empire Exhibition, Wembley, 1924. Machine cancel on cover bearing Britain's first commemorative stamps.

A 'More to Pay' marking.

special-event postmarks are used on similar occasions — examples are the British Industries Fairs in Birmingham, the Festival of Britain (1951), the annual Philatelic Congress, Chelsea Flower Show, and Wimbledon Tennis Championships.

'More to Pay'

It has always been easy, through carelessness, ignorance or neglect, to break one or other of the many Post Office regulations. These — and the postal charges — are changed so frequently that even the sorters and postmen must spend half their time checking the rule-books and amendments, while the public learn about them through trial and error. Post Office staffs have a rubber stamp for every contingency, ever since the first 'More To Pay' marks were brought into use in 1847. In addition to the large 'Pence' marks which came into use in the 1870s, there is a range of charge, instructional and explanatory marks, mostly relating to unpaid or underpaid items, both in the London and provincial offices and in the foreign section, dealing with mail from abroad.

The instruction 'To Pay' has remained constant over the years and is usually accompanied by the

'Posted unpaid' noted as a boxed marking with double postage (14p) charged by postage due stamps.

amount due, in manuscript, and an explanation such as: 'Contrary to Regulations', 'Liable to Letter Rate' (for postcards in certain categories), 'Posted Unpaid', 'Return to Sender', 'Inadmissible', also quoting the appropriate number of the regulation, and the whole mark boxed or framed. Edwardian picture postcards were constantly under fire, they were often larger than the stipulated maximum sizes, insufficiently stamped for overseas (for which the postage rate was 1d. instead of the ½d. inland rate), or were novelty cards such as the 'pull-out' or concertina types, or tinselled cards which were permitted only at the existing letter rate or under cover.

'Postage Due' adhesive stamps were introduced in Britain in 1914 and these are described in Chapter 7. They are usually attached to the underpaid letters or cards on arrival at the destination office and post-marked, in addition to the boxed regulation, number and amount due. Letters from abroad 'short' on postage usually bear a 'T' (*'Taxe')* mark.

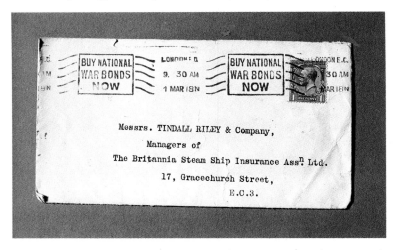

Britain's first slogan postmark – 'Buy National War Bonds Now' – introduced in 1917.

Covers

The cover collector follows a purposeful trail – he or she may be seeking a 'pre-stamp' (or 'pre-adhesive') letter or entire used in the post before stamps were invented, and filling a gap in a postal history col-lection; a flown cover – by Imperial Airways, perhaps – on a pioneer South African route; a Pony Express, or 'Wells Fargo' cover from the 'Wild West' of the United States; or merely a Post Office cover with Christmas stamps bearing the postmark, 'Bethlehem' (Llandeilo, Wales). The collector of postal stationery treads a neighbouring path – looking for the official stamped (embossed or imprinted) letter-sheets, wrappers, envelopes and postcards which date approximately from 1840.

Many stamps are rare on cover and many rare stamps are rarer still – if not unique – on the original envelope or entire. The 3d. New Carlisle Postmaster's Provisional – it is Canada No. 1 in the catalogue – printed on an envelope posted to Toronto in April 1851 fetched £31,000 at auction in 1977, having previously been sold for £220 in 1963. The only existing Bermuda 'Perot' One Penny Postmaster's stamp on an entire letter was once owned by Ferrary and Burrus, and a cover bearing two 1d. 'Post Office' Mauritius stamps,

which was originally bought in an Indian bazaar for £50, sold for $380,000 at the 'Lichtenstein/Dale' sale in 1968. These are top-level examples of the enhanced value of stamps on original covers or folded letters, and the principle applies to more humble stamps, too. A single, loose stamp, postally used, is virtually anony-mous – on its original envelope, its function can be traced from posting to delivery.

There is no problem in finding early covers – at exhibitions and fairs many dealers have boxes full of them. They feature in auctions and some dealers advertise them in the stamp magazines, offering to send covers on approval.

Postal history aside, there are numerous avenues for the cover collector in the vast field of postmarks – commemorative covers and special postmarks, machine cancellations and slogans, 'disaster' covers – mail surviving air crashes and shipwrecks – and the popular first-day covers. Some enthusiasts collect the postmarks of villages and towns in their own county or district, and such a collection forms an interesting sideline. Preferably postmarks should be collected on cover, but this is not always possible and the only alternative is to collect 'on piece' in the form of neat rectangles. Airmail 'first flights' illustrate the develop-ment of worldwide airways and the opening of new routes.

Since 1964 the Post Office has sold first-day covers specially designed and printed for most special issues of stamps; special posting facilities are provided and covers receive hand-cancelled 'First Day' postmarks. Britain's first-ever slogan postmark – 'BUY NATIONAL WAR BONDS NOW' – was launched in London in December 1917, and, on cover or postcard, is now a collector's item. Since that time, slogans have been used for government-sponsored campaigns, national publi-city, local events and, from 1963, tourist and prestige advertising. In the 1930s, the Post Office publicized its telephone service with numerous slogan postmarks, and the first tourist mark, showing 'Happy Harold', and worded 'WE'RE READY FOR YOUR INVASION AT HASTINGS' was introduced in 1963.

Scope for the cover/postmark collector embraces the world – the 'village' postmarks of Cyprus, the turn-of-the-century 'flag' cancels of the United States or the sparkling modern pictorial postmarks of Switzerland. Letters bearing coded phosphorescent dots are sought by students of mechanized letter-sorting.

Postal Stationery

Collecting postal stationery is a revival of a pastime which was keenly followed in late Victorian times – and was supported by special Gibbons' catalogues – but which declined about 1906 when Gibbons disposed of their vast stocks of British, colonial and foreign embossed and imprinted envelopes, postcards, letter-

HER MAJESTY THE QUEEN HER MAJESTY THE QUEEN   HER MAJESTY THE QUEEN HER MAJESTY THE QUEEN

Sixtieth Birthday 34p   Sixtieth Birthday 34p   Sixtieth Birthday 17p   Sixtieth Birthday 17p

FIRST DAY OF ISSUE 21 APR 1986

FIRST DAY OF ISSUE 21 APR 1986

The Sixtieth Birthday of
Her Majesty The Queen
21 April 1986

ROYAL MAIL FIRST DAY COVER

A A Barron
Room 9
New Belvedere House
White Horse Road
LONDON
E1 0ND

35   32   27   19

Pontcysyllte Aqueduct, Clwyd   Mill, New Lanark, Strathclyde   Tin mine, St Agnes, Cornwall   Ironbridge, Shropshire

FIRST DAY OF ISSUE BRITISH PHILATELIC BUREAU EDINBURGH 4 JULY 1989

FIRST DAY OF ISSUE BRITISH PHILATELIC BUREAU EDINBURGH 4 JULY 1989

INDUSTRIAL ARCHAEOLOGY MUSEUMS YEAR 1989

ROYAL MAIL FIRST DAY COVER

STANLEY GIBBONS LTD.
399 STRAND
LONDON WC2R 0LX

*Since the 1960s the British Post Office
has accompanied new stamp issues with specially
designed first-day covers. The above two
examples commemorate the Queen's 60th birthday
(1986) and Industrial Archaeology (1989).*

A 2d. Mulready lettersheet, 1840.

cards, reply-cards and wrappers. Ideally, today, unused items are eagerly sought, but postally used envelopes and cards are easier to obtain and may be interestingly stamped and/or postmarked.

The development of British postal stationery was linked to the improvement of paper manufacture in the early 1800s, when several paper-makers were busily involved in devising machines for the purpose – had they failed, supplies of cheap envelopes and writing-paper would scarcely have been adequate for the introduction of postage stamps and the Mulready envelope in 1840. One who succeeded almost beyond his dreams was John Dickinson, the paper-maker of the Apsley, Nash & Croxley Mills. In 1807, he patented cartridge-paper, well known today for its finish and strength, but originally used as a cartouche or wrapper for cartridges. In 1828, Dickinson invented his now famous security paper which had silk threads incorporated in it, and was widely used for bonds and other documents. The silk-thread paper was used in the manufacture of the ill-fated Mulready letter-sheets and envelopes, and of the superbly embossed envelopes which succeeded them.

When, in January 1840, the free franking privileges of Members of Parliament were abolished, they were issued with special prepaid envelopes inscribed 'Temporary – Post Paid' and the value, 'To be posted at

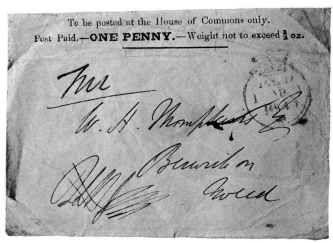

Parliamentary envelope – sold to Members of the House of Commons after abolition of their free franking privilege in January 1840.

the Houses of Parliament' (1d. and 2d.), 'House of Lords' (1d., and 2d.) or 'House of Commons' (1d.). These are scarce and interesting items for the collector – their use ceased with the long-awaited introduction of stamps and stationery in May 1840.

Envelopes or 'pockets' came into fashion in the 1830s, a time when it was still customary for letters to be charged according to the number of folded sheets they comprised – the first envelopes were counted as an extra sheet of paper. By about 1837, envelopes were being sold in flat packets, ungummed, and had to be folded and wafer-sealed. Dickinson's silk-thread paper came to the notice of Rowland Hill and he produced some trial letter-sheets inscribed 'London District Post – One Penny.' In the event, the Mulready postal stationery was printed by William Clowes on Dickinson's machine-made, silk-thread paper.

Meanwhile, William Wyon, whose famous medal commemorating the Queen's coronation was the model for the first stamps, had also produced a similar head of the Queen in the form of an embossed die, described by Rowland Hill as 'a beautiful thing'. Use of this exquisite die was temporarily shelved, but was introduced on the embossed 1d. and 2d. envelopes which followed the demise of the Mulready stationery in 1841, also printed on Dickinson's silk-thread paper. Another of Hill's proposals was the 'stamping' of private or commercial letter-sheets or envelopes for postal use. This service was introduced belatedly in 1853, when it became possible for the public to have private stationery printed or impressed with postage 'stamps'. The practice was discontinued in 1973.

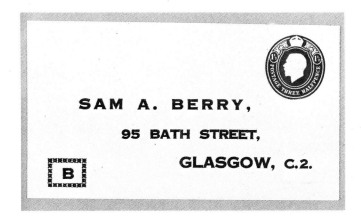

Above, right: Rowland Hill Centenary air letter had much useful philatelic information on it. Above, left: Private stationery with stamp officially embossed.

Today the British Post Office still issues postal stationery in the form of first- and second-class envelopes, registered envelopes, aerogrammes and Swiftair packs. The envelopes bear a non-value indicator stating that postage has been paid but not specifying a particular rate; therefore the stationery can continue to be used after postal rates have increased without the necessity of affixing additional adhesive stamps to make up the new rates. Each year since 1965 pictorial aerogrammes have been issued for Christmas mail and in 1989 a series of six 'Landscapes of Britain' aerogrammes went on sale – a colourful alternative to the standard issue. Distinctive designs were introduced for Scotland in 1974, usually two a year are issued. A few Welsh issues were made in 1973–6 but were not continued. Since their postal independence Guernsey, Jersey and the Isle of Man have issued a number of attractive, pictorial aerogrammes showing island views.

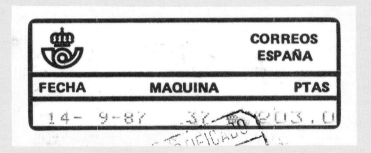

*Frama stamps or 'machine labels' from Great Britain,
Australia, New Zealand, France, West Germany, West
Berlin and Spain.*

*Non-valve indicator stamps of Great Britain, USA and
Canada.*

15
The Future of Stamps

Stamp catalogues are the barometer of stamp values and catalogue trends indicate a rosy future for stamps and stamp collecting. If stamps suddenly ceased to be issued all over the world, there would be no shortage of stamps for the collector, although there might conceivably be an all-round increase in the prices of existing stamps! Since 1840 the postage stamp has provided loyal service to the peoples of the world, and has justified its use a million times. It has survived, by its very convenience and adaptability, the immense progress of civilization and two world wars, and as yet the scientists and post office technologists have found no substitute for it (or even sought one). In this computer age, is it just possible that, perhaps by the year 2000, there could be some revolutionary change, a universal free post in which letters require nothing more than a computerised postmark? (Back to the Bishop mark!).

An International Stamp?

A more likely possibility is the ultimate solution – a world uniform currency to replace the surging ups and downs of British Sterling, the US dollar and all the other dependent currencies, and a world stamp or series of stamps. The annual 'Europa' stamps, when originally conceived, were intended to have, as part of the 'new Europe' conception, not only a standard design each year, but also an interchangeable denomination and currency, enabling the stamps to be used in any of the member countries. The project did not materialize as visualized, and it seems that mutual friendship and understanding, and a merger of national and commercial interests are the essential prerequisites for a world postage stamp.

The Universal Postal Union came near to this ideal when, on the occasion of its 75th anniversary, a proposal for a world issue of commemorative stamps was submitted by M. Herwich, Chief of the Polish Postal Administration, at the UPU congress held in Paris in 1947. Although the member countries could not agree on the idea of a universal stamp design, the original proposal for a world issue was accepted in principle, and in 1949 (or during the following year) the postal administrations of almost the entire world issued commemorative stamps for the Union's 75th birthday.

It was the nearest approach to an international postage stamp there had ever been, and it was significant – any project for universal stamps would have to be inspired and approved by the Universal Postal Union, an agency of the United Nations.

For many years the UPU endeavoured to persuade its members to use, by mutual agreement, postage stamps of certain colours for specific purposes and rates of postage – one colour for 'home' (or inland) letters, another for overseas letters and others for standard airmail charges and registered letters. Thus, to fall in line with such suggestions, Great Britain changed the colours of some of its low-value stamps in 1950-1. Our 1½d. stamp, for example, became green instead of brown; the 2d. was changed from orange to brown; the 2½d. stamp, then used for inland letters, became red instead of blue; and the 4d. grey-green for overseas letters was issued in blue. But many nations were either unable or unwilling to co-operate, so this idealistic aim was never fully integrated. Many countries use multicoloured stamps as definitives and are reluctant to change them; many also display their history, products, industries, flora, fauna and scenic beauties on their stamps – another reason why national stamps are unlikely to be entirely replaced by international ones.

Each year millions of tourists, businessmen, sportsmen and statesmen are on the move across the world – how convenient it would be for the traveller to carry with him a supply of international stamps, purchased in his own country or *en route* and valid for postage in all the countries of the world!

A 'Moon Post' is not an impossible thought for the future. The 'Apollo 11' astronauts – Neil Armstrong, Edwin Aldrin and Michael Collins – landed on the Moon on 20 July 1969 with the master die and a letter bearing a die proof of the US 'Moon Landing' commemorative stamp. Together the three astronauts 'stacked hands' and postmarked the first 'Moon letter' – a 'giant leap' for the United States Post Office!

New Types of Stamps

In recent years we have seen stamps issued for use on greetings mail, the United States PO introduced 'Love' stamps in 1982 and Ireland has issued an annual Greetings set since 1985. The British Post Office

ROYAL

GREENWICH

OBSERVATORY

HAILSHAM
15 VI 79
EAST SUSSEX

GREAT BRITAIN

00

RM 2575

POSTAGE PAID

produced its first Greetings stamps in 1989 – five designs issued in books of 10, two stamps of each design. The stamps featured a rose, Cupid, a sailing boat, a bowl of fruit and a teddy bear. Attached to the stamps were 12 labels bearing messages such as 'BEST WISHES' which could be affixed to the envelope if so desired. The issue of Greetings stamps reflects the growth in the sending of cards of all kinds.

Ever since the introduction of stamps, some users have been worried about hygiene, not finding the licking of stamps acceptable. In tropical countries there is the problem of stamps sticking together if they got too moist and in 1964 Sierra Leone introduced self-adhesive stamps. These were 'free form' in the shape of a map of the country. Many self-adhesive issues have followed from Tonga, Montserrat and Norfolk Island. Britain has issued self-adhesive airmail, registration and Recorded Delivery labels but not yet self-adhesive stamps. The first major postal administration to do so was the USA with a 10¢. Christmas stamp in 1974, issued in sheets of 50 on rouletted backing paper. Canada's first self-adhesive stamp was issued in 1989, a 38¢. value showing the national flag, sold in books of 12 at $5.

In our ever-changing world, postal administrations are striving to find improved ways of meeting customers' needs. Today we buy many things from vending machines and since the 1970s many post offices have introduced machines which vend stamps of the desired amount and some even give change. These machines are popularly known as 'Framas' after the Swiss company which produces many of them. Frama stamps, termed 'Machine Labels' in Gibbons catalogues, are now issued by many countries and are popular with certain collectors. Australia Post introduced Frama stamps in 1984 and regularly change the background pattern of the paper on which the stamp is printed; making new variations for collectors. France has a range of Frama-type stamps of rectangular shape, printed in red and black on blue-patterned paper. These

Franking by meter is widespread; though disliked generally by philatelists, meter stamps are collected by some.

and Spanish Framas are printed on self-adhesive paper. Framas from West Berlin are pictorial.

The British Post Office installed four Frama machines in London, Cambridge, Southampton and Windsor in 1984; these dispensed stamps in ½p units up to 17p. The ½p unit stamps were discontinued at the end of 1984 and the machines taken out of service in April 1985. They had not proved operationally successful and were frequently 'out of use'. The Frama stamps now command quite a high catalogue valuation and stamps genuinely used on cover are worth keeping.

In Britain stamp books, with bright red covers, are available at some 40,000 retail outlets – almost double the number of post offices. In order to simplify arrangements for retailers at a time of postal rate changes, the Royal Mail introduced Non Value Indicator stamps, designated simply '1ST' and '2ND' into these books in August 1989. The stamps were hailed in the press as 'priceless stamps' and their issue attracted a lot of collector interest. This was Britain's first such issue although non value indicators had been used on postal stationery since 1982. The first US 'non value' issue came in 1978 when the uncertainty over the postal rate increase led to the Christmas stamp being without value. Definitive stamps marked 'A' were issued in 1978 pending production of 15¢. stamps and similar issues inscribed 'B', 'C', 'D' and 'E' have followed. Canada issued stamps marked 'A' in 1981 when the rate was increased to 30¢.

Meter Franks

Meter markings, denoting the amount of postage paid, were introduced in the USA in 1920 and in Britain two years later. Today a very sizeable proportion of business mail is so marked. The machines are supplied to companies by firms licensed by the Post Office.

16
'Stamp Finder'

The identification of postage stamps – that is, of the countries issuing them – is sometimes a problem for the inexperienced collector who may be unfamiliar with foreign languages, scripts, alphabets and national emblems. Chinese writing, for example, is not unlike Japanese; Korean scripts are different again (though not so very different) and the stamps of North and South Korea have distinctive inscriptions which enable them to be distinguished and correctly classified. The great majority of 'difficult' stamps have some clue to their identity embodied in their designs, and need just a little detective work – with the help of the stamp catalogue – to establish their origins.

The catalogue is an important aid – Gibbons' *Stamps of the World* catalogue lists over 275,000 stamps and has more than 65,000 illustrations, and many a profitable and rewarding hour may be spent just browsing through it, noting the characteristics of different countries' stamps, the appearance of the various styles of lettering and any other unusual features of the stamp designs. In one respect, the catalogue is the key to identification of one's stamps, but if you are going to peruse its 2,500-plus pages in search of a single stamp (or a number of stamps), that is likely to be a very time-consuming task. It is more logical to regard identification – the recognition of a country which has issued a stamp – as the key to the catalogue. The country can then be located quickly and the required information extracted.

The *Stamps of the World* catalogue was fully described in Chapter 10. The essential information you will need, apart from the name of the country, will be the year of issue, the event commemorated (if it is not a definitive), currency and colour (if not apparent on the stamp), and the number of stamps comprising the issue or set to assist you in arranging your stamps in chronological order – and in order of value – on the album page. For 'writing-up' you will also need details of the stamp design(s) – descriptive captions will give your display added interest. Inscriptions – the country name (in particular), and other words and figures, including overprints or surcharges, are the main source of identification, but sometimes portraits of heads of state, emblems and devices may be recognizable, thus speeding up the task of locating the issuing country, especially so where stamps are without country names.

Portraits and Emblems

British stamps are not inscribed as such – they bear the likeness of the reigning sovereign and are thus easily identified – Queen Victoria (reigned 1837-1901), King Edward VII (1901-1910), King George V (1910-1936), King Edward VIII (1936 20 January-10 December), King George VI (1936-1952), and our present Queen Elizabeth II (from 1952). Now take a look at Austria in the catalogue – the early stamps showed the Austrian 'eagle' arms and the profile of Emperor Francis Joseph. The name *'Oesterreich'* ('Austria') did not appear on Austrian stamps until 1890, thus we are dependent upon the arms or the portrait (and the *'kreuzer'* or *'kr'* currency) to pinpoint the country of issue. The currency is important because similar designs appeared for Austrian post offices in Turkey and for Lombardy and Venetia. Check also the first stamps of Hungary which show a similar portrait of the emperor and bear the same figures of value. The Austrian 'eagle' appears also on the first stamps of Bosnia and Herzegovina.

Numerals – and no other means of identification – were shown on Brazil's first issues: these, as described elsewhere, were given appropriate nicknames – 'bull's eyes', 'snake's eyes' and 'goat's' or 'cat's eyes'. The Swiss arms (inscribed *'Orts Post'* or *'Local Post'*) and the figure of the 'Seated Helvetia' serve to identify the first stamps of the Federal Republic of Switzerland, while the first Swiss postage dues comprised numerals representing the face values within a circle of stars – the 22 cantons. The papal insignia of 'crossed keys' indicates the stamps of the Papal States – parts of Italy under papal rule until 1870, and the first issues of Italy should not be confused with those of Sardinia – both show King Victor Emmanuel II. If you find the head of Mercury on stamps with or without face values, these are almost certainly the early newspaper stamps of Austria. Royal silhouettes – Queen Maria, King Pedro V and King Luiz – feature on the first issues of Portugal, and various profiles of Queen Isabella II on the early stamps of Spain.

The monarch's portrait identifies stamps from Great Britain.

Queen Victoria   King Edward VII   King George V

King Edward VIII   King George VI   Queen Elizabeth II

Portraits and emblems provide corroboration of the identity of many stamps – Kemal Ataturk appears on Turkish stamps, King Baudouin, Queen Juliana and King Carl XVI Gustav are depicted on the definitive issues of Belgium, the Netherlands and Sweden respectively, Queen Margrethe on Denmark and Greenland, King Juan Carlos I on Spain. Russia's first stamps – small-size definitives – depicted the Russian arms, and Finland, a Russian grand-duchy until 1917, issued almost identical stamps in 1891. These can be distinguished by the small circles flanking the arms – between 1901 and 1911, the Russian-style designs have the different currency, *penni* and *markkaa*, for Finland. Poland's first stamp of 1860 also bore the Russian arms.

Japanese stamps issued between 1872 and 1947 constantly featured the 16-petalled chrysanthemum – the emblem of Japan's royal family. The 'sun' emblem occurs on early Chinese stamps, always with 12 rays, and portraits of Sun Yat-sen, a national hero, were frequently depicted. Korean stamps picture the cherry blossom, and the yin-yang, a circular symbol part light and part dark, is peculiar to South Korea.

Alphabets and Scripts

Many stamps bear inscriptions in languages expressed in the normal (Roman) alphabet, but many foreign alphabets have letters and characters which apparently

Stamps are quite often inscribed in more than one language.

bear no relation to our own familiar A, B, C... Some written languages – Arabic, for example – look very much like 'shorthand'; others, like Korean, appear to be formed of a mixture of letters and tiny 'diagrams', closely related to Chinese, but not so intricate as Japanese. Many such stamps show the country name in a regular style which will become familiar to the collector. The stamps of the Malay States – now Malaysia – are expressed in Malay and Chinese (as well as English); Hindi, the Devanagari script, is the official language of India; Urdu and Bengali, those of Pakistan. Urdu has many Arabic and Persian words, while Persian, with Pushtu, is also the written language of Afghanistan.

The (H)ELLAS inscription identifies Greek stamps.

Japanese stamps now include NIPPON.

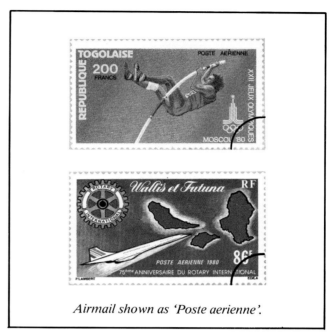

Airmail shown as 'Poste aerienne'.

The Greek alphabet has distinctive characters which soon become recognizable at sight – especially the country name, 'HELLAS', which appears, in Greek, as 'ELLAS' with a normal 'E', two characters like an 'A' without the crossbar ('L'), a normal 'A' and, for 'S', the peculiar zig-zag 'E'. The Greek currency, *lepta* and *drachmae*, or the commonly used abbreviations, are fairly easily deciphered on Greek stamps. The ancient Cyrillic language has some characters very similar to Roman shapes. Russian is a branch of the Slavonic family of languages, some of which are written in the Cyrillic alphabet, said to have been adapted by St Cyril, apostle to the Slavs, from the Greek alphabet in the ninth century. Some stamps of Bulgaria and Yugoslavia are inscribed in Roman letters, others bear Cyrillic characters; some have both. Oriental scripts will become familiar on acquaintance – in the Chinese language each character is a complete word; Korean signs represent a separate letter of the alphabet; and Japanese stamps, now helpfully inscribed 'NIPPON', have a four-character title.

'Postage' and Currencies

Clues to the identification of stamps may be found in the way that 'Postage' and similar 'purpose-of-issue'

words are expressed, and in the names of currencies.

In France and French-speaking territories, including Belgium (with Flemish), Luxembourg and Monaco, 'postage' is *postes*; a postage-due stamp is inscribed *chiffre-taxe, timbre-taxe, à payer* or *à percevoir*; and airmail is *poste aérienne* or (rarely) *avion* or *par avion*. *Exprès* is self-explanatory, as also is the word *postale* or *postaux* as an adjective. Parcel post is *colis postaux*. Pre-cancelled stamps are inscribed *affranche postes*. *Royaume* is kingdom or realm; and *république,* a familiar word on the stamps of the African French-speaking territories, is 'republic'. The French currency – centimes and francs – is usually indicated as 'c', 'F' or 'f', or in decimal form as '0.40' or '1.75'. 'RF' is the usual abbreviation for 'République Française'.

'Postage', originally *Reichspost*, is shown as *Bundespost* in the German Federal Republic and West Berlin, but is omitted in the German Democratic

(Left) 'Deutsche Luftpost' identifies German airmail; and (right) a clear country name, Österreich (Austria).

Republic (DDR). *Luftpost* is the German for airmail; *flugpost* in Austria. German currency – pfennigs and marks – is expressed in numerals, marks as 'm' or 'Dm'. Austria has groschen and schillings, indicated by 'g' or 's'. Hungarian stamps are inscribed *posta* ('Magyar Posta'), airmail *legiposta* and the currency – fillers ('f') and forints ('Ft'). The Polish currency is in groszy ('gr') and zlotys ('zl'); Bulgaria, stotinki and leva; Rumania, bani and lei; Albania, qindarka and leks; and Russia, kopecks and roubles.

'Poste Italiane' for Italian stamps.

Italian stamps ('Poste Italiane') are easily identified; airmail is *posta aerea,* postage due, *segnatasse,* and parcel post, *pacchi postali.* The currency is in lire ('L'). In Spain and the Spanish-speaking territories of Latin America, postage is *correos* and airmail, *correo aéreo.* Currencies, however, vary from the Spanish centimos and pesetas to centavos and pesos (Argentina, Bolivia, Colombia etc), sucres (Ecuador), colones (El Salvador), quetzals (named after the national bird – Guatemala), lempiras (Honduras), cordobas (Nicaragua) and balboas (based on the U.S. dollar – Panama). Chile has escudos and pesos; Peru, centavos and soles; Costa Rica, centimos and colones; and Paraguay

'Posts of Portugal'.

centimos and guaranies. In Portuguese, postage is *correio* and airmail, *correio aereo.* Portugal's currency is in centavos and escudos, Brazil has centavos and cruzeiros. Dutch stamps are inscribed in cents and florins or guilders, while Denmark and Norway share øre and kroner, Sweden, öre and kronor.

Some Help on Inscriptions

Here is a short list of the inscriptions in the normal alphabet commonly found on postage stamps. It includes the names of countries, identified in brackets, abbreviations, and 'special purpose' inscriptions and overprints.

A Açores (Azores)
Afghanes or Postes Afghanes (Afghanistan)
Afrique Equatoriale Française
(French Equatorial Africa)
Afrique Occidentale Française
(French West Africa)
Algérie (Algeria)
A.M.G.-F.T.T. (Trieste).
Allied Military Government overprints
Andorre (Andorra). French Post Offices
Archipel des Comores (Comoro Islands)
Autopaketti (Finland). Road parcels-stamps
Avisporto Maerke (Denmark). Newspaper
stamps

B B (Bangkok). British Post Office overprint
B in oval (Belgium). Railway officials
Bánát Bacska (Hungary). Rumanian
Occupation
Baranya (Hungary). Serbian Occupation
Bayern (Bavaria)
B.C.A. (Nyasaland Protectorate)
B.C.O.F. (British Occupation of Japan)
België (Belgium)
Belgique (Belgium)
Benadir (Somalia)
B.M.A. (Malaya).
British Military Administration
Böhmen und Mähren (Bohemia and
Moravia)
Brasil (Brazil)
Braunschweig (Brunswick)
British Central Africa or B.C.A.
(Nyasaland Protectorate)
British South Africa Company (Rhodesia)

C Cabo Verde (Cape Verde Islands)
Cambodge (Cambodia)
Čechy a Morava (Bohemia and Moravia)
C.E.F. (China). Expeditionary Force
C.E.F. (Cameroun). British Occupation
of Cameroons
Československo (Czechoslovakia)
C.F.A. (Réunion). French overseas
currency (francs)
Cilicie (Cilicia)
Confoederatio Helvetica (Switzerland)
Congo Belge (Belgian Congo)
Corée (Korea). Postes de Corée
Côte d'Ivoire (Ivory Coast)

D Danmark (Denmark)
Dansk Vestindien (Danish West Indies)
Deutsch-Ostafrika (Tanganyika).
    German East Africa.
Deutsches Reich (Germany)
Dienstmarke (Germany). Official stamps
D.P.R.K. (Democratic People's Republic
    of Korea) North Korea
Drzava S.H.S. (Yugoslavia). For Slovenia

E E.A.F. (Somalia). East African Forces
E.E.F. (Palestine). Egyptian
    Expeditionary Force
Eesti (Estonia)
Equateur (Ecuador)
España (Spain)
Etat Comorien (Comoro Islands)
Ethiopie (Ethiopia)
Eupen and Malmedy (Belgium).
    Belgian Occupation of Germany

F Filipinas, Filipas (Philippine Islands)
Føroyar (Faroe Islands)
Franco Bollo (Italy). 'Postage stamp'
Freimarke (Germany). 'Postage stamp'
Frimaerke Kgl. Danish 'Royal' stamp

G G (Griqualand West). Cape of Good Hope
G.E.A. (German East Africa).
    Tanganyika overprints
Grand Liban (Lebanon)
Grønland (Greenland)
Guinée (French Guinea)
Guyane Française (French Guiana)

H Haute Volta (Upper Volta)
Helvetia (Switzerland)
Hrvatska (Croatia)

I I.E.F. (India). Indian Expeditionary Force
Iles Wallis et Futuna (Wallis and Futuna)
Island (Iceland)

J Jeend, Jhind (Jind). Indian state
Jugoslavija (Yugoslavia)

K Kameroun (Cameroun). German protectorate
K.S.A. (Kingdom of Saudi Arabia)
K.u.K. Feldpost (Austro-Hungarian
    Military Post)

L L.A.R. (Libyan Arab Republic)
Latvija (Latvia)
Lietuva (Lithuania)
Lösen (Sweden). Postage dues

M Magyar, Magyarorszag (Hungary)
Malagache, Malagasy (Malagasy Republic)
    (Madagascar)
Maroc (French Morocco)
Melaka (Malacca)

N Nederland (Netherlands)
Nederlandse Antillen (Netherlands Antilles)
N.F. (Tanganyika). Nyasa-Rhodesian Force
Nippon (Japan)
Norge, Noreg (Norway)
Nouvelles Hebrides (New Hebrides).
    Anglo-French Condominium

O Oesterreich (Austria). Also Österreich
Ottomanes, Postes (Turkey)

P Persanes, Postes (Iran). Formerly 'Persia'
Pilipinas (Philippine Islands)
Poczta Polska (Poland)
Porteado Correio (Portugal).
    Postage due stamps
Portzegel (Netherlands). Postage due stamp
Postzegel (Netherlands)
Pulau Pinang (Penang)

R Rayon (Switzerland). Early issues.
Rialtar Sealadac na Héireann (Ireland).
    Issue of 1922
Rodi (Aegean Islands). Rhodes
Romana, Romina (Rumania)
Royaume de l'Arabie Saoudite (Saudi Arabia)
R.S.A. (Republic of South Africa)

S Saargebeit (Saar)
Sachsen (Saxony)
Samoa i Sisifo (Samoa)
Saorstát Eireann. 1922. Irish Free State
Saurashtra (Soruth)
Shqiperia, Shqiptare etc. (Albania)
Siam (Thailand)
Slesvig (Schleswig)
Suidafrika (South Africa)
Suidwes-Afrika (South West Africa)
Sverige (Sweden)

T Tanger (Tangier)
Tchad (Chad)
Te Betalen Port. Postage due
Terres Australes et Antarctiques Françaises
    (French Southern and Antarctic Territories)
Toga (Tonga)
Transjordan (Jordan)
Türkiye Postalari, or Cumhuriyeti (Turkey)

U U.A.R. (United Arab Republic).
    Formerly Egypt and Syria
Ultramar (Cuba, Puerto Rico). 'Overseas'

V Van Diemen's Land (Tasmania)
Vaticane, Poste (Vatican City)

W Württemberg (Germany)

Y Y.A.R. (Yemen Arab Republic)

Z Zuidafrika (South Africa)

A DESCRIPTIVE

PRICE LIST & CATALOGUE

OF

BRITISH, COLONIAL & FOREIGN

POSTAGE STAMPS,

FOR SALE BY

E. STANLEY GIBBONS,

FOREIGN POSTAGE STAMP DEALER,

15, TREVILLE STREET,

PLYMOUTH.

This List will be sent to any address in the Kingdom, post free, for 2d.; or abroad, post free, for 5d.

Plymouth:

COVE BROTHERS, PRINTERS, &c., 9, TREVILLE STREET.

Only two copies survive of this first Gibbons Catalogue, a penny price list of 1865.

17
Stamp Books and Magazines

Books are the fount of all knowledge and a philatelic library, built up lovingly over the years, is a personal and essential source of reference for the dedicated stamp collector. Probably never again will we see the like of the philatelic library formed by the Earl of Crawford which covered every aspect of the hobby as it was in his lifetime. Today the emphasis is on stamp catalogues, specialized handbooks and collectors' guides, and there is a truly vast range of philatelic publications available to the collector.

A catalogue of some kind is a necessary aid to the beginner and experienced philatelist alike, and the Gibbons catalogues (described in Chapter 10) are technical reference works of the highest order. For those who specialize in foreign countries there are numerous foreign-language catalogues published abroad, notably by Yvert & Tellier (France), Michel (Germany), Bolaffi (Italy), Zumstein (Switzerland) and Facit (Scandinavia). Scott of Sidney, Ohio publishes catalogues of United States stamps and of foreign countries on the scale of Gibbons in this country, while there are many specialized catalogues of the 'one-country' type covering the countries of Europe and the rest of the world.

Handbooks provide specialist expertise and many of them are the results of exhaustive study and research on specific issues of stamps or of one country's issues, postal history, postmarks, aero-philately, forgeries and scores of other subjects. Among the leading publishers of such books are the Royal Philatelic Society, London – for example, *The Postage Stamps and Postal History of British Guiana*, by W.A. Townsend and F.G. Howe – and Robson Lowe Ltd of Bournemouth, a typical specialized work being *St Helena: Postal History and Stamps*, by Edward Hibbert.

Sometimes philatelic handbooks go out of print and are subsequently reprinted (otherwise the books themselves become collectors' items) – examples are M.H. Ludington's famous *Postal History and Stamps of Bermuda*, originally published in 1962 and reprinted by Quarterman of the United States, and *The Picture Postcard and Its Origins*, by Frank Staff, which has made a welcome reappearance. Two luxury books on rare stamps are H. Kanai's *Classic Mauritius* (Stanley Gibbons, 1981) and T. Todd and N. Williams's *An Album of Rare Stamps* (Vallency International, 1983). Alcock and Holland's *British Postmarks: Short History and Guide* is a recognized authoritative work on the subject. *The British Postage Stamp*, by Robson Lowe, is a comprehensive historical survey of 19th-century British stamps, based on the R.M. Phillips collection in the National Postal Museum.

Stanley Gibbons publish a series of useful guides to various aspects of the hobby. These include:

Stanley Gibbons Guide to Stamp Collecting, by John Holman
Stamp Collecting – How to Start, by James Watson
Stamp Collecting – How to Identify Stamps, by James Watson
Stamp Collecting – Collecting by Theme, by James Watson
How to Arrange and Write-up a Stamp Collection, by Stanley Phillips and C.P. Rang, revised by Michael Briggs

Gibbons sell, but do not publish, two important atlases of value to stamp collectors: *The Stamp Atlas*, by Stuart Rossiter and John Flower and *The Orbis Philatelic Atlas*, edited by Kenneth F. Chapman.

Gibbons' *Philatelic Terms Illustrated*, now in its third edition, is a dictionary of philately which describes and illustrates all the different kinds of stamps, printing methods, paper, perforations etc. according to philatelic language. The principal dealers in stamp books (new and out of print) are:

Stanley Gibbons Ltd, 399 Strand, London WC2R 0LX
Vera Trinder Ltd, 38 Bedford Street, London WC2E 9EU
H.H. Sales Ltd, 25 Horsell Road, London N5 1XJ

Stamp magazines are a popular means of keeping in touch with all that is happening in the stamp world. Magazines may be grouped in three classes – those published by philatelic societies and issued to their members (sometimes on sale to non-members), commercial magazines sold through stamp shops, newsagents and also on postal subscription direct from the publisher, and those published by postal administrations, mostly giving information about forthcoming issues.

In Britain the most prestigious of the society publications is *The London Philatelist*, the journal of the Royal Philatelic Society, which is published six times a year. As might be expected its contents are of an advanced nature. The second major society, the National Philatelic Society, has published a journal, *The Stamp Lover*, since 1908; it is published six times a year and contains useful information on new issues, book reviews as well as authoritative articles. The British Philatelic Federation publishes a monthly magazine, *Stamp Mail*, which, in addition to news and articles contains reports of BPF and local society activities. Most one-country or thematic societies publish their own journals, e.g. *The G.B. Journal* (G.B. Philatelic Society) and *India Post* (Indian Study Circle). The BPF runs the British Thematic Association, which has its own journal *Themescene* and a number of specialist thematic groups also produce journals and newsletters, for example the Guild of St Gabriel (religion on stamps), the Philatelic Music Circle and the Society of Olympic Collectors (details in the *BPF Yearbook*).

Turning now to the commercial magazines, a few are still published by stamp dealers, the most eminent of which is *Gibbons Stamp Monthly* which has a history dating back to 1890 making it the longest running commercial journal (it was originally entitled *Stanley Gibbons Monthly Journal*). Amongst its most popular and best known features are the supplements to the Gibbons Catalogues, 'Stamp News in Brief', 'Philatelic World', 'The G.B. Collector' and 'Through the Magnifying Glass' (a look at varieties on stamps reported by readers). Each issue includes a 'British Stamps' section with up-to-date information on recent issues as well as specialist articles on older stamps and postal history. The 'Machin Watch' feature is especially popular.

The Philatelist and Philatelic Journal of Great Britain is published six times a year by Robson Lowe Ltd of London and Bournemouth and contains specialized articles and extensive book reviews. *The Aero-Field*, published since 1928 by Francis J. Field Ltd of Sutton Coldfield, West Midlands, is the specialist magazine dealing with aero-philately.

Other commercial magazines are the so-called 'independent' journals, not published by companies dealing in stamps but by commercial publishing houses. The longest-running of these is *Stamp Magazine*, published by Link House Ltd of Croydon, which began life in 1934 and tends to cater for the younger philatelist and the new issue collector. The monthly *Stamps* first appeared in 1980 and has been published by several companies, currently CGB Publishing of Warrington, Cheshire. *Stamp and Coin Mart*, another monthly, is from the same stable as the well-established *Exchange and Mart*.

The British Post Office publishes three magazines. The *British Philatelic Bulletin* began in 1963 as a duplicated newsletter giving details of new stamp issues and the services of the Philatelic Bureau. It is now a glossy, well-illustrated 24-page monthly, edited at the National Postal Museum in London and despatched to subscribers from the British Philatelic Bureau in Edinburgh. It is also available from philatelic counters at main post offices and from the Stanley Gibbons shop in the Strand. As well as details of forthcoming British stamps, it contains articles on older issues, postal history and thematic collecting. In the early days it gave details of forthcoming special handstamps and postmark slogans but as the number of these grew this information was transferred (1971) to a new fortnightly *British Postmark Bulletin*. This is available only on subscription from the Philatelic Bureau. The third publication, *Stamp Bug News*, is aimed at the young collector and is a bright, colourful magazine mostly concerned with recent issues. It includes a Pen-Pal feature and is distributed six times a year to members of the Stamp Bug Club, Freepost, Northampton NN3 1BR. The Club, set up in 1980, has some 70,000 members – the biggest stamp club in the UK.

Most postal administrations publish Bulletins or Newsletters, for example the Australian Post Office's *Stamp Bulletin* which dates from 1953, Guernsey's *Philatelic News*, Jersey's *Stamp Bulletin* and the Isle of Man's *Newsletter*. Details can be obtained from the relevant bureau (addresses in the *BPF Yearbook*). Some of the larger postal museums also produce regular publications as well as handbooks and guides. The National Postal Museum in London published the first of its annual reports, *Philatelic Year*, in 1989.

In the United States, 'high society' in the philatelic world is represented by the *American Philatelist*, the journal of the American Philatelic Society, and the *Collectors Club Philatelist*, published by the Collectors Club of New York. On the popular front is *Linn's Stamp Weekly* and another weekly journal, *Stamps*. Virtually every nation in Europe has one or more regular philatelic magazine – France, for example, *Le Monde des Philatélistes*, and *L'Echo de la Timbrologie*; and Italy, *Il Collezionista Italia Filatelica* – as do countries in the rest of the world, while numerous philatelic societies publish magazines, bulletins, newsletters and monographs.

18
Philatelic Organizations and Societies

World philately is in the care of the Fédération Internationale de Philatélie (FIP), the worldwide 'caretaker' organization whose principal aims are: '*The development of philately in all its branches by establishing international standards for collectors and for their displays in international exhibitions (including "General Rules for International Exhibitions under FIP Patronage"); The suppression of philatelic fraud of all kinds and all other practices harmful to collecting and collectors; To act as the official representatives of worldwide philately in relation to the Universal Postal Union. . . ; To further, and encourage, friendship and active co-operation among philatelists throughout the world, regardless of creed, race or political opinion.*'

The British Philatelic Federation, founded in 1976 by the merger of the British Philatelic Association (formed in 1926) with the Philatelic Congress of Great Britain (founded 1909), is a national organization catering for the needs of collectors, societies, exchange clubs, dealers, auctioneers and philatelic publishers. Membership falls into two main classes, Individual (business or collector) and Affiliate (company, society or junior), and the special needs of exchange club organizers and secretaries are also accommodated. It sponsors the annual British Philatelic Federation Congress at a different centre each year (and is one of the sponsors of the annual STAMPEX Exhibitions), an expertising service (operated by BPA Expertising Ltd. in association with the federation), and the annual Melville Junior Stamp Competition.

The BPF publishes an annual *Yearbook and Philatelic Societies Directory* which is a complete guide to BPF activities – Congress, BPF awards, exhibitions, philatelic bureaux, lectures and displays, affiliated associations and federations etc., and a comprehensive listing of countrywide societies, specialist societies and study circles in the United Kingdom.

In 1930, Albert Harris founded a dealers' organization to give much needed assistance to the growing stamp trade – this was the birth of the Philatelic Traders' Society which, after World War II, was reconstituted as an independent organization of stamp dealers with an elected council. The PTS is perhaps best known as one of the organizers of the annual national stamp exhibitions, STAMPEX, held at the Halls of the Royal Horticultural Society, Westminster, London. It publishes a bi-monthly *Journal* and a membership directory. The Stamp Publicity Board is concerned with publicity for the hobby.

National Societies

The Royal Philatelic Society, London, has its headquarters at 41 Devonshire Place, London W1. It has more than 1,500 members and holds meetings fortnightly between September and June. The society has its own expert committee, publishes a number of important works and plays a large part in sponsoring international exhibitions held in this country. The National Philatelic Society meets at 107 Charterhouse Street, London EC1, on the first Saturday of the month from September to June, and has more than 1,200 members. It has an extensive library, and holds auctions and postal sales, with the largest society exchange packet in the UK. Provincial meetings are sometimes held.

Local Societies

There are some 450 local societies in the UK; four have celebrated their centenaries – Plymouth (founded 1876), Birmingham (1884), Liverpool (1888) and Falmouth (1889). Most of these societies meet regularly and have modest annual subscriptions (50p to £5). The meetings are usually held at least once a month from September to June and include a full programme of talks, displays, visits to and from other societies, etc. Some of the larger societies have their own library, attract top speakers and organize stamp exhibitions and fairs. For the most part these local societies have fewer than 100 members and organization relies heavily on a few stalwarts who book the meeting hall and organize speakers etc. All welcome new members, especially younger collectors. Details of the societies, including the name and address of the Secretary are given in the *BPF Yearbook*; enquiries about local societies can also be made by writing or phoning the BPF (107 Charterhouse Street, London EC1M 6PT, tel. 01-251 5040) or contacting local reference libraries. Most of the local societies are affiliated to the BPF and to one of a number of regional Philatelic Federations. These Federations

also organize stamp exhibitions and some publish newsletters.

Specialist Societies

The third type of society is the specialist society. These are not usually locally based and have members scattered throughout the British Isles, sometimes throughout the world. There are over 120 such societies based in the UK. Some specialize in particular countries (e.g. Great Britain Philatelic Society, India Study Circle, etc.); others in particular themes (e.g. Railway Philatelic Group, etc.). Nearly all produce a regular journal; some hold auctions and arrange exchange packets. Most welcome new collectors but some tend to prefer collectors to have acquired a reasonable amount of knowledge and expertise before joining. The purpose of these societies is to further detailed knowledge of particular groups of stamps and most include amongst their members the leading specialist collectors and writers of the day.

Clubs for Young Collectors

Mention has already been made of the successful Stamp Bug Club, run by the British Post Office. Their Youth

The British Philatelic Centre in Charterhouse Street, London, houses the National Philatelic Society, the British Philatelic Federation, the British Philatelic Trust, the Stamp Publicity Board and the offices of the 'Stamp World London 90' exhibition.

Philately Section (76 Turnmill Street, London EC1M 5NS) produces interesting literature connected with British stamp issues for use in schools. Many schools have stamp clubs, sometimes organized by a teacher, sometimes by the pupils themselves. The British Philatelic Trust makes grants to school clubs of philatelic literature. Details are available from the BPT, 107 Charterhouse Street, London EC1M 6PT.

Overseas

Australia, Canada and New Zealand have their own Royal Philatelic Societies. The Royal Philatelic Society of Victoria, in conjunction with the Royal Sydney Philatelic Club, publishes a quarterly journal – *Philately from Australia*. The Royal Philatelic Society of Canada sponsored the international philatelic exhibition, CAPEX 78, the largest and most important show in Canadian history, in 1978. The Royal Philatelic Society of New Zealand publishes (from Wellington) *The New Zealand Stamp Collector*, a quarterly journal, in conjunction with the Federation of New Zealand Philatelic Societies.

The American Philatelic Society is the largest of its kind in the United States with a membership of more than 44,000. It operates a popular stamp sales division, and publishes an official journal, *American Philatelist*. Enquiries to: The American Philatelic Society, Box 800, State College, Pa. 16801, USA. The Collectors Club of New York was founded there in 1896 and its library contains one of the largest collections in the world of printed works and MSS devoted to philately, more than 150,000 items. The *Collectors Club Philatelist* is a bi-monthly journal for club members. In lighter vein, the American Topical Association of Milwaukee, Wisconsin, USA, caters for the thematic collector and publishes a bi-monthly magazine, *Topical Time*.

Round-up of Museums

National Postal Museum, King Edward Street, London EC1. 'Phillips' collection of 19th-century Great Britain; 'Berne' collection of UPU member-countries.
The British Library, Great Russell Street, London WC1. 'Tapling' collection, including many famous rarities; 'Fitzgerald' airmails; 'Moseley' Africa; Wartime Channel Islands.
Science Museum, Exhibition Road, South Kensington, London SW7. The 'Penn-Gaskell' airmails.
Bruce Castle Museum, Bruce Grove, Lordship Lane, London N17. Postal history.
Imperial War Museum, Lambeth Road, Lambeth, London SE1. World War I stamps (on application).

The famous philatelic library formed by the Earl of Crawford, which includes rare first stamp catalogues published by Oscar Berger-Levrault (1861), Mount Brown (1862) and Edward Stanley Gibbons (1865), is contained in the British Library, and can be viewed by appointment.

The Cardinal Spellman Philatelic Museum at Weston, Massachusetts, USA, is the only museum in the United States designed and built expressly for the preservation, display and study of postage stamps. The nucleus of its worldwide stamp collections is that of the late Francis Cardinal Spellman supported by the Dwight D. Eisenhower collection, bequeathed by the late President. The famous Smithsonian Institution in Washington opened its National Museum of History and Technology in 1964 which includes the Division of Philately and Postal History where philatelic treasures are displayed.

19
The Story of Stanley Gibbons

Edward Stanley Gibbons began trading in stamps in his father's chemist shop in Plymouth in 1856. He was just 16, born in the year of the Penny Black, and within a few years he established an office above his father's shop and carried on the business of 'E. Stanley Gibbons – Stamp Dealer'. When, on the death of his father, he succeeded to the pharmacy, young Gibbons turned the shop over entirely to stamp trading, and contemporary photographs show the main window full of stamps on display, and Cape triangulars in a small side window.

In fact the Cape of Good Hope stamps contributed largely to Gibbons' success and prosperity – in 1863 he was visited by two sailors who had won a sackful of stamps in a raffle at Cape Town and wanted to sell them. Gibbons bought the stamps, with alacrity, one imagines, for they were all Cape triangulars, thousands of them on the original pieces of envelope and wrappers, including the original Perkins Bacon printings, the 'woodblock' provisionals and even the rare errors of colour, 1d. blue and 4d. red stamps, worth many thousands of pounds today. But Gibbons was pleased to sell them at 8s. a gross, or 3s. a dozen for 'genuine woodblocks'.

The Gibbons Catalogue began life as a penny price list (2d. by post) of stamps, first published by Stanley Gibbons in 1865. By 1870, the price list was appearing as an embryo catalogue in book format, in which we find numerous gems at 'give-away' prices (by present standards), such as Great Britain 1d. black, unused 1s. 6d.; Canada 12d. black, unused 10s. and India 1854 4 anna, blue and red, 3d. each. About this time Gibbons also published his first stamp albums, including the *Improved*, which he maintained was an improvement on all the other rival brands of album, and the elaborate *V.R. Illustrated* album, bound in red morocco with ornate gilt lettering and a brass clasp or 'padlock' – the first album to have printed 'compartments' or spaces for all the stamps which had been issued up to the time of publication.

'Love' and Greetings stamps from the USA and Ireland. Hygienic self-adhesive issues from Sierra Leone and the USA. (see Chapter 15).

Move to London

In 1874 Gibbons moved to London, first to Clapham where he set up business in a private house, then, in 1876, to Gower Street within the shadow of the British Museum. Here during the next 16 years, he prospered as a stamp dealer and publisher and, in 1890, at the age of 50, he sought early retirement and sold his business to Charles J. Phillips, who formed a company – Stanley Gibbons Ltd – with himself as Managing Director and Stanley Gibbons as Chairman. The purchase price was £25,000.

Gibbons then lived the life of a wealthy man – travelling to France, Egypt, Algeria, India and many other places. In England he lived in a villa near Twickenham; he is believed to have had six wives. He died in London in February 1913, aged 73.

The new Managing Director of Stanley Gibbons Ltd, Charles James Phillips, was born in 1863 and came from a respected Birmingham family. By profession he was an accountant and from the 1880s onwards he developed a strong interest in stamps, founded the Birmingham Philatelic Society and became friends with many of the leading collectors of the day. He was also a keen amateur historian, a member of the Society of Antiquaries and a student of the Sackville family of Knole in Kent. Before buying Gibbons' business he had published, in Birmingham, the *Stamp Advertiser and Auction Record*, so the introduction of the *Stanley Gibbons Monthly Journal* in 1890 came as a natural development. Phillips wrote many articles based on his researches of the stamps of Brazil, British East Africa, Chile, Colombia, Italy, Mexico and West Australia. He also produced books on the stamps of Fiji, Paraguay and Mexico. In 1921 Phillips became one of the first signatories of the Roll of Distinguished Philatelists, the greatest honour in the world of philately. Phillips was more acceptable in 'high society' than Gibbons had been and his contacts with highly placed personages enabled his business to prosper. In 1891 he opened a branch office at 435 Strand and in 1893 closed the Gower Street office and moved the entire business to new premises at 391 Strand, which was to remain the company's home for 90 years. An office in New York followed in 1902 and another in Buenos Aires in 1910, although neither survived for very long. Numerous important and valuable collections were bought; for example the 80-volume W.W. Mann collection of European stamps for £30,000 in 1906 and the Breitfuss collection of British Colonies and Europe for £50,000 the following year. By this time Phillips had a staff of 50 and casual staff were brought in during busy periods. Many collections began with the purchase of stamp packets and in 1911 the company started to produce these, ranging in price from 6d. to no less than £165 for a packet of 10,000 stamps! The recognition that Gibbons had become the main British stamp firm came in 1914 with the granting of the Royal Warrant by King George V. The company still retains the warrant as Philatelists to HM The Queen.

The First World War caused disruption to the supply of stamps and the company's publications but once hostilities had ceased things gradually got back to normal and more important collections were being acquired and sold. In 1922 Phillips handled the collection of Henry J. Duveen, one of the most famous collectors of all time. However Phillips' methods of business were not without controversy and in the same year he sold his shares in Stanley Gibbons Ltd and moved to the USA, where he continued dealing and writing until his death in 1940.

Steady Growth

For the next 40 years the company prospered under various Chairmen but without the flamboyance of Gibbons and Phillips. The most significant person during this period was Stanley Phillips, nephew of Charles, who joined the company as a junior in 1906 and died, as Chairman, in 1954. During that time he had been Editor of the catalogue and magazine and Managing Director. Stanley Phillips' greatest contribution was perhaps the introduction of the *Simplified Catalogue*, now known as *Stamps of the World*. He was a man of strong opinions and high morals. His editorials in the magazine were forthright and in his famous book *Stamp Collecting* he gave sound advice to three generations of stamp collectors. He organized gifts of stamps and albums to orphanages and hospitals, readers of the magazine being invited to contribute to the Christmas Fund. He did much to publicize the hobby and was amongst the first to speak on stamp collecting on television.

In 1956 the company celebrated its centenary with an exhibition at London's Waldorf Hotel, on display were many rare stamps loaned by eminent collectors and customers of the company. The exhibition was opened by Sir John Wilson, Keeper of the Royal Philatelic Collection.

In the early 1960s there was increased interest in stamps and the time had come for further expansion. In 1962 Gibbons merged with the 'firm next door', W.H.

Wingfield of 392 Strand. The name Stanley Gibbons Ltd remained, with the company under the joint Managing Directors W.F. Deakin of Gibbons and A.L. Michael of Wingfields. Michael was as energetic as Gibbons himself and Charles Phillips and from 1968, when he became Chairman, until his retirement 10 years later the name Gibbons became a household word with numerous articles in the general press, mentions on radio and television and a rapid expansion in both stamp dealing and the publications side of the business. In 1965 the centenary of the Gibbons Catalogue was marked by an exhibition at the Royal Festival Hall, opened by the Postmaster-General (Anthony Wedgwood-Benn) with the world's rarest stamp, the British Guiana 1c. magenta on display. Gibbons played a major role in the stamp world, in the organization of STAMPEX and 'Philympia', the international stamp exhibition in London in 1970. Offices were opened in the USA and in Monaco and in 1970 the company diversified with the opening of a new department dealing in banknotes, later enlarged to include coins. Another Gibbons company was established to deal with antiquarian maps and separate Publications and Magazines companies were formed. The auction side of the business also became a separate operating company. Stanley Gibbons Ltd became the stamp dealing business of Stanley Gibbons International Ltd, which by the end of the 1970s had seven addresses in London.

Public Company

In 1968 Gibbons 'went public', the first British stamp company to do so and to much media interest. In 1973 Gibbons took over the West German stamp firm of Merkur, whose owner, Howard Fraser, joined the Gibbons board. In 1978 A.L. Michael retired to Monaco although he continued to take an interest in Gibbons until his death in 1987. The new Chairman, Howard Fraser, continued with his predecessor's expansion plans but within a year Stanley Gibbons International had become part of the Letraset group for the price of £12.8 million and 4.6 million Letraset shares. Fraser continued as Chairman of Gibbons and was appointed Deputy Chairman of Letraset. Sadly the boom in stamps was not to continue and almost immediately after the international stamp exhibition in London in 1980 stamp prices began to fall and interest waned. The diversification into other collecting interests had not proved as successful as was hoped and Letraset were forced to close certain sections of the business and reduce the number of staff. Fraser left Gibbons in 1980 and for a while Letraset executives ran the company.

During the ownership by Letraset the company celebrated its 125th anniversary with the opening of a new shop at 399 Strand and the forming of Stanley Gibbons Promotions at Ringwood in Hampshire to deal with the flood of orders for stamps marking the wedding

Top Left: The 391 Strand shop, home of Gibbons from 1893 to 1981.
Top Right: Edward Stanley Gibbons – the best known portrait.
Bottom Right: The present 399 Strand shop.
Bottom Left: Stanley Phillips, Editor of both Catalogue and Magazine,
Managing Director and Chairman of Stanley Gibbons Ltd.
Centre Left: Stanley Gibbons's original shop in Treville Street, Plymouth.

of the Prince of Wales and Lady Diana Spencer (July 1981). This event, and the big demand for Falkland Islands stamps the following year, kept Gibbons afloat during the recession in the stamp market. The Promotions business later developed into a company dealing in thematic collections and clubs for collectors interested in particular countries or groups of stamps. Late in 1981 Letraset was taken over by the Swedish company Esselte; Gibbons was put up for sale. The following June, Gibbons once again became an independent company, having been bought from Esselte by a consortium which included some of its existing management. The new Managing Director, David Stokes, continued with the rationalization of the various businesses including the move of the Publications company from London to Ringwood in 1984–5. By this time the control of Gibbons had come under various City interests, the Chairman, Ronnie Aitken, being a well-known City figure. Sadly the continued recession meant that more energy had to be given to financial rather than philatelic considerations and there is no doubt that Gibbons's reputation fell to an all-time low. A period of near isolation from the philatelic world ensued and some of the company's best-known personnel left.

The Future

Since 1986 things have improved, first under Stephen Quinn as Chief Executive (1986–9) and, at the time of going to press, under his successor Tim Yarnell. The finances and organization of the company have been overhauled and the reduced number of staff are looking to a brighter future. The London end of the market is headed by Richard Watkins, himself a stamp collector, as are his fellow directors, Ian Brushwood, Andrew Lajer, Dr Philip Kinns and Greg Todd. In Ringwood, the Publications business is headed by Stuart Northcote, with philatelic input from Peter Mollett, General Manager of the Promotions section, David Aggersberg, Catalogue Editor and Hugh Jefferies, Editor of *Gibbons Stamp Monthly*.

In 1990 the company will celebrate the 150th anniversary of the birth of Edward Stanley Gibbons, the 125th anniversary of the catalogue and the centenary of the magazine. The isolation of a few years ago is now over with representation on the British Philatelic Federation, the Stamp Publicity Board and the company planning major participation in the international exhibition 'Stamp World London 90' at Alexandra Palace (3–13 May 1990). Stanley Gibbons would no doubt be surprised not only at the growth in the interest in stamp collecting over the 75 years since his death but by the varied fortunes of the company which still bears his name.

20
Glossary of Philatelic Terms

A selection of the terms most commonly used in stamp collecting.

Adhesive. A gummed stamp, as distinct from an imprinted one.

Albino. Fortuitous omission of colour from a stamp resulting in a colourless impression of the design.

Aniline. A fugitive ink or dye causing suffusion of colour.

Backstamp. An 'arrival' postmark applied to the back of a letter.

Bâtonné. Paper watermarked with straight parallel lines.

Bisect. A stamp cut in half for separate use.

Blind perforation. A hole not punched out (blunt or missing pin).

Block of stamps. A group of four (or more) unseparated stamps.

Blued paper. Paper with a pale blue tinge, caused in manufacture.

Bogus. A pretended stamp, an unauthorized label.

Burélage. A stamp's security background: a network of lines/dots.

Cachet. A commemorative inscription or special endorsement on a cover.

Cancellation. Any authorized defacing mark on a stamp.

Cancelled to order. Stamps postmarked 'by favour'.

Centred. 'Well-centred' – a stamp design with equal margins.

Chalk-surfaced paper. Paper coated with a chalky solution.

Charity stamp. One bearing a premium for charitable purposes.

Classic. A distinction of quality/rarity in early stamps.

Coil stamp. One from a roll in an automatic vending machine.

Colour changeling. A stamp whose original colour has changed.

Comb perforation. From a perforator with pins arranged as a 'comb'.

Commemorative. A stamp marking a special anniversary or event.

Compound perforation. A stamp having two different perforations.

Controls. Letters/numbers in the sheet margins.

Cover. A postally-used envelope, letter-sheet or wrapper.

Cylinder number. In sheet margins: identifying cylinder(s) used.

Dandy roll. The wire-mesh roller used in papermaking to produce a watermark.

Definitive. A stamp issued for regular postal use.

Die. The original engraved plaque or plate of a stamp design.

Doctor blade. A steel blade which wipes ink from the cylinder.

Duty plate. A printing plate which produced the country name and denomination when used in conjunction with a Key plate.

Embossing. A form of printing (or 'die-stamping') in relief.

Engraving. The art of cutting (stamp) designs on metal, wood etc.

Entire. A *complete* envelope, letter-sheet or wrapper.

Error. A mistake in a stamp's design or production.

Essay. A trial design, differing from the issued stamp.

Face value. The denomination or value expressed on a stamp's face.

Fake. A genuine stamp/postmark 'doctored' to defraud collectors.

Fiscal. A revenue or tax stamp – not a postage stamp.

Forgery. A fraudulent copy of a genuine postage stamp or postmark.

Frank. 'Free' (of postage). Also a stamped/postmarked letter.

Granite paper. Stamp paper embodying minute coloured fibres.

Graphite lines. On backs of British stamps: aid to automatic sorting.

Gum. The mucilage on the backs of adhesive stamps.

Gutter. The space between stamps to permit perforation.

Gutter margin. The margin dividing a sheet of stamps into panes.

Handstamp. A postmark/overprint applied by hand. Also the stamper.

Harrow perforation. A means of perforating whole sheets at a time.

Imperforate. Stamps printed in sheets without perforation.

Imperf.-between. Perforations omitted between adjoining stamps.

Imprimatur. The first sheets of early British stamps 'approved', before the printing run is authorised.

Imprint. Name of designer/printer on stamps or sheet margins.

Ivory head. Clear white Queen's head on back of Q. V. blued stamps.

Jubilee line. Coloured line framing stamps in sheet margin.

Key plate. Printing plate for common use, paired with 'duty' plate.

Line-engraving. The process of steel or copper engraving in lines.

Line perforation. A method by which each line of perforations in a sheet is struck individually. This tends to produce an overlap of the holes at corners.

Lithography. Surface printing from a flat 'stone' or plate.

Local. A stamp whose postal use and validity are limited in area.

Machin stamps. The current British definitives, designed by Arnold Machin.

Miniature sheet. A small souvenir sheet of stamps.

Mint. A stamp in its original state of issue.

Mulready. Pictorial envelopes and letter-sheets issued in 1840.

Newspaper stamps. Stamps issued for postage on newspapers.

Obligatory tax stamps. Issued to raise funds: compulsory use.

Obliteration. A cancellation in the form of a heavy defacement.

Obsolete. A stamp which has ceased to be available for postal use.

Official stamps. Issued or overprinted for governmental use.

Offset. An impression on a sheet of stamps from another laid on it.

Offset-lithography. Surface printing from cylinders.

Overprint. A printed addition to a stamp. Also see 'Surcharge'.

Pair. Two unseparated stamps, joined as originally issued.

Pane. Section of a sheet of stamps separated from other sections by a gutter margin (**q.v.**). Also booklet pane or leaf.

Perforated initials. Initial letters punched through stamps ('Perfins').

Perforation. Holes punched between stamps for ease in separation.

Phosphor stamps. Overprinted/coated with 'fluorescent' substances.

Photogravure. A form of recess printing employing photo-etching.

Plate number. In sheet margins: identifying plate(s) used.

Plating. Reconstruction of a sheet of stamps from original plates.

Plug. Insertion on a printing plate – figures of value, repairs etc.

Postage due stamps. Used to collect fees on unpaid letters etc.

Postmark. Of post office origin used to indicate place of posting (usually cancelling an adhesive stamp), to indicate offices of transit, or arrival, or a special service.

Precancel. A stamp postmarked prior to use on bulk mail postings.

Proof. A trial impression taken from an original die or plate.

Provisional. A stamp issued for temporary use.

Quadrillé paper. Patterned or watermarked with criss-cross lines.

Recess printing. Line-engraving. Recesses are formed on the plate.

Re-entry. A double impression on the plate, visible on the stamps.

Remainders. Stocks of stamps on hand after an issue is withdrawn.

Reprints. Stamps printed after the issue has been withdrawn.

Retouch. A minor correction by hand on the plate or cylinder.

Roulette. A means of separating stamps by cuts instead of holes.

Se-tenant. Joined stamps which differ in value or design.

Shade. A minor variation in the colour of a stamp.

Specimen. A sample stamp, usually overprinted/perforated 'Specimen'.

Stamp money. Unused postage stamps used as coins during shortages.

Surcharge. An overprint which alters a stamp's face value (up or down).

Tab. A label or coupon attached to a stamp.

Telegraph stamps. For prepayment of telegraph charges.

Tête-bêche. A stamp upside-down in relation to an adjoining stamp.

Thematic collecting. 'Thematics'. Collecting a specific theme.

Tied. A stamp 'married' to the original envelope by the postmark.

Typography. Letterpress or 'surface' printing from relief plates.

Unissued stamps. 'Prepared for use but not issued'.

Unused. An uncancelled stamp, not necessarily 'mint'.

Used. A stamp postally used and accordingly postmarked.

Used abroad. Stamps of one country used and postmarked in another.

Variety. A stamp which is abnormal because of an error or flaw.

Vignette. The central feature of a stamp design.

War stamps. Issued in wartime and so inscribed. Also 'War Tax'. Normally issued to meet increased postal rate.

Watermark. A device or pattern, embodied in the paper.

Wilding. British definitives, 1952–68. Portrait by Dorothy Wilding.

Window Book. Booklet of stamps issued by British Post Office from 1987, on sale at post offices and retail outlets. Initial issues had 'window' cut into front cover revealing stamp contents, later issues had illustration of stamp printed on front cover – as illustration shown here.

Wing margin. An extra 'wing' or flap of margin within the stamp.

Woodblock. 'Carved on wood'. Sobriquet for Cape triangular stamps.

Wove paper. Paper with fine even texture. 'Laid' paper is lined.

Zemstvo issues. Russian local posts and stamps, 1870 to 1890.

Index